TELLING SOME TALES

TELLING SOME TALES

ANNA MASSEY

HUTCHINSON
LONDON

Published by Hutchinson in 2006

3 5 7 9 10 8 6 4 2

First published in the United Kingdom by Hutchinson in 2006

Hutchinson
The Random House Group Limited
20 Vauxhall Bridge Road, London SW1V 2SA

Random House Australia (Pty) Limited
20 Alfred Street, Milsons Point, Sydney
New South Wales 2061, Australia

Random House New Zealand Limited
18 Poland Road, Glenfield
Auckland 10, New Zealand

Random House (Pty) Limited
Isle of Houghton, Corner of Boundary Road & Carse O'Gowrie
Houghton 2198, South Africa

Random House Publishers India Private Limited
301 World Trade Tower, Hotel Intercontinental Grand Complex
Barakhamba Lane, New Delhi 110 001, India

The Random House Group Limited Reg. No. 954009
www.randomhouse.co.uk

A CIP catalogue record for this book is available from the British Library

The publishers are unable to locate the copyright holder for the front cover photograph,
but if notified would be pleased to amend the acknowledgement in any future editions.

Papers used by Random House are natural, recyclable
products made from wood grown in sustainable forests. The manufacturing
processes conform to the environmental regulations of the country of origin

ISBN 9780091796457 (from January 2007)
ISBN 0091796458

Typeset in Bembo by Palimpsest Book Production Limited,
Polmont, Stirlingshire
Printed and bound in Great Britain by
Mackays of Chatham plc, Chatham, Kent

For Uri

LIST OF ILLUSTRATIONS

SECTION ONE:

1. My mother, Adrianne Allen, as a fairy
2. My father, Raymond Massey
3. My mother and father
4. Daniel and me
5. Daniel, my stepfather Bill Whitney and Mummy. And me as a 'Cross Red Nurse'
6. My nanny, Gertrude Burbidge
7. Ann Walker, Penelope Roberts, Lady Sarah Berry (née Clifford-Turner), me and Sarah Barford playing nanny with our prams in Hyde Park
8. Me, aged ten, presenting a bouquet to Her Royal Highness, the Princess Elizabeth before the charity matinee for the NSPCC (© Keystone/Horst Tappe)
9. Me as Laura in *The Glass Menagerie* (© Angus McBean)
10. Me, my mother and my brother Daniel (© *Daily Star*)
11. My great friend Kate Whitney
12. Iris Warren, my voice teacher
13. A glamorous photograph of my mother
14. Jeremy Brett at the time of our marriage (© John Timbers)
15. David and me in fun-loving combat (© Keystone/Horst Tappe)
16. David, aged two, on the Embankment on a rainy day (© John Timbers)

17. Me as Annie Sullivan in *The Miracle Worker*. The turning point of my career (© John Timbers)

SECTION TWO:

18. Alfred Hitchcock directing me and John Finch in *Frenzy*
19. Denholm Elliot and me filming *Hotel du Lac* in Witznau in Switzerland (© BBC)
20. Taken during His Royal Highness the Duke of Edinburgh's visit to my uncle Vincent Massey's home in Port Hope, Canada
21. Daniel, my half-brother Geoffrey, David, Father and me (© *Daily Express*)
22. Me as Ariadne Utterword in *Heartbreak House*
23. Me as Queen Elizabeth in Schiller's *Mary Stuart* (© Gautier Deblonde)
24. Me as Miss Prism in *The Importance of Being Earnest*, with Martin Jarvis as John Worthing and Judi Dench as Lady Bracknell (© Zoe Dominic)
25. Artro Morris as John Goronwy Jones, Katharine Hepburn as Miss Moffat and me as Miss Ronberry in *The Corn is Green*
26. Me as Mrs Danvers in *Rebecca*
27. Me as Gwen John in *The Journey Into the Shadows* (© BBC)
28. Me filming the Buxton Mineral Water ad in the Tana Delta
29. My son David, fishing
30. David teaching my grandson to fish
31. Me and Uri on our wedding day
32. And David and Maddie on their wedding day
33. My grandson Dan
34. And my granddaughter Iris
35. Uri and me soon after we were married

ACKNOWLEDGEMENTS

The last year has been an exciting adventure for me, and there are a great many people who have helped me on the journey, and I would like to thank them, for their encouragement gave me the strength to get to the end.

So here is my thank-you list.

Alan Rickman who was responsible for getting the whole project started. Pat Kavanagh for her invaluable advice. Alex Irwin for protecting me, and for taking such care of my needs. David Hare, Peter Eyre, Howard Schuman, Corinne Laurie, Anna Benson-Gyles, and Suzanne Bertish who have helped me to remember certain anecdotes and stories along the way, and Aimee Wood for her great detective work.

Two years ago I didn't even own a computer, so I must thank my computer doctor, Rob Gordon, for his lessons and his calm when I panicked.

I would also like to say how grateful I am to Post-its, and how greatly I relied on them, and to the Internet, where I learnt things about myself that I never knew before.

My very special thank yous go to my son, David Huggins, whose help and support has meant so very much to me.

Thank you to Tiffany Stansfield, who has kept me cheerful and welcomed me to the world of publishing with enormous patience and calm.

But it has to be said that I would not have been able to write a word if my editor, Paul Sidey, had not given me his invaluable guidance. He has made the daunting task a journey of pleasure, and I thank him for his warmth and enthusiasm, and for all he has taught me.

My husband, Uri Andres, has named me 'Don Pomeranzo', a character in a poem who went on 'writing and writing', while the town and countryside around him were in turmoil. So my very special thanks to Uri, who, during my 'role' as authoress, has endured the ramblings of one obsessed, listened to every page, given wonderful notes, gone without meals, done the shopping, and proved to be the most patient of partners.

CHAPTER I

I HAVE ALWAYS THOUGHT MY EARLIEST MEMORY WAS BEING HELD in my father's hand at one month old. I was told this was an impossibility. Nevertheless I defied the doubters and gained comfort from my memory of this closeness to my father, who within the first year of my life had left our household for good.

Later I saw a photograph in my mother's album of the baby in my father's palm, and I realised the doubters were right. I had imagined myself in this lofty hold. The memory was the photograph, not the event itself.

Sometime in 1938 my father had left my mother and gone to live in the States. After a few months he asked her to join him there. He wanted a reconciliation. She went to New York and found that it was a trap. He wanted a divorce, so that he could marry a lawyer called Dorothy Luddington. One of my mother's friends recommended a law firm, and an appointment was made to meet William Dwight Whitney at the Plaza Hotel tea room. He was to wear a pink carnation, and she was to wear a sailor hat. She said she wanted to divorce her husband Raymond Massey and was citing a certain Dorothy Luddington. To this Mr Whitney said, 'You have named the one person which prevents me from taking your case. Dorothy Luddington is my ex-wife.'

Six months later my mother and Bill Whitney were married. Raymond and Dorothy married at almost the same time. So Noel Coward's play *Private Lives* had been brought to life, and a strange note to all this was that my mother had appeared as Sybil in the very first production of that play.

The two families now settled on either side of the Atlantic. I lived with my mother and Bill in England, and my father remained forever in the States. The man who once had held me in the palm of his hand was three thousand miles away.

For a while we stayed on at the house in Sussex where I was born. My mother had changed the name of this house from Hunger Hill, after the famous battle, to Rosings Farm. At the time she had been appearing in *Pride and Prejudice*, Rosings Farm being one of the houses named in Miss Austen's book. Some people believe that to change the name of a house brings ill fortune, but my mother was undeterred. She was used to changing names, and had altered her own from Gladys Allen to Adrianne Allen when she joined the acting profession.

Part of Rosings dated back to Elizabethan times, and was approached by a long straight drive lined with pine trees. I remember there were many hedged walks in the garden, and beautiful lawns where croquet was often played. I was even given a miniature mallet as a child.

My parents had met when Father ran the Everyman Theatre in Hampstead with Basil Dean, and Mother had gone there to audition for a part. They married soon after. Father had been married before to Peggy Fremantle, and had a son, Geoffrey, who had come to live with my parents at Rosings. Daniel, my brother, had been born in 1933, and I was born in 1937. But of course by then the marriage was failing. After the changing of partners, Geoffrey went to live with my father in the States, and Daniel and I stayed in England. To complete the cast there were two other members – Bill Whitney's two daughters, Margaret and Dorothy, joined my father's household in America.

So that sets the scene for my childhood. It was a fairly dramatic situation to have been born into. On the surface everyone appeared to behave well, but underneath there were enormous tensions. The key players in the drama were, of course, my mother and father. Perhaps because I never saw them in a 'wedded' context, I always found it hard to believe that they had ever been man and wife. They were such opposite personalities. Mother was fair and wilful and gregarious, and Father was dark and moody and somewhat shy. They simply did not seem to mix, and yet I think that she was in love with him until the end of her life.

Adrianne was a very original person. She had golden frizzy hair, a trim figure, and to my eyes was always somewhat overdressed, but she did possess a certain glamour. I have a photograph of her as a little girl dressed as a fairy, standing in her ballet shoes, her feet elegantly turned out. She is smiling, but her expression is so full of determination and wilfulness that 'fairy-like' is not an adjective that springs to mind on beholding this small portrait. However, she was filled with fears all her life which she concealed rather well, and I have never known a more superstitious person. Each year new 'dos and don'ts' were added to her list, and these she shared with the whole family. As a child, I accepted them all out of fear, but later in life I found that they were too burdensome and restrictive. I started to pick up dropped gloves, and to put new shoes on tables.

She was the daughter of a jeweller's apprentice who had run away to Manchester from Newport, Monmouthshire, in his early teens. He had worked hard, and in his twenties he himself owned a jeweller's shop. Later he went into real estate and bought the St James's Cinema in London. In later years it became the Westminster Theatre. He was apparently a fun-loving, gregarious man, known to his friends as 'Champagne Charlie', and his daughter certainly inherited his social charms and energies. No one enjoyed parties more than she. She was the most welcoming hostess I ever encountered. If I picture her at her happiest, it is with glass in hand surrounded by friends. Somehow all fears left her at such times. It was a form of escapism, I'm sure. Party-going and giving were her necessary diet. Acting was less important. She was a great arranger of events. Noel Coward called her Plannie Annie, and Emlyn Williams, the famous Welsh actor, called her The Iron Butterfly. Witty titles, and somewhat acerbic, but they did define her rather accurately.

I could almost count on my hands the lunches and dinners that I had alone with her. There was always a guest or a gathering. She made many friends and they all remained close. At her table you would find the most extraordinary cross section of people – a dresser from one of her tours, a politician, a countess, or some illustrious member of the acting profession, Noel Coward, Ivor Novello, the Oliviers, together with a young actor starting out on his career. People loved her. She was a famously generous friend, and she had a very original wit. Noel Coward remained one of her closest friends since the *Private Lives* days. He was my brother Daniel's godfather, and he was a frequent visitor to our house.

Mum's generosity and wit were her shining qualities. She was not a maternal person at all, and when she kissed you she remained quite rigid. Hugs and cuddles with her children were not in her repertoire. Whether she was aware of these limitations I don't know. But I do know that she tried her best.

My father I knew less well. He was extremely tall with dark brown eyes and raven hair, moving with consummate grace in his youth. He was an intensely shy man with a very bad stammer that he only managed to conquer when he was acting. In emotional situations the affliction was at it worst. Once, on one of the very few occasions when I was alone with him, we were having tea, and he tried to tell me that he loved me. His stammer was so bad that he couldn't complete the sentence. It went on for so long that I offered him a scone in the middle. I couldn't say, 'You . . . love . . . me.' It's not a line you can prompt somebody with.

He had been born in Canada. The family had emigrated from

Cheshire in the seventeenth century. Father was one of two sons. Vincent, the eldest, later became High Commissioner of Canada in London during the war, and later the Governor General. A more royal personage you could not wish to meet. He was far more of an actor than his brother on public occasions. My father was over six feet two inches tall and Uncle Vincent only about five foot four, but apart from the difference in height, they were obviously brothers. Both had somewhat protruding dark brown eyes set in rather rugged features. Their mother had died when Raymond was young and this had had a profound impact on him. I think his father had been very severe with him. In all family photographs that I have seen of him as a boy, he seems sad and rather withdrawn.

The family were part-owners of the Massey Harris firm that made farm machinery. All their equipment was painted in bright yellows, reds and blues. There is a tale that a workman had fallen into a vat of this brightly coloured paint, and my great-grandfather had had his wages docked for the amount of paint lost. Whether this story is true or not remains a mystery, but I think it shows a lack of generosity in the family, and it may account for a certain meanness in my father. For the whole of my life he sent me twenty-five dollars for my birthday. It always arrived a month late, after he had received our birthday card to him, and had been reminded. He was quite a wealthy man, but the sum of twenty-five dollars never altered. He disregarded inflation and the advancement of years or any need. He believed strongly that everyone was responsible for themselves. Perhaps his own father had believed likewise and he was only following family tradition.

The contrast between Mother's extraordinary generosity and Father's parsimony was marked. I think it must have created great tensions between them. I never was able to discuss with either any personal details of their life together, and only gleaned little pieces here and there over the years.

Father was a complex man. He had fought in World War One, something of which he was very proud. His kitbag was handed down to my son who has it to this day. Father was an Anglophile, and had immersed himself in the London theatrical world. He both directed and acted. One night he had an opening of a play he was directing, and yet he himself was performing in another theatre. He apparently darted between the two theatres during the intervals. Hard to believe that this could happen today, but of course traffic was considerably lighter then.

My mother and father were of course dominant figures in my life. Even though Father had virtually left the scene when I was a baby, his presence was still felt. But there were two other important figures in my childhood: one who taught me logic and discipline, and the other who shielded me from untold pain, and gave me all the care and love and warmth that I yearned for.

CHAPTER 2

GERTRUDE BURBIDGE WAS THE MAINSTAY OF MY LIFE. SHE HAD entered our family when my brother Daniel was three weeks old and she stayed with us for the rest of her life. Her constancy and devotion held me together until her death in 1968.

Nanny had been born in Bedfordshire and was one of nine children, four of whom had died of tuberculosis. In her early teens she had gone to work for a family as nursery-maid. Before coming to us she had only held one post as a nanny. I once asked her if she had ever wanted to be married, and she replied that one evening, holding Daniel in her arms and looking out of the window over Central Park from her room at the Plaza Hotel, she felt that she had everything she could ever want from life.

Our world in Mother's house centred entirely round the day and night nurseries, where Nanny ruled her tiny kingdom. She did absolutely everything for us. She washed and ironed all our clothes with unimaginable delicacy, organza and taffeta coming to life again under her mastery. She also arranged flowers with the greatest taste and invention. Vases would appear all over the house, each one a creation that Constance Spry would have envied. In the midst of a bowl of yellow daisies, a crimson zinnia, tall and elegant, would be perfectly placed, giving an oriental touch to the display. No one had ever taught her. She simply had a natural gift, as she also had for tying bows. These bows adorned many of my dresses as a child, and always seemed

7

to have been untouched by human hand. I had very little hair until I was four years old but the few red wisps that I possessed were decorated with Nanny's exquisite miniature bows, thus feminising my small head. We were truly cared for and cherished by her. One of my earliest memories of her was in Cornwall where we had gone for a holiday. It was late at night, and, being in new surroundings, I could not sleep. I lay awake listening to the rustle of tissue paper as Nanny carefully unpacked our clothes.

She had an ample bosom into which we could snuggle on the nights when we had earache, a malady I suffered from frequently as a child. She was not very maternal but she was overwhelmingly reassuring and you knew she would always be there. It was this constancy that was so comforting. Her cooking skills delighted us; fish poached in milk with tasty fresh vegetables would be prepared without fuss, decorated with herbs and lemon. The appearance of things mattered to her.

She was also a strict disciplinarian and never very relaxed about things, and quite unintentionally she instilled fears in us. I found it very difficult to get to sleep at night, and once I asked Nanny if one should go to sleep with one's eyes open or shut. She answered that it didn't matter, which of course led to untold problems. Our manners had to be perfect. I had the most terrible temper as a child, and my punishments I remember to this day. The hairbrush would be brought out and I was spanked quite often for my misdemeanours. Once in a shoe shop in Sloane Street I kicked a shoe right up to the top of a cupboard. I was severely reprimanded and for two or three days Nanny hardly spoke to me. This was punishment indeed, and of course I vowed to be good forever more, failing to keep my word more often than I would have liked.

I was once given a fancy dress costume of a Red Cross nurse, and Mother called me her 'cross red nurse.' My fiery nature taxed the entire family.

But Nanny ultimately, for all her strictness, forgave me for everything. When she went on holiday I cried every single night until she returned. These were true tears of anguish. Without her I just didn't feel safe. It was not that my mother was cruel. It was just that she was so often not there. Her social life and her acting kept her away. She flitted in and out of our lives with her generosity and wit and irony, the latter being somewhat confusing to a child. Even during Nanny's holidays Mother didn't look after me. We had temporary nannies who must have suffered greatly from my tears and pain.

For long periods Daniel was away at boarding school and suffered less from these breaks. He was a moody boy; sometimes full of laughter and fun, at other times morose and a little frightening, at least to a small child. When he was at home for the school holidays I tried to keep up with him and his friends, but they didn't need me for their games, so I was left out. More rejection: I think my birth, so near to the departure of his father, was very hard for Daniel. Deep down he must have resented my arrival, and been angered by my presence. All these feelings get buried in the soul and years later help has to be sought to unravel them.

In 1941 we went to the States. My mother had apparently thought much upon this, but finally decided that we should go. We stayed in a rented apartment in Hampshire House on 59th Street, over-looking Central Park. It was planned that my father would come and take me to his house on East 83rd Street for tea to meet his wife, Dorothy. When the bell rang, I was standing with Mother and Nanny in the hall. The door opened and there stood a great thin dark man, over six feet tall. Terrified, I fled to the bathroom and locked myself in. I could hear my father accusing my mother of causing this flight deliberately. My mother had never said a word against my father, and throughout her life she never did so, but that day she was accused.

9

It was Nanny who finally coaxed me out. I remember walking over the Park to my father's house and having a tense tea with Dorothy. Where Mother was warmly ironic, Dorothy was acid. She was one of the most frightening people I have ever met. She had been a lawyer, and when she married my father, she gave up her practice and devoted her considerable energies to looking after his contracts and all his affairs, thus earning him many enemies in his later years. Even my father seemed in awe of her.

Dorothy was not a beautiful woman, but she was powerful. Her best feature were her ankles, which were thin and dainty. The rest of her figure was quite fulsome. Her hair had been dyed so many times that the plot had been lost. It was a mixture of grey, red and dark brown, and often tied with a shoelace. Her skin was slightly pockmarked, and, when she smiled, she did not employ her eyes. Enormous tension vibrated in the air around her.

They lived in a tall brownstone house that was extremely dark, and ideally matched Dorothy's aura. I was too young to take in the details, but I remember many small rooms filled with antiques, lamps with heavy shades and all the walls painted in dark blues and greens.

However, that day at tea Dorothy tried to win me over by letting me go through her costume-jewellery box which she brought out from a cavernous cupboard. She gave me a brooch of a diamanté umbrella with a pearl handle, which of course did much to assuage my unease, though the deeper tensions of this visit have never been forgotten.

My father always remained the glamorous film star who lived far away with a frightening lady. No wonder nursery life with Nanny was such a comfort.

That visit to New York did not last very long. Mother felt guilty that we were away from England during the war, and we sailed back across the Atlantic on the *Mauretania* in a convoy of grey battleships, to be greeted at Liverpool by banners saying 'Welcome Home Bomb Dodgers'. From then on we stayed in England for the duration of the war. Mother toured with ENSA in the Middle East with Emlyn Williams and a whole troupe of actors, whilst Nanny, Daniel and I were evacuated to Wales, where, ironically, a bomb fell only a few miles from our lodgings.

Whilst we were staying in the Welsh hills, Nanny took Daniel and me to the cinema (known then as the pictures) to see our father in *49th Parallel*. It was a strange choice for her to make. I was barely four years old at the time. At the point in the film where Father was about to be hanged, I stood up on my seat and shouted out for everyone to hear, 'That man is our father.' I was rushed from the cinema, and not allowed to see any more films for a very long time.

A great deal of the war, though, was spent in London, where we rented an apartment at 49 Hill Street. Here Mother entertained regularly. The bombs fell around us, and many nights everyone in the entire building had to go down to the large basement for shelter. At the sound of the siren, I was woken up by Nanny and brought down in my dressing gown, to find Mother already there with her illustrious guests, all merrily holding their glasses with replenishing bottles to hand. No bombing was allowed to interrupt the fun. The all-clear signal simply meant that the party could continue upstairs.

I remember Michael Redgrave was there one evening. He was the most charming man, rather shy, and naturally he didn't have much to say to a precocious four-year-old. Many years later I worked with him at the National Theatre in Simon Gray's *Close of Play*. I found his dignity and wisdom most moving. He was suffering from Parkinson's disease at the time, but he was always alert to everyone's performances, and gave us wonderfully subtle notes in his quiet way. He had exceptional humility.

Throughout the merriment in the basement, though, Nanny tried to keep me firmly in hand, allowing no showing off. I

don't know that she was always successful, and fear she sometimes failed to rein me in.

One night, for some unknown reason, we did not go down
to the shelter, and Nanny took me to the nursery window to
see a German plane being chased in a searchlight over Berkeley
Square. It was a quite unforgettable image, but of course a very
dangerous situation. I can only imagine Nanny believed there
was no real threat to us.

Sometime after the war, I went on holiday with Mother, Bill and
Daniel to Arosa in Switzerland. Even though we were in snowy
fairy-tale surroundings with sleigh rides and hot chocolate and
magical skiing, I cried for Nanny each night. From then on I
was allowed to go away with Nanny when the others travelled
to exotic places. They went to the South of France, while we
braved the east wind at Frinton. It was a quieter, more peaceful
life, and I much preferred it. Pictures appeared in Mother's photo
album of all the famous tanned hotel guests with whom they
had shared their holiday. But my snaps from Frinton still bring
back happy memories of sugar buns relished after freezing swims,
swaddled in bright, striped beach towels.

In my teens of course I joined in the exciting travels organised by Bill, trips to Italy, France, Holland and Germany. I was
then brave enough to leave the nursery.

Nanny had given all the solace and comfort and attention that
a child could need. For knowledge and logic and application, I
turned to my stepfather, Bill.

CHAPTER 3

BILL WHITNEY WAS AN INTERNATIONAL LAWYER WHO WORKED for a large firm in New York City called Cravath, Swaine and Moore. Soon after he married my mother he was sent to London to open their European office. From 1939 onwards he travelled back and forth between the two cities, and we often followed him.

Bill had been born in New Haven, into a family of intellectuals. His aunts Marion and Emily were formidable women of a bygone era. I remember them in stern tweed suits sitting in vast panelled rooms surrounded by books. Bill's mother, however, was a Southern Belle called Josepha. She was widowed when Bill was quite young, but in her eighties had married again, her bridegroom a charming octogenarian named Harry. They both came to stay with us a couple of times in London, Josepha befrilled and chiffoned, with her hypnotic Southern accent, acting up the demanding new bride. Everyone was forced to rally to her every whim, fetching shawls and hot drinks. My mother hated her: The Southern Belle had defeated The Iron Butterfly.

Bill had several brothers and sisters, two of whom were mountaineers, Roger and Hassler. An ancestor had been a famous climber after whom Mount Whitney, the highest peak in the Sierra Nevada range, had been named. When still quite young, Roger, who was a doctor, had been killed in a mountaineering

13

accident. It was the first tragedy in the family that I was old enough to understand. Roger was a gentle soul, who had taken pains to get to know Daniel and me. He told us tales of his mountain adventures, and his smiling face and good humour brought us pleasure and warmth. We were deeply saddened by the news of his death. He had fallen down a deep crevasse, and died instantly.

Hassler was a nuclear scientist who had worked on the Manhattan Project. He was a gentle, somewhat distracted individual, who spoke with a lisp and dressed in an extremely forgetful manner − odd socks and undone shoelaces were quite usual − and his hair seldom saw a brush or comb. He married a very docile bohemian lady and, whilst travelling in Europe, their only luggage was an old knapsack. His patience was striking, and he was ready to help anyone over the smallest problem. I could never imagine him working on something so powerful and destructive as the atom bomb.

Bill himself was a kind, bespectacled man, so different in appearance from my glamorous father. Even in his late thirties when he married Mother, his hair was thinning. His looks were pleasant but unremarkable. He did have a great influence on me, though, and took his role of stepfather very seriously. I owe much to his tutelage, and however small or great the problem, he was always ready to help. He taught me how to peel an orange neatly, how to make lists, how to appreciate order, to know exactly where your possessions are, and thus avoid the constant delays we experienced whilst Mother and Daniel searched for keys and passports. He taught me at an early age the importance of listening to another person's point of view, a lesson that I did not always find easy to put into practice. Unfortunately there was a downside to his teachings, for he did instil fear, and made both Daniel and me overcautious, contemplating the risks rather than the delights of adventure. He was fanatical about health, too, and I am sure my hypochondriacal tendencies stem from observing his preoccupations with the minutest of symptoms. But I did admire his analytical mind, and he answered all my questions with patience and precision, albeit so slowly that my racing mind often wandered. He anchored me and tried to teach me to think in depth. He had read law at Yale, and, being interested in psychoanalysis, had studied Freud's interpretations of dreams. I often discussed my dreams with him, and his insights were intriguing. Little did I know in my childhood how important Freud would become in later life.

My schooling was very simple. I went first to Miss Betts' school in London. Here the punishment for talking in class was to lie under a desk in the corner of the room, which is where I frequently spent my time. No punishment seemed potent enough to stop me from talking. In the latter part of the war I went to Miss Hoten's school in Chiddingfold, Surrey. Mother and Bill had bought a house in Dunsfold. Miss Hoten ran a very small private school, to which Nanny and I bicycled four miles there and four miles back every day. I remember Miss Hoten smelt of potato crisps and she wore a greasy brown suede jacket. She was a good and patient teacher, always ready to help young enquiring minds. But the main event during my time there was the day I fell in the garden pond trying to catch tadpoles. It was a shock I shall never forget. Nanny had been summoned, and warm blankets provided. Above all I remember the shame of having done something so stupid.

My time at Miss H's was on the whole happy. Those days in the country with Nanny were, in spite of the war, very peaceful, and the daily routine very calming. Our house in Dunsfold was a little Elizabethan cottage called The Basket, and in the small garden there was an even smaller cottage called The Little Basket where guests stayed. Mother and Bill came at the weekends with many friends, and then the rhythm changed.

One of the guests was Alan Campbell, a charming American, whose face made me think of a facetious monkey. He always arrived in his army uniform. He was the man that the famous wit Dorothy Parker had married and divorced three times. He told us wonderful stories which he made up as he went along, leaving us with beating hearts till the next instalment.

It was in Dunsfold that we heard the doodlebugs with their frightening ticking sound, and their even more frightening silence before the deadly explosion. Each night Nanny and I counted the planes that went out from RAF Dunsfold, and in the morning we counted the returning aircraft, praying the numbers would tally.

A great many of Mother's friends had joined the RAF during the war, and they often used to come and stay when they were on leave. It was quite a romantic period, tinged, of course, with tragedy. How aware I was of this as a child I don't really remember, but I do remember the feeling of people determined to have a good time. And Mother was a person who supplied that in abundance.

I had learnt to read at Miss Hoten's. *Miss Fox's School* and *Black Beauty* were my first books, read and reread with untold pleasure and tears.

After the war, we returned to London and I went to a small school in Eaton Gate run by Lillian and Dorothea Mitford-Colmer. There were many children of diplomats there, children from many different countries: India, Pakistan, China, Japan, North and South America. It was an interesting, cosmopolitan mix. The teaching was sound if not spectacular, and the classes small. Dorothea taught arithmetic. She looked like a kindly witch, and used to lean over your shoulder with a permanent drip on the end of her nose. Lillian, the younger sister, taught geometry and they made their subjects very exciting. I longed to find out what 'x' meant, and geometric puzzles became as exciting and absorbing as a thriller. They taught us logic in a unique way, and this has stood me in good stead for my whole life. Other subjects were not taught so rewardingly. History ended with the death of Queen Victoria, and even today I am ashamed of my lack of knowledge of the two great wars of the twentieth century.

I stayed at Mitford-Colmer School until I was fifteen, taking my school certificate there and achieving good grades. I had of course a few periods away, once when I went to a school in New York, and another time when I had a governess there who tried to keep me abreast of my English syllabus.

There was also a short jaunt to a school in Lausanne. This only lasted one term. I was so homesick that Mother asked Dirk Bogarde to send me a card and a photograph of himself to cheer me up. Mother had met Dirk when she was in a revival of Noel Coward's *The Vortex*, starring Isobel Jeans. They became great friends, and Dirk was a frequent guest at her parties. He was the most delightful person to me in my youth. He treated me like a grown-up and was warm and giving, taking time to talk to me which meant a great deal. Once we went for the day to the country house that he shared with Tony Forwood, who had been married to Glynis Johns. We played endless parlour games, which all the adults seemed to enjoy very much. Laughter and pleasantries prevailed at these social gatherings. Serious conversation was not on the menu, although Dirk had a contemplative and darker side to his character, which his later writings reveal. He was also a very good painter. Mother bought one of his watercolours, an abstract of subtle hues, which she treasured till her death. Of course I developed a huge crush on him. When I met him again many years later, towards the end of his life, after Tony Forwood died, I found that he had become rather embittered and inclined to speak maliciously of people. I think he was unhappy; certain goals had not been attained, or perhaps some other grief plagued him. But my stock rose greatly at my boarding school when I received the photograph of him with his horse, warmly and thoughtfully inscribed.

However, my homesickness persisted, and after many, many letters and a very expensive telegram, I persuaded my mother to let me finish my schooling at the Mitford-Colmers'. Once again I was back with Nanny and nursery food.

CHAPTER 4

MOTHER LOVED TO MOVE AND AFTER THE WAR WE LEFT HILL
Street for a house round the corner in South Street, Mayfair. It
was a perfect little eighteenth-century house with exquisite
panelling and many small rooms. Nanny and I had to share a
bedroom and bathroom on the second floor. This was
constraining, and prevented me from developing any sense of
independence. I remained far too reliant on her.

The war was over. Ration cards were still needed and there
were severe food shortages, but with Mother there always seemed
to be a party feel in the air. She had friends everywhere and our
table was always laden with tasty treats. We were very, very lucky.
We even acquired one of the new television sets, but unfortunately the screen was so small that we had to place a magnifying
glass in front it, which distorted the picture.

In 1947 we all went to Sweden for a summer holiday.
Apparently the exchange rate had made this possible. We took
a ship to Gothenburg, and during the trip I was dreadfully seasick,
but not even those horrors could dim the excitement. We took
a train to Bstaad, a resort on the coast, where all the Swedish
tennis championships were held. The hotel was most comfortable and, after our wartime rations, the food was like attending
a permanent feast. The Earl and Countess of Athlone were fellow
guests and we used to take tea together. The Countess, Princess
Alice, was birdlike and dainty in her silk print dresses, with her

little handbag hanging on her arm, and the tall and gentle Earl always at her side. It was the first time we had met members of the Royal Family. They had only existed before in fairy tales. Nanny and I were overwhelmed, but their grace and charm soon beguiled us. They used to take their morning coffee just outside our bedroom window, which looked onto a courtyard. Nanny was so embarrassed by their proximity, that she was unable to go to the loo until they left.

During the war we had seen neither chocolate nor real ice cream, so the delicious patisseries we feasted upon in Bstaad held a special significance. Sitting on the dunes overlooking the sea, guzzling coffee cream and chocolate fudge cakes was a very different experience from eating Lord Woolton's meat pies and watery ice cream made by Nanny from powdered milk.

The years spent in South Street were probably the most informative of my life. I was installed at Mitford–Colmer School and did well there. I often came top of my class, but it was a struggle and made me nervous. The competitive seed was being sewn. Rivalry can be stimulating for the confident, but if you lack that assurance, the feeling that you have to excel in every-thing takes away the joy of learning, and knowledge becomes a burden. If I ran a school I would abandon the marking system for young pupils, remembering the maxim 'a child's mind is a fire to be kindled not a vessel to be filled'. Not only was the competitive spirit nurtured at school, but my mother and Bill also encouraged it between Daniel and me. This was something that led to much heartache later in life. During this time Daniel was only at home for the holidays, and there was little time for bonding. Nevertheless I looked up to him, and all my life I craved his approval. Habits formed when you are ten years old are very hard to break.

Life at South Street was very social, I remember. The house was a magnet to the world of post-war show business. Hugh Beaumont was a frequent visitor. He ran HM Tennent Ltd, the enormously successful theatre production company. His friends always called him Binkie. One night, after returning from the dining room where she had been serving at table, Nanny announced that she had accidentally nudged her arm against Binkie, and that he was wearing a corset. Nanny was quite surprised by this and, looking back, it was also puzzling to me, and added to the list of painful questions which went unanswered until much later when analysis would help me to unravel them.

Other guests at South Street were the famous Australian ballet dancer, Robert Helpman, and Norman Hartnell, the Queen's dress designer. He was a big bear of a man, with frizzy hair and a high-pitched drawl. He made several pastel, tulled and sequined ball gowns for Mother, which I personally found too busy. The composer and actor Ivor Novello was a favourite guest. He was a gentle man with romantic, dark good looks. His musicals of course were sweet and sentimental, with songs like 'We'll Gather Lilacs in the Spring Again' becoming great hits with the public. He also composed the famous World War One song 'Keep the Home Fires Burning', which over the years must have earned him a fortune. He still looked very youthful in the late forties, surrounded by an adoring entourage. We often went to stay with him in Englefield Green. It was a cosy house enclosed by an enormous wall, which was perfect for Ivor as he was a sun-worshipper, and used to sit by his small swimming pool scantily clad, catching the sun's rays even if they appeared only momentarily from behind clouds. His gentleness and good humour warmed everyone around him. He was not in the least bitchy or ironic, and was extremely supportive of all his friends. I always felt relaxed and happy in his company, and called him Uncle Ivor.

Lynn Fontanne and Alfred Lunt took a house nearby one year when they were in London to appear in Noel Coward's *Quadrille*. They were a devoted couple, whom everyone treated like royalty.

But in their own home they behaved like a very comfortable domestic pair. Alfred did all the shopping and cooking, whilst Lynne lay down and relaxed. She appeared ageless and sported a tremendous set of false eyelashes. I remember how Alfred told Mother that he had found a wonderful little food shop, which she was to keep a secret. It was called Harrods.

Another famous visitor at this time was my godfather, John Ford. He came to see us in the late forties, which was the first time I had ever met him. When I was born, Raymond was filming *Hurricane*, directed by Ford in Hollywood, and he had learned of my birth whilst he was on the set. My father turned to the first person he saw on hearing the news, and that person happened to be John Ford. He asked him to be my godfather, and Ford accepted. I had to wait quite a few years before I met the great director, but what a charming man he was. He looked rather like a larger, softer version of Popeye, his creased face folded round his pipe. He had the most kindly yet penetrating gaze, and I immediately felt in some way 'related' to him. He made the role of godfather seem special. He gave me a photo-graph of himself. In it he was dressed in naval uniform, wearing his famous eyepatch. It was in the most beautiful silver frame inscribed warmly to his goddaughter. (Many years later he was to give me another present, the role of Jack Hawkins' daughter in his film *Gideon's Day*. But I will talk of this episode in a later chapter.) His wife was delightful too. She had raven hair and was swathed in the most luxurious alpaca coat. They both exuded warmth, and I felt at once that they were a caring couple, utterly ungrand and devoted to their family.

My father once told us a fascinating story of the time when he was filming *Hurricane*. The climax of the movie was the hurri-cane, and, whilst the great storm raged, there was an interior scene round the dining-room table, with numerous shots of everyone reacting to the havoc that was taking place outside. This scene was filmed early on in the shoot. Later when the

whole movie was assembled, it was clear that everyone had dras-
tically underplayed their reactions, imagining gentle rainfall
instead of the mighty heavens opening, and so the whole
sequence had to be shot again. Even great masters sometimes
get it wrong.

Once, I remember, Father and Dorothy came down to our
cottage in Dunsfold for the day and a tense time it was, with
everyone on their best behaviour. I somehow felt that I was
'acting' the daughter for him. There was an unreal feeling when
we were together. Although I had never met John Ford before,
my short relationship with him felt far more rooted and simple.
With my father, so many emotions were drifting in the air —
guilt, love, and a certain sadness, a sense of profound loss maybe.
That day they had given Nanny and me a lift back to London
in their sleek chauffeur-driven car. I was only used to rather
ramshackle vehicles, and the smoothness of Father's limousine
made me feel very car sick, but I was too frightened to say
anything, and just survived until I reached home.

Father was an extremely elegant man and exuded the afflu-
ence of subtle chic, certainly compared to Bill, who was not the
snazziest of dressers. I used to feel that Father and Dorothy's life
was far more glamorous than our life in England. Of course I
was wrong, as I later found out. They shared an extremely
secluded existence with very few friends. Dorothy, the ex-lawyer,
when dealing with Father's film contracts, had become most
unpopular, demanding chairs on the set and refusing to remain
in the background. This had not encouraged lasting friendships.
Why Father tolerated such behaviour, I do not know. Dorothy
was always right in his eyes.

We were now in the late forties, but there was a feel of the
thirties in the air whenever my father was around. Men still
wore flared trousers with turn-ups, waistcoats, and large felt hats.
Fashion for men took longer to change after the war.

On the other hand, my mother was one of the first to purchase a New Look suit by Dior. The skirts were full and long, profiting from new supplies of cloth. The jackets were tailored at the waist, and most women wore undergarments that nipped in their waistlines to accentuate the wasp-like effect, chic but very uncomfortable.

My mother came to collect me from school one day, sporting the new Dior suit and wearing a pink hat decorated with red and purple cabbage roses. As I returned from the Brownies in a crocodile, I heard the girl behind me say, 'What does that woman think she looks like?' I was so ashamed. All the young want to do is to conform, and here was someone flaunting something original, even if a little gaudy. The girl who had spoken out in the crocodile was Marika Hopkinson, who later became the famous cookery writer, Marika Hanbury Tennison. I am sure she never knew what consternation she had caused me. I certainly never told her.

For Bill, Mother could do no wrong. He doted upon her. He never criticised her dress sense. Perhaps he knew it would be a waste of time.

My wilful mother really ruled our lives. Bill was a kind, uncritical consort. I once heard him argue an antitrust law case in a New York court, and was impressed by his remarkable precision and debating powers. Answering my questions he was more long-winded. He had phenomenal patience, which, alas, he did not pass on to me. However, I was so fortunate to have been guided by him, for Nanny of course could not cope with intellectual demands at all.

I remember once being given a holiday assignment from school. This was to read an abridged version of Dickens' *The Pickwick Papers*. Nanny went through the text with me. When I returned for the autumn term we were tested on all the verbs, Dickens being a great and imaginative user of verbs. I failed miserably. Where Dickens had written 'remonstrated', Nanny had substituted 'said'. All the words that she did not comprehend she had changed to something simple. Naturally I never blamed her nor was cross with her. I loved her without reserve and understood her. But I often felt frustrated and insecure at school. The teachers tried to calm and guide me towards confidence, but there was really no one I could turn to. Not even Bill could cope with these insecurities.

All my life I've suffered from a lack of confidence. I speak of an inner confidence that can only be nurtured and encouraged in very early life. To be secure within myself proved to be an unattainable goal. The world in which I lived was hectic, and the people in it largely self-involved. Nanny of course was quite the opposite, but she did not have the knowledge to assuage the deeper fears and neuroses that were developing in me. She coped with our daily needs and comforts supremely, but anything of a darker nature she shunned, simply shutting the door. So I developed ways of coping with my 'demons' myself, but of course there would come a time when I had to seek professional help. For the time being I was a nervy, passionate eleven-year-old, at times driving the household mad. My school reports were on the whole good, but often expressed concern about my lack of confidence, and one particular report even admonished me for becoming overexcited at netball.

There were distractions and treats of course. I had learned to enjoy travel without Nanny. Mother and Bill took us on a trip to Germany. Bill's cousin, General Noce, was based in Heidelberg after the war, one of the generals in charge of US High Command. He had a very comfortable large house situated in woods outside that romantic university city. He also had the use of the train used by Goering during the war, equipped with every possible comfort and luxury, including gold taps in the bathroom. We travelled all over Germany in this train. Many of the cities and towns we passed through were still in ruins. The rebuilding programme was only just beginning. In Munich we went to see Mozart's *The Magic Flute*, the first opera that I ever saw, and I remember thinking that it was like a sumptuous pantomime. After the opera we returned to our very own private train, moving off the following morning to Garmisch. I remember seeing the shell of Hitler's house in Berchtesgaden. It was hard to imagine evil in such a breathtaking landscape. A profound depression descended on our little group that day.

To lift our spirits a trip was planned to Salzburg, where we visited Mozart's house. I was struck by the smallness of everything. His desk appeared to be that of a child, exquisite but minute. After the grandeur of *The Magic Flute*, it was like visiting a doll's house.

From then on I went on journeys whenever Mother and Bill invited me. My appetite had been whetted. Florence was the next treat. Hours were spent on the Ponte Vecchio gazing at the little shops, and even more hours in the Uffizi Gallery and the Pitti Palace, where I could have spent the whole of the holiday. Even wandering around with forty-nine painful mosquito bites could not diminish the pleasure. We visited the famous historian, Harold Acton, who lived with his parents in La Pietra, the magnificent villa on the outskirts of Florence, set in very formal gardens. His father was rather a stern tweed-suited Englishman and his mother a small, grey-haired, birdlike American. They seemed unlikely parents for Harold, who was a rare individual. He fascinated me. His looks were slightly oriental. He was an expert in Chinese, spoke the most precise, rather affected English, and talked brilliantly of all the treasures and sights we were visiting, enriching the whole experience.

We also visited Bernard Berenson, the great American art critic, in Vallambrosa. He was old and frail, wrapped in many blankets, and confined to a wheelchair. But a great mystique surrounded him. The view from his terrace took your breath away, Tuscany spread out before you. We spent the whole visit outside taking tea and never entered the villa. His secretary bustled around exuding warmth and energy, serving us delicacies, whilst Mr Berenson remained somewhat aloof in his multi-layered woollen cocoon. Daniel and I stood outside the circle of guests, looking over the Florentine landscape, eating miniature Florentine biscuits: I have always regretted that a small shower had not fallen from the heavens, then perhaps we would have been invited inside to see his formidable collection, but that was not to be.

These journeys formed part of my education in a quite original way, feeding my imagination, and allowing privileged insights into other private worlds. I am eternally grateful to Mother and Bill for their generosity in letting me join them on their travels.

CHAPTER 5

ONE OF THE MANY PLEASURES AS A YOUNG CHILD WAS DRESSING up in my mother's clothes. She had an extensive wardrobe which she always bedecked with real and costume jewellery. I never understood why she did this. Her maxim was always 'More is beautiful'. Anyway, she never minded my rummaging through her cupboards and parading myself in front of her mirrored doors playing little scenes to myself. Sometimes these playlets would be performed whilst Mother was having a massage. She and Mrs Mac, the masseuse, were a good audience. In-between the scenes, I would quiz Mother about the guests she'd entertained the night before. I had counted the wine glasses in the drawing room, and if the numbers didn't tally, poor Mother had to rack her brains to supply the name of the missing guest. Detective work has always intrigued me. It is of course a vital part of acting; searching for all possible clues to your character.

Another small example of my prowess in detection took place in Harrods. In December of each year Nanny took me to the children's department on the fourth floor to visit Father Christmas to proffer my usual list of cravings. These secrets were whispered to the white-bearded old man whilst seated upon his knee. One March day after two or three years of these Yuletide visits, Nanny took me to the soft materials department on the ground floor, and whilst she was making some purchase and chatting to the gentleman who was serving her, I said quite loudly, 'You are Father Christmas.' The gentleman, who had brown hair and sported neither white beard nor whiskers, was taken aback. He said that each year he was indeed Father Christmas on the fourth floor, but that never before in all the twenty years that he had been performing this role had he been recognised in the store during the other eleven months. I had quite simply remembered his voice. Thus my dreams of Father Christmas were shattered, but my skills as a budding Miss Marple were much enhanced.

As I paraded in Mother's high-heeled shoes, flaunting her satins and tweeds, I never questioned her dress sense. It took me many years to find my own style. The 'Body Image' is a vital part of everyone's life, but Mother had superimposed her own taste onto me, and I was too young and insecure to resist. Many years later I broke free, and 'Less is more' became my personal maxim. In later years Mother always hated my taste, and this was the cause of much tension between us.

I am sure the little scenes I explored in those days sewed the seeds of acting as a career, at least superficially. The content of the scenes was not as important to me as the visual aspect. I had no idea of the enormous demands real acting presents. My mother's career was on the whole in boulevard, popular theatre. But in the war she did make a great success in Terence Rattigan's *Flare Path*, in which she played a cockney barmaid. I had been allowed to sit in the fireplace on stage, hidden from the audience, to watch the play unfold. It was a fascinating experience for a five-year-old.

Dressing-room life was important to Mother. After each performance there were always visitors who were offered tea or drinks, and I sometimes wondered if for her this was perhaps the most important and enjoyable part of the enterprise. Much later on I went on tour with her, acting as her dresser. She knew people in each city or town, and friends flocked to her dressing room, where she played the perfect hostess.

Mother was always fun to be with. She found it easy to raise people's spirits. I think she had learned this from her father, 'Champagne Charlie'. Following his example, at an early age we were allowed, and indeed encouraged, to drink a little wine. Before I was four years old I was given a pewter and crystal sherry glass, not much bigger than an acorn cup. Once, my sherry had been watered down, and I announced (unable then to pronounce 'w's and substituting 'm's), 'There's mortar in my mine'.

Despite Mother's generosity, sadly I never got close to her, and we never shared our inner thoughts and feelings. From these she ran away in fear, to the theatre, her friends and her social whirl. She shunned the world of analysis, and considered that people only went to psychiatrists because they had 'bored their friends to death'. I never could change her mind on this subject. Mother was too rigid in her preconceptions. This is even stranger when you consider that Bill was an avid follower of Freud. But he never tried to influence her. By the time that both Daniel and I were in analysis, Bill had died, and our would-be defendant was not around.

But the fun side of Mother was powerful. She was a crossword addict, and taught me to enjoy them at an early age. We were driving in a car once returning from a seaside holiday, and Mother was trying to solve a particularly difficult clue. 'I wish I had the Morse code,' she said. 'I have it in my little case,' I replied, and produced it at once. I was a Girl Guide at the time, and took the maxim 'Be Prepared' very seriously. I only wish the Morse code had solved the clue, but, alas, it didn't.

In the late forties we spent some months in the States. Bill's work had taken him there, and the family followed. Daniel went to boarding school at Eaglebrook, where he learnt to ski with great panache, but I fear not much else. I went to a small private school in New York where my studies were equally unsuccessful. The English and American systems were not very compatible, which is why on a subsequent visit it was decided that I should have a governess who would follow the English syllabus.

During this visit, Nanny, Daniel and I spent a long weekend with Father and Dorothy at their house in Connecticut. By this time Father had become a naturalised American, having given up his Canadian citizenship.

Their house was called Honey Hill Farm. It was big and roomy, decorated in dark reds and greens and full of Father's theatrical memorabilia. The dark colours struck me as a great contrast to Mother's light blues and pinks and early English china. Both families had professionally decorated houses that personally I dislike. For me houses should simply evolve representing the essence of the owner.

At Honey Hill Farm, photographs in heavy glass and silver frames reminiscent of the thirties were displayed in every room. There were several pictures of Father dressed in his Abraham Lincoln costume. Because of his striking resemblance to the great President, Father had played him both on stage and in the film *Abe Lincoln at Illinois*. The character had for a while, I believe, taken him over. Photographs of Father as the wicked Chauvelin in *The Scarlet Pimpernel* were also on display, one with his great friend Nigel Bruce, who had played the Prince of Wales in the film. Father adored Nigel, or Willie, as he was affectionately known to his friends. He used to make Father laugh by referring to the ballet, 'as a lot of buggers jumping'.

There were also many pictures of Gregory Peck, who Father said was his closest friend. The large white dog, Bunga, that bounded around at Honey Hill was a gift from him. I once had dinner many years later with Father and Mr Peck in London. He was extremely charming and rather formal and talked about the world and life and not about himself. I found this very refreshing. He had the most courteous manners, though he seemed to lack an easy sense of humour. Father did have a sense of fun in him, but often managed to conceal it, particularly when Dorothy was present. Sadly Mr Peck shared Father's political beliefs, and in the seventies both of them had supported the extreme right-wing Republican, Barry Goldwater. This saddened me greatly. I tried to avoid all political discussions with Father. We would have got nowhere.

Father had a carpentry room at Honey Hill Farm. This was not just for display. He found great pleasure in designing pieces of furniture. He made a little bench for me that I have to this day. It is perfectly constructed, and ideal for putting our feet on whilst watching television.

This visit with Father and Dorothy was perhaps the most relaxed time we ever spent with them. We watched a lot of Father's old films, such as *A Matter of Life and Death*, titled *Stairway to Heaven* in the States, as the word 'death' was banned for commercial reasons. Michael Powell, the director of the film, was a great friend of Father's, and perhaps this was one of the reasons why early on in my career he cast me in his now renowned film *Peeping Tom*.

Father was very much the actor. He was amazingly self-involved, but in a rather naïve way. There is a tale that illustrates this perfectly. He had three children, Geoffrey, Daniel and myself. All of us, regardless of sex, have Raymond as our middle name. My mother apparently had fought for my second name to be Lee, but she failed. Anna was the name of his mother, so that was chosen automatically, but Raymond had to follow even though I was his first and only daughter. The egos in both families were quite pronounced, and I know that I can behave extremely egocentrically at times. I was taught by masters.

Later during this same trip to the States we went to stay with Father and Dorothy at Ponte Vedra in Florida, at the time a well-known golfing resort. The tensions during this visit were fierce.

Geoffrey, our half-brother, was with us as well, and he, Daniel
and Father played golf every day. Nanny and I once followed
them round the course. By the twelfth hole the mood of the
players was so dark that the game was abandoned. The three of
them stalked off in a rage. Nanny and I completed the course,
without clubs, naturally, mesmerised by the crocodiles that swam
in the many watery hazards waiting to catch wayward golf balls.

Dorothy did nothing to smooth things over later that evening.
She revelled in the awkward atmosphere. She was frantically
jealous of anyone or anything that could lure Father away from
her, and so she embraced all disharmony. She would have been
ideal casting for the wicked witch. One of her habits was to
intercept our letters to him. This was how desperate she had
become. Of course such jealousy always breeds disaster. In his
later years Father did meet a very charming lady. We got to
know her slightly, and she was warm and generous to us. But
Dorothy found out and Father went running back terrified.
He asked us to keep in touch with his mistress, which we did
over a long period. He was really heartbroken by this affair,
but Dorothy's hold over him was phenomenal. He was a weak
man, and he was sentimental, a dangerous combination. The
power of the weak is often more persuasive than the more
overt demands of the strong; and the battles that he and Dorothy
fought out with each other must have been painful experiences. Thankfully we were not a permanent part of their household. Nevertheless divorce, drama and infidelity were woven
into the fabric of our family life, and they were disturbing
influences.

It was soon after this visit to Florida that Father and Dorothy
sold Honey Hill Farm and moved to Los Angeles where they
were to remain for the rest of their lives. So Dorothy became
The Wicked Witch of the West, and Father started on his long
stint as Dr Gillespie in the *Dr Kildare* series.

★   ★   ★

During this New York stay Mother of course did her usual amount of entertaining. I met some very fascinating personalities. One of the most intriguing was George S. Kaufman, the famous writer who had collaborated with Moss Hart. Both these witty, comic giants were frequent guests at Mother's table. They could not have been more different. George was morose and rather lugubrious. He looked permanently sad with his hangdog face. He always wore the most beautiful mohair jackets that I used to love to touch. At this time he was courting Leueen McGrath, the Irish actress who had appeared with Mother in Rattigan's *Flare Path*. They were to marry. But even this happy event in his life didn't seem to cheer him up. He continued to carry the cares of the world on his interesting crumpled face. Shortly after their marriage, Leueen started to speak with a strong American accent, which always amused me. Moss Hart, in contrast, was ebullient and warm. George and he had written some of the most famous comedies together since the thirties such as *You Can't Take It With You* and *The Man Who Came To Dinner*. I suspect Moss provided the perfect antidote to George's gloom. Moss Hart was married to the actress and vocalist Kitty Carlyle. She was a vibrant and compelling person. They entertained very lavishly in their spectacular Upper East Side apartment. Kitty always dressed in very grand ball gowns, with masses of make-up, and I think Moss might have worn a little make-up too. But they were the most welcoming hosts. The New York theatre world thronged to their gatherings: Mary Martin, David Niven, Edna Ferber, the author, and any luminaries who happened to be in town at the time. I seemed to stand amidst a whirl of satin and velvet, false and real diamonds and fearsomely energetic banter. It was quite a circus to find myself in. The room was full of egos, many of whom wrote their own notices as they shook your hand. But Moss and Kitty took time to talk to me, a visiting English schoolgirl barely in her teens. I was very touched by this. Many years later Kitty Carlyle persuaded her husband to write his autobiography. *Act One* by Moss Hart is a little gem. I treasure it to this day.

We returned to London after this New York stay in one of Howard Hughes' TWA constellations. After stopping at Gander, Newfoundland, we took the trip across the Atlantic to Shannon in extremely comfortable bunk beds, donning our nightclothes, pulling our curtains, and sleeping peacefully for the ten-hour flight. But unfortunately we had to make an emergency landing. The light on the control panel failed to confirm that the undercarriage was locked in position, so the pilot jettisoned most of the remaining fuel over the Shannon Estuary, and prepared to make a crash landing. We could see fire engines and ambulances waiting for us on the runway. As though this was not dramatic enough, Danny Kaye, who was on the flight, decided to entertain everyone by walking up and down the aisle making jokes. We were a most unappreciative audience, almost everyone either being ill, or quite simply terrified. At last we made our descent. The plane skidded and there was a great deal of noise, but there were no casualties. Apparently the light on the panel was at fault, and the undercarriage had been in place all along. The experience was one that took some time to forget.

It was not long, though, before we crossed the Atlantic again. Mother and Bill had rented a wonderful apartment at 270 Park Avenue. It was right by Grand Central Station, and the apartments were built round a courtyard, which meant they were very quiet, which is unusual for New York. Mother painted all the rooms in different colours, bright greens and mauves, yellows and shocking pink, revelling in the creation of a genuinely startling environment where she would entertain lavishly and frequently. The great Alexander Wolcott, who had ruled at the famous round table at the Algonquin Hotel, had once befriended

Mother, and many of the members of that unique set still kept in touch. Those who were still alive came to her parties during this visit, Dorothy Parker being of course the most celebrated. She was petite and dark with an urchin haircut, and at that time bent her elbow rather too frequently, but there was always a friend in tow to take care of her, and to see that she got home safely. It was strange to know that blistering wit and irony came from this, in some ways, childlike figure. Edna Ferber was another round-table member, who had been a friend of Mother's since her divorce. She was a powerful person, about five feet tall, with a golden heart. She gave me my first handbag, and I used to love her forthright statements about the world and the way she included me in her conversation, always sensitive to the frailties of an adolescent. The beaver coat that she nearly always wore reached her diminutive ankles, and bon mots dripped from her lips. One of her most famous quotes was, 'Writers should be read and not seen, for they are rarely a winsome sight.' She was well aware of her plain looks, but used this knowledge with wit and fortitude. She had won the Pulitzer Prize for her novel *So Big* in 1924, and *Giant*, published in 1952, was one of my favourite teenage reads.

Other guests at 270 were the Gish sisters, Dorothy and Lillian, exquisite doll-like creatures, who captivated us all with their charm and gentleness. They were known as The Girls. Fame had not gone to their heads. They talked softly, and were interested in everyone around them. They always came to Mother's parties together, dressed almost identically in printed chiffon dresses, and seemed to be a great support to each other. Lillian was the more beautiful, but Dorothy's manner was most appealing.

Another guest was the actress Constance Collier. She used to coach Katharine Hepburn for many of her stage appearances. It was fascinating to hear Constance talk of the theatre. She told me how demanding a profession it was, and how much study and research each role needed, and how the journey towards creating a character had to be charted with infinite detail. She warned me of the many hazards, but I was probably too young to pay proper heed. Towards the end of her life she was nearly blind, and one day she took me to a matinée. Just before the curtain rose, she whispered in my ear, 'Isn't the set dreadful?' I thought it wisest to agree with her.

Richard Rodgers, the composer, and his lyricist, Oscar Hammerstein, were often around at Mother's gatherings. They came with their wives. Dorothy Rodgers was neat and petite, always sporting a velvet bow in her hair. She frequently brought her tapestry to work on during the parties. I think it must have calmed her, for she had a rather nervous disposition. I didn't get to know Dick Rodgers very well, but Oscar we saw much more of, and I found him a charming, gentle, shy man, and I always felt that he would rather have been somewhere else. We once visited him at his country home in Pennsylvania, and in this environment he seemed to blossom, surrounded by his family. His wife too was called Dorothy, but she could not have been more different from Dorothy Rodgers. Dorothy Hammerstein was Australian, and one of the warmest women that I have ever met. She adored the social life, and she and Mother remained friends until her death. She left Mother the most generous legacy. Mary Martin, the star of Dick and Oscar's *South Pacific*, was also a good friend of Mother's. She would come to the apartment with her husband Richard Halliday and their daughter Heller, and her son by an earlier marriage, Larry Hagman, who later became the famous JR in *Dallas*. She was at the time the toast of New York, but her two dainty feet remained firmly on the ground, and success certainly never seemed to go to her short curly head, as each night she sang that she was 'going to wash that man right out of her hair'.

On this particular New York trip I had a governess, who valiantly tried to keep me abreast with my English syllabus. For French, though, it was decided that I should have a proper French teacher, Madame Muscanto, who also taught at a private school in New York. One day she decided to introduce me to one of her pupils from this school, as she thought I needed friends of my own age. She was absolutely right. The company I was keeping was rather too exotic for a thirteen-year-old. This was how I came to meet Kate Whitney, who was to become my very closest friend. Kate was the daughter of James Roosevelt, and the granddaughter of Franklin and Eleanor Roosevelt. Her mother, Betsey Cushing, was now married to John Hay Whitney, the philanthropist, venture capitalist and publisher. They owned the most beautiful estate on Long Island called Greentree, where they went most weekends, and very often I was asked to join them. The mansion was vast and set in secluded grounds in Manhasset. It was built in the colonial style with a large and welcoming portico. But Kate's mother Betsey had that rare gift of making this mansion as cosy as any house that I have ever been to. There were many, many rooms decorated with immaculate taste. On the walls were some of the greatest paintings in the world. Van Gogh and Gauguin self-portraits hung in the same room. This could all have been overwhelming and daunting to an English teenager. But everyone was made to feel utterly at ease. Betsey spoke more gently and quietly than most people. She was extremely witty, but you had to be alert to catch her humorous and pithy observations, as they were uttered with the delicacy of a butterfly. Kate and I had our dinner separately, but at lunch the family and all the guests sat at a large round table, and shared a sumptuous feast. There were indoor and outdoor tennis courts, and indoor and outdoor swimming pools. We even watched the latest movies in their private cinema. I think these weekends were some of the happiest times of my life, not because of the grandeur of the setting, but because Betsey, Jock, Kate and her elder sister Sara were so warm and welcoming. Sara was a little older than we were, and I was slightly in awe of her sophistication. We laughed a lot and played word games, and it was a treat to leave the bustle of New York City. All through the years I have kept in touch with Kate and all her family. We have seen each other through the good times and the bad. I am also pleased that her three daughters, Laura, Andrea and Camilla have also become my friends. Kate and her family have given me great strength at moments in my life. Friendship of this depth is rare and precious.

Jock Whitney was one of the twentieth century's great philanthropists. The John Hay Whitney Foundation supported the development of promising leaders, most of them from groups excluded from the mainstream of American life, and their grants assisted disadvantaged groups to achieve social and economic justice. When Jock died in 1982, Betsey organised the Greentree Foundation. Sara, Kate and Kate's partner, Frank Thomas, were also very involved in the creation of this foundation, which is the current manifestation of the family's long-standing philanthropic impulse. Greentree has become the centre for international meetings devoted to the furthering of peace and human rights, and, since 2000, the United Nations and other organisations dedicated to these issues have been meeting there.

When Betsey died in 1998, many of the great Impressionist and post-Impressionist paintings that hung on the walls at Greentree were donated to the National Art Gallery, the Museum of Modern Art and the Yale University Art Gallery. It is warming and rare that a family has shared its wealth with their country in this way. Greentree had given such pleasure to us all, and now, thanks to this unique family, it continues to nurture mankind.

When I returned to England after this New York sojourn, I missed the buzz of the life there. It was 1951 and I was back in the old routine at Mitford–Colmer School, trying each week to be top of my form, and of course still clinging to Nanny for emotional stability. London might have been less hectic and less glamorous than New York, but my insecurities still clung to me even in this quieter atmosphere.

CHAPTER 6

IN 1952 WE MOVED TO A BEAUTIFUL CAROLEAN HOUSE IN Highgate, No. 2 The Grove. Samuel Taylor Coleridge had once lodged at No. 3. In fact it was the house where he was lodging when he died. All the houses in The Grove had been built for the mistresses of the court of Charles II. The Great Fire of London and the Plague had persuaded the courtiers to find fresher, healthier surroundings for their loved ones.

No. 2 was a magnificent house with all the original oak panelling and exquisite fireplaces. Mother and Bill bought it for £6,000. She later sold it to Yehudi Menuhin, who in turn sold it to Sting and Trudie Styler. It had an enormous garden overlooking Kenwood, and was a true paradise. Alas, Mother got to work on it and much of the panelling was painted. The library walls became Adam green, and my bedroom was transformed in blue and white. No one could stop her doing this, but even though my room no longer had the original panelling, it was at least now my own room. I no longer had to share with Nanny.

There was a little conservatory overlooking the garden, and Oliver Messel, a close friend of Mother's, was commissioned to do the murals. So we sat in a very theatrical setting of flowers and grapes and balustrades, and a tiny portrait of our Siamese cat, Foxy, stared out at us from a corner. On one of the walls there was a large mirror, perfect for some of the guests to preen themselves in.

At The Grove Mother gave many, many parties. It was a perfect house for entertaining, and she made full use of its charms. Here politicians, actors, members of the legal profession and all her friends of old thronged. How Bill tolerated it all surprised me. He was a quiet man. I had many meals in the kitchen with Nanny and Millie, our cook, as I could not face the endless gatherings, particularly as I was studying for my O levels, and needed to concentrate.

Millie had started out in our household as a maid. It might sound very grand talking of maids and cooks, but in those days wages were very small and everyone who worked for Mother became part of the family. It didn't feel grand at all. At The Grove Millie took on the role of cook, and she excelled in the kitchen. She and Mother invented recipes together. Around this time Mother and a friend of hers called Marjorie Salter co-wrote a cookery book. It was called *Food for Thought*. Many of the recipes were Millie's invention. Noel Coward wrote the foreword and Oliver Messel did the illustrations. Mother's friends were always loyal to her. The recipes were rich and delicious, Manhattan pudding being my favourite. It was an upmarket ice cream with frozen orange juice and walnuts blended together with cream in a most magical way. No one thought of cholesterol in those days.

Two of the guests who I did enjoy meeting at this time were Rebecca West and her husband, Henry Andrews. Bill had met Rebecca after the war at the Nuremburg trials where he was part of the American legal team and Rebecca was reporting and researching. I had been told of her formidable mind, and expected someone with a gigantic head to walk through the door. In fact she was a stout woman with a perfectly normal head. I never spoke to her other than the formal greetings and social niceties. I think I was too in awe. After 'Would you like some more fruit salad?' I just dried up. But her husband was charming, and he once sent me a case of ginger beer in beautiful stone china bottles.

Not long after our move to Highgate, it was decided that I should go to school in Switzerland and finish my studies there before taking my O levels. I have already said how desperately unhappy I was at this school. It was called Brillamont, and was situated in its own beautiful grounds above Lausanne. We had to speak French all the time, and as most pupils' knowledge of the language was as poor as my own, everyone resorted to a kind of Franglais. I made very little progress with the language during the three months that I was there, and it was practically impossible to keep up with my English school certificate syllabus. I missed the discipline of Mitford-Colmers.

But the three months at Brillamont were educative in other ways, and not without drama. I shared a dormitory with two American girls, called Liesel and Jody. I felt very much the third party, and yearned to be included. They had become best friends and were quite a formidable pair. Jody was a tall blonde girl, extremely neurotic, who gnashed her teeth at night so loudly that it woke us up. Liesel was small and stocky with raven black hair cut extremely short, and brown eyes the size of saucers. Of the two she was the most sympathetic.

Chocolate was a very precious commodity at the time, given the paucity of our pocket money. A great deal of thieving went on, and our chocolate ration had to be carefully and craftily hidden. I enlisted Liesel and Jody to help me secure a safe place in my cupboard with a series of keys hidden in special places. Imagine my astonishment when one afternoon I returned to our dormitory to find Jody helping herself to my hard-earned chocolates. She said quite calmly, *J'étais stealing de vous.'* She showed no guilt whatever. I was horrified and completely thrown by this event. There was no one that I could turn to. So I wrote yet another letter home, followed by a telegram, begging them to let me finish my schooling in London.

However, one good thing did come out of my Brillamont days. I had been woefully ill-prepared before setting off to a boarding school, and knew absolutely nothing of the facts of life. I suspect everyone at home had been too embarrassed to broach the subject. Anyway, one evening a group had gathered together in our dormitory, Jody and Liesel of course, and some Italian girls, all of whom were well aware of all matters sexual. The question being asked was, 'Have you ever been to bed with a man?' One of the Italian girls had, and was consequently much revered. In those days such precocity as this was rare for a fifteen-year-old girl. My own reply to the question was, 'Yes I have.'

'Who with?' they asked.

'My brother,' I replied.

'What did he do?' they asked.

'He snored,' I said.

Much laughter ensued. I had clearly not been deflowered. I had simply shared a twin-bedded room with my brother Daniel for one night on our way to the South of France.

They now explained to me very gently and very carefully the facts of life and how we all came into the world. I was rather shocked at the time, and thought privately that my mother would never have let my father do THAT. But looking back on that night, they told me everything with great warmth and tenderness, and probably with far more ease than my mother would have mustered.

Nevertheless the shock was profound. My periods ceased for some months, and medical advice had to be sought. Everything eventually settled down and my adolescence proceeded more peacefully.

Brillamont was a very formal place, and there were no teachers with whom you could discuss your problems or share your thoughts. It was more like a university, where you were left to your own devices for much of the time. This worked for some pupils, but I wasn't ready for such independence, and required more nurturing. Nanny and the nursery had left their mark. Finally my pleas to abandon Brillamont were successful, and that autumn I resumed my studies in London. The relief was enormous.

We now of course lived in Highgate, and the Mitford-Colmers' school was in Eaton Gate off Sloane Square. So every day I took the 137 bus there and back, one-and-a-half hours each way. But that journey was worth any suffering, anything to be away from Brillamont. I felt safe again, or relatively safe as my O levels were fast approaching. I had never found lessons easy, and was not a natural student. To gain good grades I had to struggle. Each night we had at least one-and-a-half hours' homework to prepare for the following day. So it was a stressful time, but I locked myself away in my room and worked while the social life in the house roared on around me.

I took my school certificate in the first year of O levels. The matriculation system had just been abolished. I achieved good grades in the mathematics papers, which was the subject I most enjoyed. At this stage of mathematics there were few choices; the answer was either right or wrong. In other subjects it was harder to know how you'd fared. Apart from certain facts, you depended on the personal criticisms of the teacher or adjudicator. I did all right in history, geography, French and English grammar, but just scraped through English literature. Here my insecurities prevented me from letting my imagination fly.

After these exams, Mother and Bill took me to Majorca as a treat. Here I unwound and swam from a pine-clad beach. I have always had a special feeling for this island that soothed me after the rigours of my schooling. Gentle mountains bathed by the softest light surrounded the bay where we swam. I have returned there often when in need of tranquillity. The sea has a particular magic that enables you to swim far out with no fears. That summer I ate paella for the first time, and Bill taught me to dance on the moonlit terrace. All this seemed so very far away from the stresses of coming top of the form or getting ten out of ten.

My schooling, however, was not deemed over. I was to be 'finished off' in Paris and Rome. Further education of a serious kind was not considered for me. From a very early age it had always been assumed that I would join the acting profession. College and university were not on the agenda. My education had not been geared for that, and I think my lack of confidence would have prevented me from obtaining a place at a university even if I had continued my studies. In the early fifties it was, I believe, mainly the bluestocking academic girls who went on to the universities.

Thomas Carlyle said, 'The true university is a good collection of books.' With the guidance of good friends, I must say that books have been the university of my life.

My European studies started in Paris. I spent six months in a 'pension for young ladies' in the seventeenth arrondissement on the Boulevard Berthier. It was run by Madame Verlet, who was straight out of central casting. She was very embonpoint and very stern and cold, and a more snobbish woman I have never met. She was aided by her equally stern and snobbish daughter, Françoise. The house reeked of polish and unhappiness. No one ever spoke of the late Monsieur Verlet.

Secretly I hoped he'd run away to happier climes. The food at Maison Verlet was, however, superb. All the girls were on diets, but battles were lost when such delicate and tasty dishes were put before us.

French was spoken at all times. I took lessons in sewing, but they were soon abandoned. They were designed for those whose aim was to work in some major fashion house, which was certainly not my calling. Now I am left only with the ability to sew on the occasional button, or otherwise cry for help.

In the mornings I studied at the Alliance Française. The rest of the time was set aside to study French theatre. Mother had arranged for the wife of a drama critic to accompany me to the theatre three or four times a week. Madame Lerminière was a lively companion, and guided me through the plays at the Comedie Française, and also to the boulevard theatres and art-house productions. We usually read the texts of the plays beforehand so that I could understand more fully what we were to see.

Among the highlights of these expeditions, I remember the hypnotic Gerard Philippe performing at Jean Vilar's great TNP (Théâtre National Populaire) at the Trocadero. Philippe was playing in Victor Hugo's *Ruy Blas*, and he had come to the front of that enormous stage to deliver a soliloquy where he dried stone dead, the actor's greatest nightmare. On this occasion he had taken a prompt and continued to enthral us. The dry had mattered not one jot. Gerard Philippe had that rare ability to take you to the heart of a character with perfect ease and economy. It is rare to find actors who are equally at home on stage and on film. In that vast TNP auditorium, he gave you the detail of a close-up on camera.

We also saw Jean Louis Barrault, Madeleine Renaud and Edwige Feuillière in Claudel's *Partage du Midi*, an unforgettable performance of delicacy and precision. Madeleine Renaud was frail and petite, dressed all in white, and Feuillière startling in black. The way she donned her leather gloves I will remember to this day. She took the whole of a long speech to perform the action, caressing each finger with sensual pleasure, a brilliant display of action exposing inner feelings.

Little did I know at this point in my life that one day I would appear in a film with the great Fernandel, talking in French. The film was called *Voyage à Biarritz*, and the other star was Arletty who had so enchanted the world in *Les Enfants du Paradis*.

I never encountered Arletty on set, for all my scenes were with Fernandel; but a dinner was given at Maxim's for the whole cast, and then I did meet her. By this time she was almost blind, but she looked beautiful, dressed with true Parisian chic, and wearing a large grey fur hat. She kept looking in her compact mirror, which was a touching gesture and showed her great frailty. She and Fernandel never spoke to each other during the entire evening, and apparently they had not spoken a word to each other during the filming. It was quite strange that they had turned up at the dinner. I don't know if this was a long-standing estrangement, or whether it had only happened recently, but that evening they played a scene of detached froideur to perfection. The food of course was superb, but Fernandel just had an omelette, and sat grumpily communicating with no one. A great air of depression surrounded him, this great French comedian.

Despite the fact that I saw an inordinate amount of plays in Paris whilst I was being 'finished off', and spoke French most of the time, I still lacked fluency. My accent was good, but my vocabulary was sparse. Many years later when I was working with Isabelle Huppert at the National Theatre in Schiller's *Mary Stuart*, Isabelle said, 'Anna you speak French almost without an accent, so one expects you to be far more proficient in the language.'

I understood her perfectly. To immerse yourself in any language you must read it prodigiously and practise it whenever you can. After my Paris sojourn I failed to accomplish either of these aims. I came away with a love for the city, its beauties, its architecture and its history. But I never got to know the Parisians. I was only invited to their houses on one or two occasions, and these were always rather formal strained affairs. I always return to Paris as a tourist even when I go there now for work or for pleasure. The city invites you, but not the people.

When I went to Rome it was completely different. Here I stayed, not in a pensione, but with the Grossi family. Signor Grossi was a lawyer and a friend of my stepfather's. He had a lively little wife who adored cooking pasta. They had three children, Laura, Lallo and Grazia. Laura was the eldest and a year older than me. She was to be my escort around Rome.

She was ravishingly beautiful and witty, and a born flirt. In fact she took the art of flirting to new heights. My eyes opened in wonder.

The village atmosphere of Rome was so welcoming after the formality of Paris. Rome embraced a sixteen-year-old girl in a special way, and Laura was the perfect guide to the social delights of the city.

For cultural delights, Mary Cavaletti became my tutor. She lived in an ancient palazzo on the Via Appia Antica, and two or three times a week she took me on tours of Rome. The cata-combs, the Forum and the Colosseum were vibrantly brought to life by Mary's lectures, but we also went to unexpected places off the tourist track – little temples and museums tucked away in corners of the city, treats that appear in few guidebooks. I also took Italian lessons with a professor twice a week. So my life was very busy and interesting.

But my real lessons were with Laura and her group. Here I learnt to speak the language fairly fluently. The content of our conversations may have been somewhat flippant, but I did start to dream in Italian, which I had never done in French. I also began to flirt outrageously. Once or twice this got me into quite serious trouble, but on each occasion I was saved from any real shame. It was a period when we wore tight belted dresses with very full skirts and masses of petticoats, delightful to swish about in, and high, high heels with pointed toes were the footwear of the day, flattering but hugely uncomfortable and ruinous to the feet. But it was a good time in which to be a burgeoning adoles-cent, for it was an extremely feminine fashion and everything was fun to wear. We all donned lots of make-up too in those days. Maria Callas and Audrey Hepburn had taught us to put a black line on our eyes, going into wings at the sides. This fashion lasted for some time, but over the years, personally, I've put on less and less make-up. The unadorned face is far more inter-esting, even if less flattering, but it requires courage, which at sixteen I sadly lacked. Nowadays facelifts prevent the map of people's lives from being seen, and collagen-padded lips enter rooms long before their owners. This saddens me. A face without smile lines is utterly spiritless. But in Rome in 1954 such thoughts did not enter my head.

I remember Rome mainly as my romantic baptism, getting in and out of tiny Fiats, wandering around the streets by moonlight, and visiting nightclubs for the first time.

We bathed at Ostia and Fregene, and once we went skiing in Cortina d'Ampezzo in the Dolomites, where the sunsets are strangely purple, a colour I have seen nowhere else in the world. And the whole time we flirted till our senses ached. Rome with its crumbling beauty exerts a power unlike any other city. It does not allow you to feel alone.

I returned home late in 1954. It had been vaguely planned that I should go into a repertory company the following year, so I now started voice lessons, again arranged by my mother. At first the teachers were rigid disciplinarians, demanding what they wanted rather than coaxing something original from their pupils. I look back on these lessons as a hindrance; they neither freed one, nor fired the imagination. It took me a long time to find a teacher who inspired and delighted.

Alongside my voice lessons I studied English literature with the writer Hester W. Chapman. She was a most amusing and original teacher in the way she guided me through works that were hitherto unknown to me. I soon realised how limited my schooling had been. Biographies, Restoration drama and novels were eagerly devoured and discussed with Hester. From this time on reading became one of the greatest sources of pleasure in my life.

One day Hester invited me to lunch to meet the novelist Rose Macaulay. This was a special treat. *The Towers of Trebizond* was one of my favourite novels. Hester lived in a small eighteenth-century terraced house in Clipstone Street in Bloomsbury. It was like stepping back in time. The furniture was all eighteenth century, and rather dilapidated. The kitchen appeared to be the perfect setting for a period drama, cobwebs gracing every corner. Neither dusting nor cleaning were high on Hester's list of priorities. Indeed she herself had but a nodding acquaintance with the flannel. She dressed flamboyantly in deep maroons bedecked with enormous pieces of jewellery. But none of this mattered. Her vitality was so infectious and transcended every household lapse.

Miss Macaulay was already seated at the dining table when I arrived, and all through lunch I supposed her to be a tiny little person, but when she rose from the table she seemed gradually to unfold, and finally appeared to be very tall and spidery. I wish I had been able to see more of her. She had the palest grey eyes, gentle and intense at the same time, and spoke on all subjects with piercing insight, quietly drawing you into her thoughts. Conversation was always sparky at Hester's gatherings. Her cooking was adventurous and sometimes a little dangerous, but thoughts and ideas bounced around in her house and energised the brain cells. Sometime later when I was married to Jeremy Brett, he and I would go to dinner at Hester's, knowing that we would suffer from her gastronomic endeavours, and probably come home quite sick. But her conversation was like warm burgundy, and the maladies incurred seemed trivial in comparison.

Apart from Hester, I have been very lucky to have four friends who have continuously guided me through the literary maze. These mentors are David Hare, Peter Eyre, Howard Schuman and Christopher Hampton. They have steered me toward books that I would never have found on my own, and they have provided the backbone of my library. Now of course my husband, Uri, has become another literary detective, finding us unimaginable treasures to read from unexpected sources.

But at the beginning of 1955, Hester Chapman held the match

that set my reading life alight. My studies continued quietly, a gentle rhythm was established, until one day in the spring of that year, my life was to change forever.

CHAPTER 7

LOOKING BACK NOW IT SEEMS THAT I HAVE HAD SEVERAL LIVES. The first of course was childhood and schooling. In 1955 my second life began. It was to be the year that I 'came out'. I was to be a debutante and presented at court. It was a daunting prospect, which involved going to many cocktail parties and dances and being incredibly social, and mainly meeting the same people in different settings each day. I had never really considered the demands in depth. Again it was something Mother had planned for me. At all social functions to date I had been rather a wallflower, finding myself dancing with the kind uncle of the household, all the pretty and glamorous girls having been chosen by the young swains. I can remember at one particular dance given by the late Margaret, Duchess of Argyll, for her daughter Frances Sweeney, sitting by the front door waiting to be collected an hour ahead of time, so embarrassed and saddened was I to be constantly sitting on the edge of the dance floor. However, all that was soon to change.

I had gone to dancing school from the age of five until I was about eleven. I started out at Madame Vacani's Dancing Academy in Brompton Road, and had moved on to Miss Ballantyne's dancing classes when she opened her own school. My stage appearances had been confined to the annual charity matinee that she organised each year in a West End theatre. I was rather a pet of Miss B's, and she gave me starring roles in her shows, which were always in aid of the NSPCC. One year, Princess Elizabeth came to the matinee, and I was chosen to present the bouquet, something that caused me more fear than performing the sketches.

My only other theatrical experience had been many years earlier when I was five. Noel Coward had written the script of the film *In Which We Serve*, which was to be directed by David Lean. Noel was to star in the film with Celia Johnson playing his wife. It was decided that Daniel and I should audition for the roles of their son and daughter. So off we went to the studios. Daniel did his test and I followed. Mother had made me wear a fancy-dress costume, based on one of Holbein's paintings. When the crew came into the room where I was sitting, I started to scream and did not stop until they were forced to retire. I never did the test, and went home in disgrace. Daniel on the other hand was given the part of the son. I have sometimes thought that perhaps my screaming that day was my small inner voice warning me about the acting profession, but of course I was too young to pay true heed.

1955 started off quite normally with voice lessons and English literature classes. The main event was a marvellous present from Bill. He gave me a small green Morris Minor which was a real bonus, as living in Highgate people were never too keen to give me a lift home. I had to take forty-eight driving lessons before the test. My examiner was a nervous man who asked me if I knew that I'd driven through a red light. I told him I thought it was green, and he said, 'Fair enough,' and passed me. I was really not prepared for the demands of driving, but soon gained confidence, and started to feel independent.

In March Mother took me to the RADA Annual Matinee. It had been decided that I would not go to a drama school, but straight into a repertory company in the autumn. After the show, Mother and I and a few friends were talking on the pavement

My mother,
Adrianne Allen,
as a fairy

My father, Raymond Massey

My mother and father

Daniel and me

Daniel, my stepfather Bill Whitney and Mummy.
And me as a 'Cross Red Nurse'

My nanny, Gertrude Burbidge

Ann Walker, Penelope Roberts, Lady Sarah Berry (née Clifford–Turner), me and Sarah Barford playing nanny with our prams in Hyde Park

Me, aged ten, presenting a bouquet to Her Royal Highness, the Princess Elizabeth before the charity matinee for the NSPCC

Me as Laura in *The Glass Menagerie*

Me, my mother and
my brother Daniel

My great friend Kate Whitney

Iris Warren, my voice teacher

A glamorous photograph
of my mother

Jeremy Brett at the time of our marriage

David and me in fun-loving combat

David, aged two, on the Embankment on a rainy day

Me as Annie Sullivan in *The Miracle Worker*.
The turning point of my career

outside the stage door. We were joined by the author William Douglas-Home and the theatrical producer Jack Minster, always known in the profession as 'Jolly Jack', since he seldom smiled. They had been at the matinee looking for young actresses to play in Willie Home's new play *The Reluctant Debutante*, which Jack was to direct.

I don't think anything was mentioned that afternoon about my auditioning for a part, but the following day they rang Mother to ask if I would go to the Q Theatre and read for the epony-mous role. So later that week I went along. When I arrived they said that I was to read for the part of Clarissa, the much smaller role of a fellow debutante. I did as I was told and went home. The next day I was offered the part. Mother said that to do the smaller role in a long run would not be a good idea at the start of my career. So we turned down the offer. They came back and asked if I would audition for the reluctant debutante herself. Off I went again. After much discussion, it was agreed that I would be given the role on approval, and that, after a week of rehearsals, they would have the right to fire me. They felt they were taking a big risk, as I had done no stage work before. They were absolutely right. They also retained the right to replace me after the week in Brighton, where the play was to open before coming to the West End. So I had two big hurdles ahead of me.

Celia Johnson and Wilfred Hyde-White were to star in the play as the debutante's parents. No one could be more blessed than to have had their theatrical baptism playing with Celia. She was one of the great geniuses of the profession. Her economy was stunning, and everything about her performances seemed effortless, spontaneous, deeply felt and truthful. In *The Reluctant Debutante* she displayed a comedic timing that took your breath away. It was extraordinary to be on stage with her, because her concentration took you right into the world of the play, and enabled you to focus with great precision. I have only met two other actors in my career that had this enviable gift, Anthony

Quayle and Alan Rickman. There is great reassurance in the air when you act with such players. They prevent stage fright.

The two tests I had to pass in the rehearsal room and during the first week of the tour were great ordeals. I did get through them, but they took their toll. On the first night in Brighton I think everyone was more frightened than me. No one knew if I would simply collapse in front of a live audience or walk out of the theatre. Jack Minster elected to play noughts and crosses with me in the wings. I found this diversion even more difficult than going out on stage.

Emlyn Williams, the great Welsh actor, had told me to think of the size of the universe, and then think of the piffling size of myself in relation to it. I think this might have helped a little. Anyway, just before my entrance, Celia had to call out to me offstage and ask a question. This question received a huge laugh from the audience, which thank the Lord I timed to perfection. From this moment on everyone breathed a sigh of relief, and the whole evening was a triumph.

Afterwards everyone went back to our hotel for dinner. The compliments abounded, but Nanny brought me down to earth by saying simply, 'Very nice dear, but take your elbows off the table.'

During the first week on tour I got progressively more nervous. When you've done no theatre before, you simply don't believe that things can go wrong. Things did go wrong inevitably, like Wilfred Hyde-White drying and doors not opening. These events increased my anxiety, because I had no formal training on which to fall back. However I got through the week, and now everyone was gearing themselves for the big First Night in London. My father was flying over from the States. He always seemed to turn up for events when the spotlight was on me. I found this very difficult, because there was a great tension between him and Bill, vying for first place in my affections. Curiously, Father gave me an opal fan for the First Night. Opals are renowned for bringing bad luck, so the fan had to be sent straight away to the Ivy restaurant for safekeeping. We were opening at the Cambridge Theatre just down the road from the Ivy, so it seemed a perfect spot to leave the gift. As my whole family were extremely super-stitious, it was imperative that the fan be removed from my dressing room. My father never knew of this escapade, and I never retrieved the fan. When the Ivy was refurbished many years later, I asked if by any chance my gift had been found. The answer was, 'No.'

The First Night was a resounding success. The audience laughed and cheered, and went on doing so for the next twenty-two months. That is how long I had to stay in the play. As it was my first job there was no question of a get-out clause. I was trapped.

The first few months of the run were extraordinary. We were the biggest hit in town. The season was in full swing and everyone wanted to see the play. There were headlines in the press about my performance that said, 'A star is born.' All heady stuff. But I think I kept my balance because I found the whole experience so incredibly nerve-racking and demanding. The skin on my hands peeled from fright, and the strain increased rather than decreased. People were expecting so much from me. Celia was the most tremendous anchor. I am sure she knew the pain I was sometimes in, though we never discussed it. She made every-thing so simple on stage, and her blazing honesty prevented anyone from forcing their performances. Many years later I was to be directed by Celia in one half of a double bill by Hugh and Margaret Williams, called *Double Yolk*. She told me to find my character's walk. She said this was what she always worked on first with any part. I have never forgotten this, and have followed her advice ever since. It is a route that takes you to the centre of a person.

That year I was also a debutante in real life. In the spring my godmother Lady Anne Holland-Martin took me to Buckingham

Palace to be presented to the Queen, and earlier I had attended Queen Charlotte's annual ball dressed all in white. After the play opened I was no longer a wallflower. Young men queued up to dance with me. Suddenly Cinderella was mobbed. I only went to one or two dances a week because I was too tired to go out every night, and it was a really good feeling to be working and earning my twenty pounds a week. I felt there was purpose in my life.

The highlight of the social season for me was the dance that Mother and Bill gave at No. 2 The Grove to celebrate Daniel's twenty-first birthday and my official launching. It was a very grand and jolly affair. The theatre world gathered along with Dan's and my young friends, and all Mother's and Bill's political and literary coterie. Everyone joined in the feasting and dancing until the small hours. A tent had been erected in the garden, sumptu-ously decorated with deer's heads festooned with pearls and earrings. Tommy Kinsman's band played away and the champagne flowed. It seems to me now that this all happened in another lifetime, so far away from it do I feel.

Apart from the dances and the performances, I did manage to lead a busy social life during that summer of 1955. One evening Sir Kenneth and Lady Clark invited me to dinner in the private room at the Arts Council to meet Willie Somerset Maugham. It was fairly late when I arrived there after the play, and we soon sat down to a delicious dinner of cold grouse in an elegant eighteenth-century room, painted in dark green, which enhanced the magnificent paintings that adorned the walls. Nobody was talking very much but busily munching when Lady Clark said, 'Anna, say something to Willie.' I was horrified, but before I could find any words, Somerset Maugham saved me. He said with his tremendous stammer, 'Please let the child eat in peace. She's tired and hungry.' I loved him from that moment on. It made me remember that he was once a doctor. He was dressed in elegant tweeds and seemed quite detached from the whole evening, except when he came so gallantly to my rescue.

That year I went to the first *Evening Standard* Awards dinner, hosted by Sir Malcolm Sargent. Dorothy Tutin won the award for her haunting performance in Graham Greene's *The Living Room*. I remember that during the evening, quite spontaneously, Frankie Howerd had risen to his feet and made a speech that made us laugh until we cried. For the next few years this became a regular event. He had earned his special slot. Only forty or so guests attended that dinner in 1955. Nowadays of course it is a much larger affair. I personally miss the intimacy of that evening.

Another social event I remember with pleasure and awe was my weekend at the Oliviers. Larry's son Tarquin had taken me down to their house in Oxfordshire, Notley Abbey. Vivien Leigh was his wife at that time, and she and Larry were the most elegant hosts. Notley Abbey was an old baronial farmhouse, nestling in hilly countryside and decorated with superb taste, which I suspect was Vivien's. I felt as if I were on the set of a play. Everyone was quite giggly. You felt the curtain could have descended at any time, and the decorum would have crumbled. Larry was dressed like a country squire with yellow silk kerchief, tweed hacking jacket and corduroys, not quite the jodhpurs, nor the monocle, which would have completed the portrait. They had exquisite paintings and also a huge new television that excited everyone, as most people still only possessed very small sets at this time. Vivien was the wittiest of women, with brilliant comic timing. Her mood swings, which were to torment her so painfully later on, did not manifest themselves then, and during the weekend of my stay she delighted us all.

Larry was the host at another event that I shall never forget. It was a party given outside London to celebrate the start of shooting *The Prince and the Showgirl* with Marilyn Monroe, which Larry was to direct and to star in. It was a warm starlit night, and there was a gazebo set up in the garden. Perched on three chairs were Miss Monroe and her new husband, Arthur Miller, and Dame Sybil Thorndike, the two actresses dressed in their costumes for the film, which struck me as rather strange, as shooting had not yet begun. Marilyn glowed with love and beauty and sex and fragility, clad in her sparkling figure-hugging cream chiffon robe. Mr Miller wore an elegant grey suit, and looked somewhat bemused behind his large spectacles. Dame Sybil seemed to be performing the role of the duenna, in her tiara and full Ruritanian court regalia. We all filed by the trio in awe, uncertain whether we should curtsey or not. What Mr Miller made of the evening would have been interesting to know, but nobody spoke very much. Simply to be present at this unique event provided ample pleasure. Larry hovered over the whole proceedings as though he had already donned the hat of the director, anticipating the filming with relish. How sad that it ended in tears, and proved to be such an unhappy time for all concerned. Marilyn suffered dreadfully from fear and frequently did not turn up for filming, or was incredibly late. This upset Larry greatly, who felt unable to help her. Arthur Miller also had not been able to avert the problems. The entire shoot was fraught. But that evening in the garden, none of this was imagined, and magic hung in the air.

These outings were exciting and restorative interludes from the rigours of the long run. Night after night to do the same text with freshness and spontaneity was almost impossible. Peggy Ashcroft always said that you could go on developing a perform-ance for three months, and for the next three months you could repeat it with a certain freshness, but after that there were very few evenings when the performance could be truly alive.

Celia stayed in the play for nine months, and when she left I found the whole experience strange. She had held us all together, and I had no technique to guide me through the huge demands of a long run and playing with different actors. Now I believe all play contracts end after a year, but in 1955 'run of the play' meant run of the play. It was like prison.

Then one day I saw a way to escape. *The Reluctant Debutante* was being mounted on Broadway. Edna Best and her daughter Sarah Marshall were to star in it. Then Edna fell ill and the role of the mother was offered to my mother. After a lot of complicated wrangling, it was agreed that I could be released, on the condition that I agreed to do another play for Jack Minster. Off I went to New York with Mother.

But it was a nightmare period in many ways. I had completely lost my original performance. I was just reciting lines, and if I dried, I thought they were prompting me in Chinese.

It was also very difficult acting with Mother after Celia. They were so entirely different. We both found the experience a strain. A large part of acting is to create the new world of the play, to create the background of your character down to the smallest detail. When you walk on stage and see your own past, with your own real life parent, the whole creative process is shattered. This was the problem, and it made my performance feel very superficial. For great acting couples like the Lunts, the process is different. They create their new world together from the start. This was not the case for Mother and me. The play was not a success, and only ran for a couple of months. When the end came, it was a relief for everyone.

The highlight of the whole New York run for me was the night when Willie Douglas-Home took us to the El Morocco nightclub, and I danced with Senator Jack Kennedy. This was indeed a thrill. What a charming and flirtatious man he was. Alas, I was so in awe of his glowing chivalry that I trod on his toes and ruined everything. Jackie Kennedy was there too, utterly gracious and rather regal, her beautiful moon-shaped face aglow. Already there was an energy and electricity about this formidable pair. It was only 1956 but they were shining stars.

One day Mother took me to visit the great American actress Katherine Cornell at her house in Sneden's Landing overlooking the Hudson River. She was a most friendly person, wearing slacks and a pullover at a time when most people dressed up for social gatherings. She spoke openly of her stage fright, which I found most endearing in such a big star. She said she always ate a steak and green beans and fresh pineapple at four o'clock in the afternoon on the days when she was performing at night. She found this steadied her, and later she was too tense to eat. I was touched that she took the time to share these thoughts with a young actress just starting out on her career. Katherine Cornell (known as Kit to her friends) was married to the director Guthrie McClintock, and was the daughter of the man who had invented windscreen wipers. It was said that every time it rained, Kit earned 'Pennies From Heaven'.

My other great thrill during the New York run was to be photographed by the great Richard Avedon for the cover of a glossy magazine. I wore a dress patterned with huge yellow sunflowers with a large sun hat in the same fabric. It was not the most beautiful of dresses, but the Maestro made it look quite stunning. I was of course photographed against his, by now famous, white background. The most extraordinary part of the session was its speed. You always imagine a photographic session will take hours. But with Avedon, I sat for about twenty minutes. He knew exactly when he had got what he wanted.

Another occasion when I was photographed by a wizard with the camera was my session with Cecil Beaton. This was in London, and it was a disaster. I had thought the time arranged was eleven o'clock in the morning, but apparently it was for ten o'clock. Mr Beaton was furious. I don't think anyone had ever been late for a session with him before. He made me look like a convict on parade, even though I was wearing a glittering green sequined strapless gown. I have never been late for anything since. Photographs depend so deeply on the mood of the moment. The mood was dark that morning, and Mr Beaton took two uncomfortable hours to capture the 'convict'.

★　　★　　★

I made good friends during my New York stay. Americans are most hospitable hosts. I was of course able to catch up with my closest friend of all, Kate Whitney, and once again I spent weekends on her family's magical estate at Manhasset. One weekend a new friend of mine, Nonie Phipps, invited me for the weekend to her parents' place on Long Island. On the Sunday evening her aunt gave an informal party at her house nearby. It was a very relaxed affair, with all the guests dressed in the most casual gear. When the buffet supper was announced, Merle Oberon, the famous film star of the thirties and forties, appeared from upstairs. She was a houseguest, apparently, but spent most of the time resting in her room, emerging only for meals. Word had obviously not reached her that this particular evening was very, very informal. Merle drifted into the room dressed in a glamorous green evening gown that was fit for a soirée at Versailles. She was dripping with magnificent diamonds, and, even though she was only five foot two inches tall, her presence dominated the room. She had a magnetic glow about her that all truly beautiful women seem to have. The young men in the room flocked to her side and tended to her every whim. Her beauty was unimpaired by the years, and although her life was supposed to have been quite fiery, she exuded a great serenity. I have always felt that in early life the beauties on planet Earth have many advantages over the plainer folk. Everything seems to be done for them, and they have to spend little effort to get their own way, whereas the less good-looking have to battle for recognition right from the start. But in later years the situation changes. The plainer ones have nothing to lose; their looks might even get more interesting with time. The beauties suffer as the lines appear. Their habitual 'magnet' is impaired, and they must seek drastic ways to allay the wrinkles. I speak of course as a fully paid-up member of the plainer folk. No botox for me, and no facelifts. Merle Oberon, though, seemed to have defied Father Time. I felt I was taking part in some old Hollywood film in which the star is all dolled up and the extras wear subdued costumes and flit around in supporting roles. Miss Oberon shone that night and all the youth merely flickered around her.

My social life during the New York run was fun. The writer George Plimpton took me out to a nightclub in Harlem, which made me feel quite grown up. He was an amusing and generous man, one of those people who would know someone on the Moon if ever he visited there. He was extremely gregarious and revelled in the social whirl that he created about himself. He took me to a party once where I met Truman Capote. I shouldn't really say I met him for we did not exchange one word. The diminutive Mr Capote sat on a large sofa talking very quietly to those around him, and I did not dare intrude upon his chosen and protective circle.

The New York run of *The Reluctant Debutante* ended and Mother and I returned to London, which seemed very quiet after the electric pace of the Big Apple.

Several plays were sent for me to read, but nothing that was any good. We were just about coming to the end of the time when Jack Minster had to find me something, and I was jubilant at the thought of being free and able to study some more, when a script arrived that Mother thought was possible. It was called *Dear Delinquent*, a comedy about a lady burglar. If only I had had the confidence to say, 'No, this is not for me,' I would have been spared a mammoth setback to my career. This choice of play did my reputation great harm. From then on people thought of me as a lightweight comedy actress with no depth or substance, and it took a very long time for me to alter that opinion.

Dear Delinquent was a very insubstantial, frivolous piece, and my critics were justified in their assessment, but *The Reluctant Debutante* was a very different matter. Many years later I was asked to play the role of the mother of the debutante on the radio, with Helena Bonham-Carter as the daughter. I realised then what a superbly crafted play it was. The dialogue was at times as sharp as a Restoration play, and demanded enormous breath control and vocal technique. The subject matter may be dated now, and even at the time was perhaps inconsequential, but the craftsmanship was superb. Willie wrote with great delicacy and wit. Charm and humanity pervaded all his work.

I was in the run of *Dear Delinquent* at the Westminster Theatre in London for a whole year. This was the theatre that my maternal grandfather had owned when it was called the St James's Cinema. This second long run at the start of my theatrical life did me no good. I developed bad habits, and when I should have been deepening my acting skills, I was really wasting valuable time.

But Fate had other surprises in store for me. I left the play in the spring of 1958, and in May of that same year I was to be married.

CHAPTER 8

DURING MY TWO LONG WEST END RUNS, I HAD APPEARED IN ONE television film. It was called *The Green of the Year* and was directed by Robert Hamer. He was responsible for many of the famous Ealing films including the great *Kind Hearts and Coronets*. He was the most sensitive director. He was working with quite a few newcomers in this film and guided us through it with great kindness. Unfortunately he was not well at the time and was taken ill during the filming, and had to step down for a few days. I fear the demon bottle haunted him during his last years, but I really enjoyed my time working with him, and would love to have had another opportunity.

The other film I made during my West End runs was John Ford's *Gideon's Day*. He very kindly gave his goddaughter the role of Jack Hawkins' daughter. I played a young musician, and Andrew Ray played my boyfriend.

Working with Ford was fascinating. Having worked as an editor he only shot what he needed. He never did any cover unless absolutely necessary, and he never did more than one take. He edited as he filmed. His manner was easy and congenial.

He had no henchman around him. He knew what he wanted and went about achieving it with the minimum of fuss. The crew were in awe of him. His directions to them and the actors were simple and precise. The shot would be set up with crew and cast, and then the actors would retire while the lighting was worked on. When the actors returned, we rehearsed until Mr Ford felt everyone was completely prepared before we started shooting.

On the first day, though, there was some tension. Andrew Ray had a bad stutter when he was nervous. It was an unusual stutter insofar as he didn't have any facial contortions, nor did he make any sounds. He simply stopped speaking and it appeared that he had dried, which of course is exactly what Ford thought he had done. Nobody had thought to warn him of Andrew's affliction. So initially, Ford got really annoyed, which only exacerbated Andrew's problem. By evening there was a very awkward atmosphere. However, overnight all was explained, and from then on it was the happiest of shoots.

One weekend Ford and his wife invited me to tea at Brown's Hotel, and whilst we were enjoying the cream cakes, who should stroll in but John Wayne. He was dressed as though he had just come off the set of a cowboy film, even carrying his Stetson, and he behaved exactly like one of the characters he so frequently portrayed. That is to say he was phenomenally attractive, but hardly said a word. There was obviously a great rapport between him and Ford, dating from *Stagecoach* days.

I was by now intrigued and entranced by filming. To have been directed by John Ford was indeed a very special baptism. My next exciting cinematic event was to meet the great Alexander Korda, creator of London Films. I went off to his luxurious offices in Piccadilly, decorated with large pieces of furniture, splendid rugs and wonderful paintings, none of which dwarfed the enormous personality of Korda himself. After communications with my agent and a lawyer, I was offered a three-picture deal, which was to start with my playing Tweenie in Barrie's *The Admirable Crichton* with Kenneth More. All the papers were signed and the contract was to begin in a month's time. No one could have been more thrilled than

I was. Then tragedy struck. Korda died very suddenly, and, as the contract was a personal one with him and not with London Films, it was rendered null and void. So my film career was put on hold.

When I had been in *The Reluctant Debutante* in New York, I had met briefly with the cast of the Old Vic Theatre who were performing *Troilus and Cressida* on Broadway. Jeremy Brett was playing Troilus, and like most of the young girls who came into contact with him, I fell under his spell. At this stage I didn't get to know him well, but his charm and enthusiasm were very powerful attributes. Soon after our meeting I came back to London and Jeremy remained in New York. For the time being I was preoccupied with work and beginning the tortuously long run of *Dear Delinquent*. There was no time for romance of a serious nature.

However, during the run I did meet up with the dashing Jeremy again. He came to a party that Mother gave at The Grove. I met him the following day and out of the blue he said, 'You must find somewhere to live where you are not under your mother's dominance.' I was amazed. No one had ever spoken to me on this subject before, but Jeremy had seen the situation clearly in the course of the evening, and had dared to speak out. He was quite right. I was completely dominated by Mother's will and her tastes and plans for me. I had to get out and fend for myself. Nanny was there too of course with her will and her ways. It was a formidable entourage from which to extricate myself.

Jeremy was the most complex of men. He was eccentric and often embarrassing in his outspokenness. In later life he became very deluded, but at this stage when all was going so well for him, he could get to the core of a problem effortlessly. He saw my difficulties at home and helped me find the initiative to break away. This was some feat, for I was frightened and still needy of the nest for creature comforts. But I did break away.

I found myself a room in Ebury Street. This liberated me to a certain extent, and allowed my romance with Mr Brett to blossom. But I must stress that our romance was of the purest kind. We could have been in a Jane Austen novel. In fact I suspect there was quite a bit of play-acting in the air. When Jeremy embarrassed me with his exuberances, I simply thought to myself, 'I can change him.' What very dangerous territory I was entering.

I think I must have been one of the last virgin brides. It was largely accepted in those days that young girls saved themselves for marriage. I saved myself simply from fear.

I had flirted up until this time, kissed and held hands, and had romantic friendships, but had fled from any serious commitment. It was Jeremy's intuition that enabled me to break through that barrier and unleash my feelings. He did not know what strong emotions he was releasing.

So I was to marry Peter Jeremy William Huggins, for that was his real name. He had chosen Brett out of the telephone book, as he felt Huggins was insufficiently glamorous. We had a very big, showy wedding at No. 2 The Grove. We were married in St Michael's Church opposite, and the reception was given in a marquee in the garden. Of course it was not entirely a fairy-tale wedding. My father had flown over, and had expected to give me away. I was torn in two. Bill was paying for the wedding, and it was he who had been around for most of my childhood. Naturally he had expected to do the honours. But of course Father was my father, and he had come to play his part. To tell him that Bill was replacing him would be a shattering blow. Mother naturally wanted Bill to walk up the aisle with me, and she did try and persuade me, because she knew that he would be equally shattered to relinquish the role to Dad. What to do? It was something that no bride wants to have to cope with just before her Big Day. But that was the painful situation I found myself in, and the two male protagonists did not ease matters. They fought their duel silently with velvet weaponry, and left me to make the choice. I wish that I had been original and suggested that they could both take me up the aisle, one on each side. But I expect not even that solution would have satisfied them. Finally there was a scene at Claridge's, where Father was staying. I told him that I had decided to ask Bill to give me away. I tried to explain this as gently as I could, but Father blew a gasket, and Dorothy declared that they would leave immediately for the States. The insult was more than Father could bear, she said, and plainly she was right, for Father's right eye became furiously blood-shot, which seemed to demonstrate the inner anger that he had been reining in. He and Dorothy returned immediately to Los Angeles, where he was now living. I don't think that he ever really forgave me, although the matter was never again discussed. It was difficult for him to accept, but he didn't appreciate my dilemma at all. Bill had generously offered to give me the wedding reception, and he had been around all my formative years, guiding me unobtrusively throughout my schooling. To have deprived him of that walk to the altar would have been too bitter a blow. Father only seemed to turn up when the spotlight was shining.

If only one of them had whispered to me that they didn't really mind, or had offered to step down. But I was given no such respite. A cloud was cast over the whole proceedings.

The other cloud was caused by my mother telling me on the evening before the great day that she would cancel the whole thing if I wanted her to. She did not want me to marry Jeremy, but had never said so directly. I think by saying that I could get out of it even at this late hour, she showed how deeply she felt about it all. But, I didn't flee like the heroine in Anita Brookner's *Hotel du Lac*, and the wedding proceeded with pomp and ceremony. Anthony Armstrong-Jones took the photographs. It was not long before he was to have a far more auspicious wedding himself when he married Princess Margaret. The Bishop of Coventry officiated, and I remember him saying in his address that 'our paths may not always be strewn with roses', and thinking how wrong he was. I was certain that our paths would always be romantic and peaceful. The Bishop was proved absolutely right, and I'm sure much sooner than even he had anticipated.

But the day itself was a very happy one, filled with children and laughter and hope. Jeremy was in Terrence Rattigan's *Variations on a Theme* with Margaret Leighton at the time, and had to leave early for the evening performance. I spent the evening at another theatre with my voice teacher, Iris Warren, until I met Jeremy at the Savoy for our Wedding Night. The world of show business, society, politics and close friends had attended the celebrations, and it was nice to spend some quiet time with Iris before the romantic night ahead of me.

Iris was a renowned teacher, who for many years was to play an important part in my acting life. She delivered me to the Savoy, and I waited for Jeremy in the suite that had been recommended by Moss Hart and his wife, Kitty Carlyle.

Looking back on this episode, I feel that Jeremy and I were like two actors waiting to play the most important romantic scene of their careers. It didn't feel completely real. However, the weekend passed very happily, and Jeremy played his part with tenderness and understanding. The bride was radiantly content.

We returned to Jeremy's little house in Chelsea after two days, hoping to settle down to domestic bliss. This was not to be. One day soon after we had returned from honeymoon, Jeremy had been bending over the record player, and in a playful mood I had thrown a cushion at him, which hit him on his bottom. He turned round sharply. I had expected a warm riposte. Instead he shouted at me in the most irrational and violent way. He said I was never to do such a thing again, making out that I had done something humiliating. From this moment I knew in the deepest part of me that our marriage was doomed. I told no one of what had happened, but the deep uneasiness never left me. To the outside world, though, we were a happy young married couple.

CHAPTER 9

JEREMY AND I WERE INVITED TO MANY SOCIAL GATHERINGS. ONE
of the more memorable of these was when Fleur Cowles, the
American writer and painter, and her husband Tom Montagu
Meyer invited us for Sunday lunch at their beautiful Surrey
retreat, an Elizabethan house tucked away from the world in
rolling green hills and surrounded by a ha–ha, a true paradise.
Fleur's paintings adorned many of the walls, and there was always
her current work on the easel. That particular day the chief guest
was Cary Grant. What a gallant and charming man he was. He
spoke extremely softly. His manners were impeccable and he was
amazingly unself-centred. After lunch we were all sitting in the
garden having coffee, when a swarm of bees flew over us and
one stung me on my shoulder. Who jumped to his feet and led
me to the kitchen? Mr Grant, and there he found bicarbonate
of soda for my wound, and I was immediately relieved of my
pain. It was carried out quietly and with the minimum of fuss,
so unusual for illustrious personages, but totally heart-warming.
He has always been one of my very favourite screen actors –
such economy, truth and precision. He began in Hollywood at
the same time as my mother. She had gone there on a starlet's
contract, and found herself sitting in a carriage on a set with
young Archie Leach. He stayed on to become Cary Grant and
Mother returned home. I never told him this little story, but I
often wish I had.

We were also invited to the wedding of Anthony Armstrong-Jones to Princess Margaret, and to the ball given at Buckingham Palace a few days before to celebrate the occasion. This was a very grand event attended by the whole Royal Family, and yet it also managed to be an extremely relaxed affair. The Queen Mother was there in a sparkling blue and silver ball gown. She stayed until the end, hardly missing a dance, even though her tiara had slipped a little during the waltzes.

Around this time the twist came into fashion and changed dancing forever. Now everyone was whirling away without set partners on the dance floor, and you found yourself twisting with new people all the time. One night Jeremy and I were at Buddy Greco's nightclub in Hanover Square, and lo and behold we were being given dancing lessons by Buddy himself, and twisting with Judy Garland and her final husband. Miss Garland was swathed in black velvet and an enormous feather boa, with a gash of scarlet lipstick and a pound of make-up on her tiny face. She was a veritable bundle of nerves, despair and courage. A nightclub was the perfect setting for her, dimly lit amidst swirls of smoke. Daylight was too strong for her fragile carapace. She took guidance from Buddy extremely seriously, but you could feel the great effort it cost her to be bright and cheerful. I wondered if she was ever able to relax and be herself. Maybe by this time 'herself' was too deeply buried, and the carapace was all she could present.

Soon after my honeymoon was over, I started rehearsals for T.S. Eliot's *The Elder Statesman*. Paul Rogers was starring and I was to play his daughter. Eliot had just got married to his second wife, Valerie. They used to come to the rehearsals and sit in the second row holding hands, obviously very much in love. He was most courteous to everyone, but the director, E. Martin-Brown, forbade us to ask him any questions, which I must say was quite frustrating. It was during the rehearsal period of this play that I began to realise how painfully ill-equipped I was to approach a serious role. I floundered, and there was nobody who could help me. The problems were within myself. I lacked confidence and my inexperience loomed large. When we opened at the Edinburgh Festival, I suffered agonies of stage fright. Somehow I got through and we proceeded to London, where we had a short but respectable run. One of the best things that came out of the experience was my friendship with Alec McCowen. He played my brother quite brilliantly. His wit and offbeat sense of humour kept us all from despairing. He has remained one of my closest friends, and we have both seen each other through good and bad periods in our lives. Alec has that unique quality of making people feel better with the minimum of effort. He has a supreme lightness of touch. I have worked with him often on television and radio. Even performing the gigantic role of John Tanner in *Man and Superman* on the radio, he managed to imbue the event with laughter and cheer.

During *The Elder Statesman* I leaned heavily on the talents of the voice teacher, Iris Warren. She had that rare gift of letting each pupil find their own voice. I began to feel vocally free, and this helped me to liberate my imagination. I owe so very much to Iris, and to this day I do the exercises she guided me through. She gave me so much to think about that she succeeded in alleviating my stage fright for a while.

When *The Elder Statesman* finished, I found out that I was pregnant. So for the next few months I became an actor's wife, and pottered about the house enjoying the domestic peace. Jeremy was working so I spent a lot of my pregnancy alone. I remember it as one of the calmest periods of my life.

David was born three days after my twenty-second birthday. No one could have had a more perfect gift. We were thrilled with him. But when he was just three months old, Jeremy's mother was tragically killed in a car crash in the Welsh mountains. It was the most enormous shock for Jeremy, and from this time on, our marriage suffered greatly. I was filming *Peeping Tom*, and was not around to give him essential support. But, looking back, I doubt that I would have been of much help. His mother's death released Jeremy from past restraints. He changed, and our relationship never really recovered.

The filming of *Peeping Tom* was an absorbing time for me. My father's old friend Michael Powell was an extraordinary man. He came to the set each day immaculately dressed, a distinguished ferret in a tweed suit and a bow tie. He thrived on tension. I have never known a more electric atmosphere than on the set of *Peeping Tom*. Before each take he had to have a row with someone, and it was usually the camera operator, Gerry Turpin, who was the target of his wrath. He liked to do tremendously long and complicated takes, so everyone's nerves were already on edge without the added friction provided by the director.

The tale of the photographer who films his victims, hoping to capture their final terror on celluloid, was macabre, and there was a feeling of great unease on the set each day. I have often been asked how I got the part. I think the fact that my father had worked with Powell on *A Matter of Life and Death* must have had an influence. But I think there was another reason. Powell for many years had conducted a clandestine relationship with the actress Pamela Brown. Pamela and I looked extremely alike. We could very easily have been related, and I have always thought this was his main reason for choosing me to play the heroine, Helen. It was the most wonderful part, full of emotion, warmth and innocence. Her journey was indeed frightening, and often on set I was genuinely scared, even though the crew were around. The lighting was extremely low-key and atmospheric, and I often felt quite isolated and threatened. I am sure this was Powell's intention.

Like John Ford, Powell believed in setting up the shots carefully, and then, when the crew were ready, the actors would return. We would rehearse and rehearse until Powell was satisfied that he could get his shot in one take. We never did more than two. Some of the takes were eight or nine minutes long, involving extremely intricate tracking. I learnt an enormous amount about filming from Michael Powell. He was not easy to work with, but he was a true original and a taskmaster. I think he enabled everyone to give of their best. When I saw the film recently in a sparkling new print, I thought how fresh and undated the acting was. *Peeping Tom* was the last film Powell ever made. It received the most dreadful reviews, and it took many years for people to rediscover it as a masterpiece. The script was by Leo Marks, another fascinating man. He had been one of the major code breakers in the war. I was very fortunate to meet these strong and interesting individuals so early in my career. Our lighting cameraman was the great Otto Heller who had lit many of Marlene Dietrich's films. He had the most delightful and bubbly personality, not dimmed at all by his age. He adored women, and used wonderful blue filters to flatter them. Every time I came on set I whispered to him, 'Otto, give me the blue,' and often he did.

After finishing *Peeping Tom*, I was at home enjoying my beautiful new son, and trying not to dwell on my marriage, which was not in a good state. I kept all my fears and doubts about this to myself, for there was no one I could comfortably confide in. I dreaded Mother or Bill or Nanny saying 'I told you so'. I kept hoping that perhaps everything would work out in some magical way. I was not being rational of course. I think that one of the main problems was that Jeremy had released enormous passions in me, and these were a great and insurmountable burden for him. He had really wanted to make the marriage work, but my emotional demands were too much for him. We both needed to talk to someone, but in those days that was not easy like it is today. So we battled on, each of us growing unhappier as the days went by.

★   ★   ★

In the spring of 1959 I was asked to play the role of Ralph Richardson's daughter in Enid Bagnold's *The Last Joke*. John Gielgud was to play Ralph's brother and Glen Byam Shaw was to direct. I felt very torn. Part of me wanted to be at home with my son, David, and the actress in me wanted the challenge and excitement of acting with Ralph and John. The actress won. It was a unique opportunity to work with these two great knights of the theatre. Sir John was the most famous classical actor of his generation, with the most mellifluous and haunting voice. He always said that an actor could only submerge ten per cent of his own personality in a performance. On the other hand Sir Ralph was one of the greatest character actors of his genera- tion, and I'm sure he felt that he could submerge a far greater percentage. It was said that of all the greats Ralph was able to play the man in the street, but that when he was in the street, he was the only man in the street.

These two giants of the stage had very different ways of working. John was all instinct, and Ralph worked out everything beforehand in the minutest detail.

It was an extremely demanding and difficult play about the art world. Ralph had based his character on the millionaire Nubar Gulbenkian. He had so many whiskers, false eyebrows and props that everyone felt his performance was getting lost. Gradually during the long tour prior to the London opening, he was stripped of his mask, and in the end only Gulbenkian's orchid remained. When Glen Byam Shaw left us in Liverpool, John Gielgud tried to take over the direction, and gave us all copious notes each night, sometimes even during the performance. One night Jeremy was waiting for me outside my dressing room when John G appeared and knocked on Ralph's dressing room door, which happened to be next to mine. 'Who is it?' Ralph said.

'It's me, Johnny,' came the reply.

'Oh no more notes tonight, cocky,' said Ralph in tired and fractious tones. We were all getting desperate with the rewrites and suggestions. The tour seemed endless, and the London First Night loomed in the distance. When at last it came, it was a fiasco. The audience booed, although when Nanny came round afterwards, and I said, 'Oh Nan, the audience booed,' she replied, 'No no, they shouted bravooooo.' I didn't believe her, but appreciated the comforting words. The reviews were dreadful, and we only ran eight weeks.

It was during *The Last Joke* that Jeremy left me. I was devastated, and could hardly summon the energy or the will to go to the theatre each night. I told no one in the cast except Robert Flemyng, who was dear and kind to me. He gave me the strength to carry on. When the play ended it was an enormous relief to us all. The next day a gigantic and elegant bouquet of flowers arrived. I read the card. It was from John G, written in his immaculate miniscule handwriting, saying how much he had admired my bravery and dignity during the last difficult weeks. I burst into tears. I had no idea he had even known of my troubles. He was the kindest man and he had a delicacy about him that was very rare. I was to work with him again, and we remained close. I valued his friendship very much.

Soon after *The Last Joke* ended, Jeremy returned. It was a fragile reunion, and I felt I was being tested. I desperately wanted to make the marriage work, although I don't think Jeremy was very hopeful.

In the late autumn of 1960 I was asked to audition for Donald Albery and Peter Coe. They were casting *The Miracle Worker* by William Gibson. The play was the story of Helen Keller, the blind and deaf child, and her Irish teacher Annie Sullivan. It was a formidable piece and required tremendous performances from the two main characters. The role of Annie Sullivan was as far as could be imagined from *The Reluctant Debutante*. I didn't think I stood a chance, but I went along to the audition well equipped with my Irish accent. I was told fairly quickly that I had not got the part, and Jeremy and I planned a trip to Tenerife to try to patch up our marriage. As we walked into our room at the hotel, the telephone rang. It was Donald Albery saying that they wanted me to play Annie Sullivan after all. What drama this caused. In the end it was decided that I would stay for a week in Tenerife, and return for rehearsals. That was the death knell for my marriage, but also the turning point of my career.

Knowing what I was soon to know, my marriage would have ended no matter what career moves I made. But the next few months were to be the hardest and most painful of my life. The rehearsals for *The Miracle Worker* were phenomenally arduous. There was a fight between Annie and Helen in the middle of the play that lasted ten minutes and demanded immense physical strength and concentration. It was the climax of the evening. On top of that there was the accent to cope with, and the pressures of succeeding in a role so different from anything I had attempted before. I felt people were expecting me to fail. The strain was at times almost unbearable.

Life at home was far from easy, so it was a relief when we went off on tour. We opened in Stratford. The play was an instant success. The audience were completely held. They laughed and they cried, and they cheered our fight. Janina Faye played Helen Keller. She was wonderful in the part and really convinced that she was blind, not an easy task. I very much enjoyed playing with her. We had a second week on tour in Streatham, and then we opened at the Royalty Theatre in Kingsway. This had been built originally as a cinema, and the acoustics were appalling. The sound only seemed to go one way. The audience reaction was somehow delayed. We missed the warmth of the proscenium theatres, where the atmosphere is so alive.

However, the play was a hit. We received rave reviews, and at last I seemed to have buried the upper-class comedy image. My reviews could have been written by my mother. It was only the demands of playing each night, and trying to keep the whole performance fresh, that forced me to keep my head. For the second night of the play I had ordered a taxi to take me to the theatre, and as I got in I said, 'The Royalty please.' The driver took me to a strip club in Soho. He had never heard of the new Royalty Theatre in Kingsway. After a few weeks we moved to Wyndham's, back to the beloved proscenium arch, where you can hear an audience breathe, and their reactions spur you on. We heard laughter in places for the first time. It was a magical experience. When I started out in the theatre we used to have footlights, which were not only flattering, but also they enabled you to create your own world with much more ease. Sean Kenny had designed the set for *The Miracle Worker* with a new thrust stage that didn't allow for footlights, and made you feel much more exposed.

One night during the run we were in the middle of the fight when I felt even more exposed than usual. All my petticoats and bloomers had become unattached and gradually descended to the floor. What to do? I calmly stepped out of them and continued the fight as though nothing had happened. This is of course what you would do in real life. Friends came round afterwards and hadn't even noticed what had happened. When an audience is completely involved, they will accept almost anything.

It was during this run that Jeremy left me for good. He had gone to Switzerland for a holiday, and when he came home he told me that he had found someone else, a man he had met in Montreux. It was the most enormous shock, but somehow deep down I had suspected it. In a way it was also a great relief. Jeremy was honest with me, and told me as gently as he could. We parted, and David, Nanny (who had come to live with us when David was born) and I were on our own. I had to get through the play each night, which was not easy, but it was also a distraction from the pain.

Music was a great help to me at this time, and one night Jascha Heifitz came into my dressing room. His playing of the

Brahms violin concerto was one of my most treasured records. What a sensitive man he was. He was immaculately suited, and looked at you with his piercing, sad owl eyes, and words seemed almost unnecessary. He had come round to the dressing room with Margot Fonteyn, who was a most generous person. She of course could express herself so eloquently with movement and gesture. Between the two of them silence would have revealed all. However, Margot did compliment me about the way I used my hands in the play, which thrilled me. But, for a few nights, I was rather self-conscious. Compliments can sometimes be as damaging as savage criticism, which is why now I never read reviews until the run of the play has finished.

The Miracle Worker ran for nine months. Friends were an enormous help and comfort to me then. Lots of people came to see the play, but when the notice eventually went up saying it was to close, I was grateful. I needed a break, and I needed time with my little David. We planned to go and stay with Mother and Bill in Switzerland. They had just moved there to a chalet in Glion overlooking Lake Geneva. Mother gave us a warm welcome as always. The chalet was decorated in her usual light and busy style. Gone were the original dark wood walls and floors. Carpets were everywhere and the walls were papered in bright floral patterns. The Swiss locals were quite surprised, I'm sure. All her antique furniture had been brought over from England, and many little tables were placed around the rooms with enamel boxes and Dresden figurines adorning them, a hazard when a two-year-old is darting about the place. But I must say Mother was quite good-natured if a mishap occurred.

In Glion she had a team of helpers from around the area, led by Mathilde and Madeleine. Mathilde cooked succulent feasts even when there were no guests. She had a magic touch, and I still remember baby artichokes surrounding tiny parcels of pork in a sauce that I wish I'd recorded. Madeleine was a large russet woman who lifted heavy pieces of furniture as though they were dusters. The chalet literally gleamed under her supervision. Much later, Mother and Bill had to move to a small apartment in La Tour de Peilz on the lake. The staff of helpers dwindled as Bill's finances suffered. But that was not until the late sixties. For the time being the chalet was a hive of social activity.

It was wonderful to escape the stresses of the last few months. The weather behaved in the correct Swiss way. Snow fell, and everything looked like a picture postcard. Noel Coward lived on a nearby hillside in his fabulous 'Chalet Coward'. He invited us to lunches and dinners, and visited us too. He was the most perfect host. His chalet was wonderfully comfortable, and filled with photographs and memorabilia of a very grand kind. Noel had been photographed with all the members of the Royal Family, and almost every famous person you could think of. These photographs were informal, not the usual posed studies one sees in the press. You felt you were being embraced by his life. I remember the banisters were covered in red velvet. Noel loved colour and this was reflected everywhere in the chalet, but all was executed with restraint and taste. Many of his own paintings adorned the walls, colourful oils of Jamaica, where he owned a house and spent much of his time. Looking back I see Noel surrounded by colour. He and his chalet glowed in a swirl of golds and reds, and his wardrobe reflected this too. He always wore brightly patterned kerchiefs with blazers and slacks of vivid hues. This suited his personality of course. Sombre was not a word he would appreciate, certainly not sartorially or in interior decoration.

My spirits lifted when we went to visit Noel, and when he came to see us in Glion. He was like a zestful cocktail. Wit and irony usually dominated his conversation. I remember he was once asked if he was superstitious. 'Only about thirteen in a bed,' he replied. Once, at a time when several of his friends were dying, he said, 'I feel lucky to get through lunch.' However during this stay he was very kind to me. I had not expected this. He knew of course that my marriage was over, and I suspect he understood the reasons for the break-up. But he never talked about that specifically. His tact was amazing, and the caustic humour disappeared when one evening we had a long talk together in a little room away from everyone else. He was sympathetic and realistic. He told me that he thought it was impossible for an actress to have a good and lasting marriage, and that on the whole they are doomed to be unhappy in love. He told me of the countless times he had seen Gertrude Lawrence suffer from tragic affairs, and how she always revived, almost drawing strength from the drama surrounding her. This was of course a harsh view of the situation, and extremely pessimistic, but I think he meant it kindly, and I trust he hoped to make me feel that I had not failed, but was simply 'doomed' like every actress. In retrospect, I utterly disagree with most of what he said. Actresses are not 'doomed' to be unhappy. All they need is a lot of good fortune to find a sympathetic partner, and in my opinion, so does the whole of mankind. But Noel really had tried to comfort me in his way, and I was extremely grateful. He showed me a side of himself that I suspect few people knew existed. I came away from that stay liking the rainbow-hued wit much more than I had done in the past.

We stayed with Mother for six weeks, and then came back to London. I met up with Jeremy once or twice, and, against everyone's advice, we decided to get back together. It seemed only right to try again, now that I knew everything. The reconciliation lasted six weeks. There were no rows, but we realised we were really ill-suited as partners. Jeremy was restless and never read a book, nor could he have a conversation. I needed to discover myself and to start to study and read again. He was a kind man but always in flight, and so, to my enormous relief, he took wing once more, this time never to return. A chapter was closed. We went through an extremely amicable divorce, managing against the lawyers' wishes to keep in touch and remain friends. We felt that for David this was absolutely essential. And indeed I always knew that Jeremy would be there for us if we were ever in great trouble. He was a gentle and caring person.

I shall never regret my first marriage, but I regret that Jeremy had been forced to feel guilty. We were living in 1962. A year later the Wolfenden Report was published. Perceptions were changed forever. I hope that he felt released from the tension and pain that had haunted him.

CHAPTER 10

NO DIVORCES ARE COMPLETELY SMOOTH, OF COURSE. THERE was one small note of drama during ours. I had formed a close relationship with Jeremy's lawyer, Peter Chettle. He had in fact been a friend of ours prior to the divorce, and the proceedings brought us closer together. He immediately withdrew from the case, and everything continued with no further difficulty. Peter was a good and kind friend to me, and helped to restore my shattered confidence.

It was also good to get away from the world of theatre. Peter introduced me to a new group of people. I used to walk round golf courses with him and his friends, and their conversation was both interesting and stimulating. I started to read again and felt the world to be a larger place than the West End theatreland. But it was not long before an offer came my way, and I found myself back at the Haymarket. This time I was to play Lady Teazle in Sheridan's *The School for Scandal*, directed by John Gielgud. Ralph Richardson was to play Sir Peter Teazle, and John Neville and my brother, Daniel, the Surface brothers.

Margaret Rutherford was Mrs Malaprop. She suffered the most dreadful nerves each night, and battled bravely to say the correct text. One night, as Ralph came off into the wings, he said to those of us standing around waiting to go on, 'It's rough weather out there tonight.' I felt for Margaret coping with such terror every evening.

Only once before had I seen such dreadful stage fright, and that, believe it or not, was with Bob Hope. We were doing a big theatrical charity show called 'The Night of a Thousand Stars'. I was in a chorus line-up waiting to go on with Tyrone Power, who was to sing 'Chattanooga Choo Choo'. Bob Hope was the act before us. He was pacing up and down, on fire with nerves. You felt he was about to collapse, and then his theme tune, 'Thanks for the Memory', struck up, and he sauntered on stage as cool as forty cucumbers. I don't think it was an 'act'. I think his terror was genuine, but suddenly he was focused, and his calm restored. He gave his usual effortless performance.

Acting with Daniel in *The School for Scandal* was not a happy experience. I was going through my divorce and felt quite edgy, and Daniel, for some reason known only to himself, had decided not to speak to me. This made things extremely difficult. As a small child I hero-worshipped him, and when he was home for the school holidays, I craved his attention. This must have been very irksome for him. He was prone to dark moods as a young boy, and they could last for two or three days. They affected the whole household. At other times he was the brightest, most amusing, charming person you could wish to meet. His laugh could affect a whole room, and at these times he exuded an incomparable gaiety of spirit. I loved him dearly, but he was a complex man. He was in many ways an innocent, but his innocence was mixed with mammoth egocentricity, which inevitably created tense and fiery situations. I think he had been deeply affected by Father leaving Mother when he was only four years old, and his relationship with Bill was not an easy one. I am sure he resented Bill's arrival on the scene. He had known Father well, unlike me, for I was barely one at the time of the break-up. To suffer your father's departure and the arrival of another sibling at the same time must have been traumatic for him. In the late thirties no therapy or help was even considered, so the poor little boy battled on, dealing with his demons alone. He had no control over his feelings. At times of crisis, he would just clam up, and shun those around him. During *The School for Scandal* he was obviously going through a difficult patch, and I was the one he chose to shun. No explanation was ever given to me. The portcullis simply descended.

The only moments I was really close to him were at times of tragedy, when he was always there for me, and during his marriage to Penelope Wilton. She encouraged a feeling of family unity in us all, but, when the marriage ended, Daniel drifted away, and, for the next twelve years until his death, he did not speak to me. This break was far more serious than any previous ones, for during these years he also stopped all communication with Mother, and in fact never spoke to her again during her life. He never told her why he refused to talk to her, but someone once suggested that his anger was so deep and out of control that he feared he might physically harm her if he saw her. I do not know how true this was, for I was never in a position to discuss it with him. All I know is that his inner pain and wrath took him over completely. From the outside his behaviour appeared very harsh and cruel, but I think that the agonies he endured rendered him incapable of rational conduct.

However in *The School for Scandal*, Dan did resume talking to me after a few weeks. I think Laurence Naismith, with whom he shared a dressing room, had urged him to end the silence that had puzzled and upset the whole cast.

So the run went on, but not happily for me. I found the play very demanding, and felt somewhat at sea. John Gielgud was an instinctive director, not a teacher, and sadly he lacked patience. I floundered and he could not help me. He waited for you to give him something, and would then proceed to build from that. He did have innate taste though, and encouraged economy in performances. He once told me of an actress whom he didn't admire. He said that he dreaded her characters getting bad news on stage, for she would make such a meal of it.

Ralph played Sir Peter extremely sympathetically, which made Lady Teazle's task much harder. He didn't rant and rave at his wife as most Sir Peters do, but greeted each of her wilful caprices with hurt looks and a gentle, but aggrieved, acceptance. I found it very difficult to retain the humour in our scenes, and not to appear harsh and ungrateful. One day during rehearsals Ralph took me and Pinkie Johnstone, who was playing Maria, out to lunch. He felt we were not giving enough voice to our roles. But his way of explaining this to us was uniquely 'Ralph'. He started by saying that all theatres were like women, and needed to be wooed and flattered. He proceeded to give us a little show of how he achieved his goal. It was a breathtaking piece of theatre, his sensuality and humour shining through. No lesson has ever been more fun.

John Gielgud also changed his mind all the time. We were forever incorporating his new ideas, often gleaned from casual acquaintances. When these new ideas didn't work, he changed everything yet again. If nothing else, it was a learning experience.

During the run Ralph tried yet again to help me. He invited me to his dressing room in the interval one evening. Mac, his dresser, had laid out tea in a silver teapot with some small chocolate cakes. We sat by a blazing fire in this perfect eighteenth century theatre. Dressed in our period costumes it almost seemed that we had been swept back in time. Ralph proceeded to demonstrate a point he wished to make about a certain scene. He asked me to sit upon his knee, and acted out the section that he felt was not right. Mac was our only audience, and I understood precisely what Ralph wanted, but each night on stage I seized up, and failed to perform with the delicacy that was required. I let Ralph down and I let myself down. I never felt at home in Sheridan's world. When my contract came to an end I left the production, grateful for free evenings and a little fun.

I remained good friends with Ralph and his wife Meriel

Forbes, known as Mu to her friends. She had played Lady Sneerwell in the play. Ralph was a great letter writer, and these letters were small works of art. Unlike John Gielgud's miniscule script, Ralph's writing was large and generous. He had worked in bookbinding when he was young, and he was a consummate artist. Some of his work adorned the walls of their house in Kenwood. He wrote his letters diagonally across the page, and at the end there was always a drawing of a bunch of flowers or a bottle of champagne, or of some subject relevant to the note. They were mementoes to be treasured.

One evening Ralph and Mu asked me to dinner at their house. It was a dinner to honour the great American director, William Wyler. I had greatly looked forward to this evening. Ralph and Mu were elegant hosts. Their house was modern, built in mock-Georgian style, set in a beautiful garden, but somewhat uninspiring from the outside. Inside, however, was quite a different matter. It was filled with exquisite eighteenth-century furniture and remarkable oil paintings and watercolours that Ralph had collected over the years. His study was a treasure trove of sculptures and antiques. This was the room where he kept his pet ferret, a fierce little creature, very prone to nipping his guests on their shins.

Driving to dinner, I heard on the radio the terrible news that President Kennedy had been assassinated. I stopped the car by the side of the road. The sense of loss was profound.

The evening at the Richardson's proceeded, and everyone gathered together. The Wylers were utterly charming. Naturally the talk was entirely about the tragedy that had taken place in Dallas. Gradually during dinner all conversation ceased. Everyone was in a state of shock. William Wyler said immediately after dessert that he felt everyone should go home and be with their own thoughts. A dark cloud hung over the world that night.

The following day I went to a matinee of *Uncle Vanya* at the Old Vic, with Laurence Olivier and Michael Redgrave giving utterly brilliant performances. The afternoon had held the audience spellbound. We were transported to Russia and Vanya's world. At the end of the performance we were perched to express our enthusiasm and gratitude to the cast, but Sir Laurence stepped forward and stopped us. We had a minute's silence for President Kennedy, and then all of us quietly left the theatre. It was a strange feeling. The afternoon had helped us to forget for a little while a tragedy that had shattered the world, but we also felt disappointed to be unable to thank the cast for this rare achievement. I am sure Sir Laurence had done the correct thing, but never have I been so aware that applause really can express feelings in an incomparable way.

The next play I did in the West End was *The Right Honourable Gentleman*. It was about the Member of Parliament for Chelsea, Sir Charles Dilke, and his supposed affair with Virginia Crawford. It was real-life Victorian melodrama. Anthony Quayle played Dilke, I was Nia Crawford, and Coral Browne was my mother. Glen Byam Shaw directed. After a short tour the play opened at Her Majesty's Theatre, and was a great commercial hit. I felt much freer on stage than ever before. This was largely due to Anthony Quayle, who was wonderful and generous to act with. He was completely spontaneous and drew you into his world. If there were nights when concentration wandered, Tony drew you back and focused you in a very particular and penetrating way. He was such a truthful actor. I remembered seeing his Falstaff at Stratford when I was a teenager, and being moved to tears and laughter almost simultaneously.

Coral Browne was a huge personality, known of course for her famous irony and wit. I once overheard her say to someone whilst looking at a photograph of me in some newspaper, 'What's Anna Massey looking for? Her chin I shouldn't wonder.'

When she knew that I had heard her, she was mortified. When her wit took hold of her, she couldn't control it. But she was extremely kind to my son, David, and to me, and she had a gentle side that few but her closest friends saw. During rehearsals for the play we had all had lunch one day in a fish restaurant in Shaftesbury Avenue. Coral was very critical of the miniscule portions that we had been given. On leaving, the rather sycophantic head waiter had asked Coral if she had enjoyed her meal. She announced, much to his amazement, that she would be returning the next day to feed the fish.

The run was fun, but after about six months, we all got the usual fear of forgetting our lines. There is little you can do to fight this. The brain just seems to get tired of the repetition. The fear passes after a week or so, and calm is restored, but while it lasts, it takes all the joy out of acting. One night while we were all going through the agonies, Coral was waiting to go on, and I came up to her and saw a lot of writing on her arm. I said, 'Coral what is that?'

'My lines,' she replied. She had indeed written large chunks of the script out on her arm. She had to take her spectacles on stage with her so that she could read her promptings. This illustrates just how frightened one can get.

We all stayed in the play for fifteen months, but I never got bored, and found fresh things in my part right up to the end.

During the run of *The Right Honourable Gentleman*, I was asked to do a recording of *Henry V* for an American company. Richard Burton was to play Henry and I was to be Katherine. I was much looking forward to it, and practised my French accent endlessly, annoying all my friends. I had met Richard once or twice before with my mother when he was playing in *The Lady's Not For Burning* in New York. But this of course was before he had become a film star. At the time of our recording he had just finished filming *Cleopatra*, and had just started his much-publicised romance with Elizabeth Taylor.

The day started shakily. Richard worried about his voice, because it had been some time since he'd been on stage and used his full vocal range. However, all was well and during the day his voice warmed up magnificently, and his lyrical Welsh phrasing enthralled us all. At teatime Elizabeth Taylor arrived. I had met her once before with my godmother, the ex-Gaiety Girl, Gertie, Countess of Dudley. She was a wonderfully fat and generous old lady who lived in Chiddingfold in Surrey. She was a friend of Mrs Taylor who brought her daughter Elizabeth over for tea. This occasion had been very memorable for me as I had recently seen *National Velvet*, and it was a thrill to meet the star, who was utterly charming, extremely beautiful and unspoilt. The star that came to tea twenty years later to meet her lover, Richard Burton, was equally charming and even more beautiful. She glowed and her blue eyes shone, but she was dressed rather strangely for afternoon tea – she had apparently broken something, and had to rest her weight upon a crutch. Her hair was done up very ornately, and decorated with diamond pins. Even the ebony shepherd's crutch she held had a bejewelled handle. She wore a vivid blue dress that was almost hidden by a vast black velvet cape trimmed in ermine. Our informal little tea party hardly merited such sartorial effort. The two lovers gazed upon each other and made the rest of us, the cast and crew, feel somewhat de trop. After a mammoth pause when no one dared to speak, I heard myself say to Miss Taylor, 'I love your crutch.' No one laughed.

I do not think I have ever before or since that day been in the presence of two people who were so mesmerised by each other. They thrived on their love alone.

Around this time I was asked to be in the film of *Bunny Lake is Missing*, a thriller to be directed by Otto Preminger. Keir Dullea was to star with Laurence Olivier, Noel Coward and Carol Linley, and the great Martita Hunt in a cameo role of a bedridden invalid. The story was about a child who goes missing from a nursery school. Carol played the mother and Keir her somewhat unbalanced brother. I was in charge of the nursery school. Most of my scenes were with Olivier who played the detective. Poor Larry had a dreadful time with his lines. They were full of details of bus times and probing non sequiturs. We ended up doing extremely short takes. He felt defeated. Otto Preminger was wonderfully patient with him and totally in awe. But I found him one of the cruellest and most unpleasant directors that I have ever worked with. I think Keir did too. He nearly suffered a nervous breakdown during the filming. Preminger was brutal in his approach to him and completely undermined his confidence. Keir wanted comfort, and one day he went down to see Stanley Kubrick in his country house in Buckinghamshire. Keir had quite recently starred in Kubrick's *2001: A Space Odyssey*. He took me along with him. The Kubricks gave us the warmest of welcomes. We chatted away by a roaring fire eating a cosy farmhouse supper cooked by Mrs K. I could quite see why Keir had sought Kubrick out for reassurance. He had that rare gift of listening, of genuinely caring about other people and their problems. He was a gentle man. It was refreshing to be away from Preminger's monstrous ego, and to be bathed in the warmth and normality of the Kubrick household.

On my last day on *Bunny Lake*, Preminger said he wanted to speak to me. I assumed that he was going to thank me for my services. Not at all. He said that I was a stage actress, and that I had used far too much voice, and would have to post-synch my entire part. I was horrified, and left the location in a great depression. When the time came for post-synching, I realised he had just been taunting me. I had only to dub half a line.

The run of *The Right Honourable Gentleman* came to an end. My affair with Peter Chettle had finished some time before, and I had started a relationship that was to last for the next two years. It was a passionate affair. We never lived together, and it made neither of the 'participants' particularly happy. It was too turbulent, and ultimately disruptive. I craved domestic peace, a calmness to come home to at the end of the day, someone to comfort you, and equally someone to comfort. How elusive these desires proved to be. I had to wait a long time before such happiness came my way.

CHAPTER 11

UNTIL 1967 THE WEST END THEATRE WAS TO BE MY HOME. I was now asked to play Laura in Tennessee Williams' *The Glass Menagerie*. It is perhaps my favourite of his plays. The great dramatist gives four actors heartbreaking roles – Amanda, the spoilt Southern belle still hanging on to her fading youth, Tom, her son yearning to fly the nest, Laura, the painfully shy crippled daughter, and the gentleman caller, unaware of the havoc he is creating. They are all characters that demand the subtlest performances. The play burns with Williams' own youthful frustration and pain. Vivian Matalon was to be our director, and this turned out to be another turning point in my career. Gwen Ffrançon-Davies was going to play Amanda, Ian McShane was Tom, and George Baker was the gentleman caller. Vivian Matalon was a great teacher as well as a wonderful director. Broadly speaking there are two types of directors – those who teach and under whose direction you learn, and those who inspire you without specifics. Until now most of the directors that I had worked with blocked the play very quickly, that is to say they worked out where everyone should be on the stage in a very technical way. There was little investigation of character. 'Light a cigarette on this line', 'Move to the window on that line' were the sort of directions you were given. You had little to cling on to.

But Vivian was a master. He had studied with the great American teacher, Sandy Meisner, and, for the first time, I learnt how to approach a part in great depth and detail. Vivian enabled you to create your inner world, and prevented all form of demonstration. Laura in *The Glass Menagerie* is painfully shy. Vivian did not let me demonstrate this fact. One of the greatest sins in acting is to 'tell' an audience anything too overtly. A shy person's 'action' or 'intention' is to overcome their shyness, not to display it. He helped me to portray Laura with infinite delicacy and subtlety. Laura is partially crippled, and I had to limp each night on stage, and sometimes I continued to do so after the performance. We all became so involved with our roles. Vivian explained that we should play 'off the line'. Basically this means not overemphasising the line but giving it its true weight. When we speak in life we frequently think of many things whilst we are speaking, which instils naturalness in our speech. With a part you have to create the character's world to enable you to do this. Stanislavski and the great American actress, Uta Hagen, have both written extensively on this subject. Each actor has to make this 'journey' their own. Vivian was the instigator of this process for me. Over the years my methods have deepened, and later I will discuss in more detail how this approach helped me to overcome stage fright and pure panic.

We toured for five weeks before coming to London and opening at the Haymarket Theatre. I learnt so much, and it was most rewarding working with Gwen Ffrançon-Davies. She was over seventy years old at the time, but her sheer joy and spirit made you believe that she was in her early fifties. Gwen suffered all her life from the most dreadful eyesight, but she never let this impede her. She had a blazing inner honesty. We became close friends for the rest of her life. Once many, many years later when she was nearly a hundred years old, I visited her in her country cottage in Suffolk. Alec McCowen and I drove down together. After tea, sitting by a roaring fire, Gwen started to recite from memory one of Agatha's monologues from Eliot's *Family Reunion*. It was so spontaneous that for a moment neither Alec nor I were aware that she was quoting from a play. We thought that she was speaking directly to us. It was a uniquely moving experience. She slipped from *Family Reunion* to Juliet, and in an instant she was fourteen years old, her voice and posture had lightened. She had a most remarkable talent.

The Glass Menagerie received wonderful reviews, but was not a hit. After a few weeks we closed, and for the very first time at the end of a run I felt sad. Normally I rejoiced at the sense of freedom, but this time I was bereft and longed to be back in Tennessee's world of intense emotional fragility.

After a few weeks' catching up with my social life, I received a surprise invitation. My Uncle Vincent, as I have said, became the Governor General of Canada after the war. I think he enjoyed the role to the hilt. He now invited me to spend a long weekend at his house in Port Hope, Batterwood, outside Toronto. He was to entertain Prince Philip, and wanted me to act as his hostess. His wife had died some years earlier. I accepted the invitation, and flew to Toronto. There had been a little difficulty as to who was to pay for my ticket. Uncle Vincent was not the most generous of men, and had expected me to pay for my own flight. But in the end he did buy my ticket, rather grudgingly, and met me at the airport. I arrived late in the afternoon Canadian time, which was about midnight British time. Nevertheless, Uncle Vincent insisted on taking me all round the city, showing me all the sights – Massey College and his old school, even the outside of the house where he and Father had been born. It was at this time a restaurant, but prior to that had been a high-class brothel. I never asked my father what he felt about this, but Uncle Vincent appeared quite amused. Finally after all the sightseeing and dinner, we reached his house at midnight, which was five in the morning by my personal clock. I was barely able to speak.

The next day I was taken through all the royal protocol, such as backing out of the dining room when the ladies left after dinner. You sensed Uncle Vincent revelled in all these details. When Prince Philip arrived, the atmosphere eased greatly. The Prince was far less royal than Uncle V, and when all the ladies backed out of the dining room, he laughed and told us not to be so formal. We all spent a charming and relaxed evening talking by the fireside. His Royal Highness retired early, and left immediately after breakfast the following day. The whole visit was over in a flash. But despite my jet lag, I remember everyone laughed a lot.

On my return to London, I was asked to take over from Vanessa Redgrave in *The Prime of Miss Jean Brodie*. I accepted and immediately regretted my decision. Taking over a role denies you the time to make a part your own. The play has been moulded to someone else, and you never can forget that. All that Vivian Matalon had so painstakingly taught me went out the window. Peter Wood, the director, whipped me into a state of frenzy. He talked a great deal, when I needed to be calmed. I panicked and only just got through my own First Night. The Brodie girls were terrific and helped me as much as they could, but it took me a long, long time to settle in. I always felt I was Vanessa's inadequate ghost. I took over once more in my career — from Penelope Keith in Michael Frayn's *Donkey's Years*. It was the same experience. Why hadn't I learnt? I think my decision this time was largely financial, never a rewarding move.

After I left *Jean Brodie*, I did a light comedy by Hugh and Margaret Williams called *The Flipside*. It was directed by my good friend, Robert Chetwyn, and felt like taking a holiday. It ran for a year and the audience laughed a lot. For a time everything seemed all right. But then disaster struck. Nanny had for the last two years been suffering from breast cancer. She became very ill and had to go into hospital. For nine months she fought the disease, but in March 1968 she died. The grief was overwhelming. She had been my life support from birth. She had shielded me from so much pain. For a while I managed to carry on, but eventually I broke down, emotionally and physically. At last I had to learn to face life on my own.

CHAPTER 12

I BELIEVE SOCRATES WAS THE FIRST PERSON TO SAY, 'KNOW thyself.' Many have quoted him since. To know oneself is not an easy task, as we are all prone to self-deception. In 1968, I was completely 'blind to my own nature'. I had never even considered who I was. I relied upon everyone else for their opinions. I could make no decisions for myself. I was completely unaware of my talents, abilities or potential. I was like a raft on stormy seas, being blown in all directions. I circulated in the great big world, but I came home each night and there was Nanny. She had come to live with me when David was born, but she of course continued to look after me too. We were her two charges. Her death was like losing both parents on the same day. My mother had once said, 'You love Nanny more than you love me.' This was true, for it had been Nanny who had given me tenderness, warmth and strength when I was young. She was not maternal but she was giving and constant. Without her, in the practical sense, everything fell apart. She had run my home, had organised all the menial tasks, and when I came back from the theatre each night, she would have turned down my bed, laid out my nightgown, and in winter, she would have given me a hot-water bottle. All these deeds performed with no fuss and with no requests for thanks. She knew we loved her, and I knew she loved David and me, profoundly. Such selflessness is rare. Nanny was quite irreplaceable. There was a howling void in our lives.

David was now at a boarding school in Sussex. We had decided to send him away to school because Nanny was already quite ill, and with me working all the time, I felt that with fresh country air, and lots of friends of his own age around, he would have a healthier and more normal existence. He never wanted to go, and suffered dreadful homesickness the days before he was due to return to school after the holidays. Once he was there I think he did settle in quite well, but I shall regret the decision to send him away to school for the rest of my life. Home and family are vital to a child's development, and I deprived David of this right. Holidays with one parent or the other is not a way to raise children. It gives them no sense of security. When Nanny died, I can only say that I was in no fit state to look after anyone. I suffered inconsolable grief, and there were days when I couldn't even get out of bed. Once I lost the sense of feeling in my legs. It was only temporary, and all my symptoms at this period were simply manifestations of inner pain and panic at having to face life on my own with a small son. My brother Daniel was around a bit and tried to help, but really there was only one person who could do that, and that was me, and I had neither the strength nor the insight to go about the task.

For the first holiday that David spent at home without Nanny, I got a young girl to help out and take him around while I was at the theatre. This was a disaster. No one could replace Nanny, and from then on I abandoned replacements, and I coped as best I could. Jeremy helped when he was free, and he did take David on several trips, and I turned down work as much as possible during the school holidays so that I could be with my son, but I know that I offered him too little comfort. I was drowning in despair and anxiety.

When David went back to school each term, I started working again. I did a lot of television at this time. This is a medium I love. The demands of filming and television are quite different from those of the theatre. Your evenings on the whole are free, and the commitment is not so long.

I did a television performance at this time of Ibsen's master-piece, *The Doll's House*, playing the childlike Nora, who grows up during the play and abandons her husband and small children to find herself in the great outside world. It was a strange and painful play to be working on, for there were so many parallels in Nora's and my life. Torvald, her husband, had shielded Nora in much the same way that Nanny had shielded me. How aware I was of these parallels at the time, I am not sure. I think I was too troubled to think so clearly. In the course of the play Nora finds out about herself, and also finds the strength to act upon her discoveries. She leaves Torvald, whereas in my life, Nanny had 'left' me.

The Doll's House is a drama where life can be telescoped. In real life self-discoveries take a great deal longer, and it is much harder to find the strength to face the world alone. I found working on this play extremely disturbing. Ibsen pares his texts to the bone. He gives you the mountain peaks, and leaves you to discover the subtext for yourself. Everyone's journey is superbly crafted with the minimum of explanation. Sometimes you have to take great leaps of faith. The mood changes are sudden and often difficult to make appear spontaneous. I would love to have had the chance to play the part again when I was in a fitter and more rational state. But alas that opportunity never came my way.

The year after Nanny's death I was in an extremely destruc-tive relationship with an actor. We both seemed to be punishing ourselves inexplicably, so unsuited were we to each other. If you know nothing about your real self, it is impossible to know anything of other people, and so to have a loving, equal rela-tionship is an unachievable goal. This was a truly unhappy affair. We never lived together, and after little more than a year, we went our separate ways.

It was shortly after Nanny's death that I started to develop anorexia. This is a word that is frequently used incorrectly. It is an umbrella title for eating problems. I simply did not want to eat, and of course if you don't eat you perish, so my form of anorexia was a slow wish to die. The more people urged me to eat, the more impossible it became. The wisest friends found subtle ways of getting me to lift a knife and fork. They diverted me as you would a child. One day I weighed myself, and found to my horror that I was six stone nine pounds. This was frighteningly light. I will never know why I reacted to this discovery so positively, but it is true to say that from that day on, I started to eat again, not enormous amounts at first, but bit by bit I began to put on weight till I reached seven stone twelve pounds. This was the weight that I retained for many years, although I have to confess that at all difficult times in my life, eating is not easy. Stuffing myself from the fridge for comfort has never been my problem. Getting the fridge door open at all was my difficulty. The frightening thing about my form of anorexia, and I know countless people suffer from the same affliction, is that you have absolutely no control over yourself. You are taken over by the illness, and no amount of rational thinking helps. It has always surprised me that I conquered the disease by myself without professional help, and when I went into analysis some years later, my anorexia was a matter of the past. Once I started to eat again, I found more energy to cope with life, and when I was offered a part in Cy Enfield's film about the Marquis de Sade, I accepted, packed my bags and flew to West Berlin.

De Sade was to be played by Keir Dullea. It was good to meet up with him again after our *Bunny Lake* jaunt. I was to play Keir's wife, and Senta Berger, the Austrian film star, was to play my beautiful sister, with whom de Sade was really in love. There was a scene where de Sade is signing our marriage contract when he fantasises for a moment that he is to marry my sister. He looks up and sees the plain sister who is to be his bride, then flies into a tyrannical rage, railing against my appearance. I was playing the ugly duckling. Cy had gathered together a really strong cast. Lilli Palmer, the famous German actress who had been married to Rex Harrison, was to play our mother, and John Huston, the director, was to play the priest. He was full of wonderful Irish charm, with a droll sense of humour, and during our canteen lunches he was interested by everyone and everything that was going on around him. He was warming to be near and we needed to be cheered, for the studio where we filmed was extremely gloomy and depressing. It had been a prison during the war, and it was rumoured that gas had been used there. It was a difficult place in which to work. Spandau gaol was also a few minutes from the studio, the gaol where Rudolph Hess was imprisoned.

Lilli Palmer longed to find out at the end of each week that she had not been paid, so she would have the right to leave the film and return to her beautiful Swiss mountain retreat. But the cheque always arrived on time and she had to complete her role. Lilli was an exquisite woman, as tiny and delicate as a piece of Dresden china, with the softest and most seductive of voices.

During the filming, Cy Enfield suffered a mild heart attack and had to withdraw. Roger Corman was flown in to replace him. The film now changed gear. The psychological atmosphere that had dominated Cy's film was replaced by Corman's own personal view of the story, less delicate, but certainly more colourful and robust. He asked me if I would be prepared to strip to the waist for a dream sequence, which he promised would be shot with a prismatic lens, preventing full exposure. If I agreed to do this scene, he said I could go home three days early. By this time I was so disenchanted with West Berlin that I agreed. It was the first time in my career that I had been asked to take off any part of my clothing, and I have to confess I loathed every moment of it, romping around on a bed with nine naked men and women from a Berlin nightclub. But Roger

Corman was true to his word. He did use a prismatic lens, and when I saw the film, I hardly recognised myself. It was all done with great taste. Roger had called it a dream sequence; I remember it more as a nightmare.

Throughout the filming I tried to find some member of the cast to accompany me to the eastern sector of Berlin. They were a timid bunch and no one had accepted. So, before I went home, I decided to make the journey on my own. It was quite an ordeal in 1969. Passports and documents were required, and the officials were harsh and unfriendly. Finally I arrived in the East German sector feeling extremely brave and adventurous. I went straight to Brecht's old theatre where his Berliner Ensemble performed. It was a grey day and the theatre doors were locked. I was sad, for I had wanted to pay homage to this great man whose company, under the leadership of his wife, Helene Weigel, had recently visited London, and had held us spellbound in *The Resistable Rise of Arturo Ui*. The production was charged with an electricity that was new to us. The sets were monochrome. It almost felt as though you were watching a black and white film, and the acting was precise and choreographed down to the minutest detail. This was political theatre, the theatre of a left-wing writer. I sat there absorbing it, enthralled. I had been reared in a conservative household, and my political beliefs were changing rapidly under the influence of new friends, and the theatre of Brecht provided much food for thought.

When Helene Weigel was not acting in a production, she sat in a box surveying all, white-faced and dressed in black. She was in charge of everything. You felt the ghost of Brecht sat with her. Alas, I never saw her perform during their London season.

Having failed to enter the Berliner Ensemble Theatre, I made my way to the art galleries, where some of the great paintings of the world hung in almost deserted rooms. The wondrous colours of the French Impressionists contrasted wildly with the stern ladies in black who guarded the galleries. How unwelcome they made you feel. It demanded courage to press on, but press on I did. So transported was I by the paintings that I completely lost track of the hour. I suddenly realised I barely had enough time to catch the last train of the day back to West Berlin. Coming out of the gallery, my sense of direction failed me. I was utterly lost. I found myself running frantically through dark deserted streets, when all of a sudden a little Fiat car pulled up beside me, and the driver wound down his window and asked me in perfect English if I needed help. I nearly cried with relief. He offered me a lift to the station. I leapt in. Sitting next to the driver was a woman. She immediately reassured me that I would catch my train. She lived in the eastern sector of Berlin. The driver was her lover who lived in the German Democratic Republic, and who was only allowed to visit her once a year for three days. It seemed the most tragic and romantic story. I felt guilty that I had robbed them of time together, so precious must these three days have been.

West Berlin in 1969 was also a strange place. Walking down Kurfurstendam, I sometimes felt that I was on a film set, and that, behind the facade of the buildings, one would find nothing but the studio walls. There was an unreal feeling in the air. During the film I had stayed in a hotel on a lake just outside the city, very peaceful and very secluded. It was modern and held no memories of the war. But nevertheless one was always conscious of the Wall. Twenty years were to pass before it was torn down.

My time in Berlin had certainly been interesting, but I was very pleased to come home. I wasn't back for long before Peter Dews, the director of the Birmingham Repertory Theatre, asked me to play Ophelia in Alec McCowen's *Hamlet*. I agreed, and once again I packed my bags, but this time I wasn't going to a divided city, but to the Midlands.

Peter Dews had originally mounted the production for Richard Chamberlain. Gemma Jones had played Ophelia. So in many ways this was a takeover, but with a difference, for the whole cast was new to the production which was also to be restaged. It was good to be with Alec again and watch him tackle this formidable part. He arrived at rehearsals completely prepared and could have opened almost immediately. The same could not be said for me. *Hamlet* is a mammoth play about family, revenge and death. At this moment in my life, I could not immerse myself in this world of despair. The verse frightened me, and instead of relishing the richness of the language, I panicked, and all my worst habits came to the fore. I went on stage each night in a carapace of fear. I look back in shame at the superficial performance I gave in Shakespeare's masterpiece. The detailed work that I had learnt from Vivian Matalon again deserted me. Each night I felt completely adrift.

However, life off stage was full of surprises. Quite unexpectedly romance appeared on the horizon, and a painful time was transformed into a most enjoyable experience.

In the cast of *Hamlet* there were many young actors playing many small parts. We all got on extremely well together, and went around in a happy group, laughing a lot and generally having fun, something I had not experienced for a long time. No particular member of the group attracted me during rehearsals. They were all attentive and humorous, and I thought of them collectively. But just before we opened, all the men had to have their hair cut. The production was set in the early 1900s, and demanded short back and sides. One day I became aware of a devastatingly good-looking young man called George Fenton. He had been hidden previously by long brown hair that had hung over his large and beautiful green eyes. I was immediately smitten. But there was a small problem. George was twelve years younger than me. I was thirty-two and he was barely twenty. The problem was overcome. Soon after the play opened, I moved out of my hotel, and joined George in his digs in Handsworth. Our families knew nothing of what was happening in the Midlands, and it gave us time to get to know each other.

When we came back to London, we broke the news gently to everyone, and George moved into my flat.

During the run of *Hamlet*, all I thought about was coming off stage to find a note from George pinned to a piece of scenery. He was playing various roles, a soldier in one scene, and the sailor in another. He always managed to find the time to write me a little love poem. Ophelia goes mad from the guilt of betraying Hamlet, and from his cruel treatment of her. I did not experience the enormity of this anguish. I failed in the role completely, for apart from my fear of the verse, my mind was elsewhere. For a while I felt all that mattered to me was the fact that I was in love.

George was the only man I ever invited to live with me after my marriage had ended. I was determined not to subject David to my romances, unless they were important and hopefully permanent. I knew a romance with someone so young was probably not destined to last forever, but George had an inner calm about him, and he and David got on really well. George was nearer in years to David than he was to me, and they struck up a friendship that has lasted to this day. They used to play football every weekend in Hyde Park, and at last I felt I was giving David a more stable home life. It had not been so easy to start with, for naturally David had felt threatened by George's arrival on the scene. He said he wanted to leave me and go and live with his father. But George helped me to explain to David in the most thoughtful and gentle terms that he did not want to share my happiness, only my unhappiness. David understood this, and soon everything settled down, and a peaceful domestic phase began. George and David became good friends. Our flat was filled with young people and much merriment. George's youth and outlook affected both David and me. I started to wear hippy clothes. I permed my hair and felt relieved to abandon the Audrey Hepburn look: the little suits copying Givenchy, and the white gloves and neat handbags. Now I carried colourful satchels, wore wedge sandals, and followed every young fashion trend. George was a musician, and he played the guitar with enormous charm and had the lightest of singing voices. He and a group of his friends recorded an album while we were together. It was interesting for David and me to enter this world for a while.

Eventually, of course, George abandoned his acting career, and became a famous film composer, writing the scores for countless British and Hollywood films, and winning awards on both sides of the Atlantic. But in 1970 he was with David and me in our London flat.

Soon after we got back from Birmingham, George was given the role of the student in Simon Gray's play *Butley*, directed by Harold Pinter, and starring Alan Bates. This is when I got to know both Simon and Harold. I was to work with them many times in the future. I was quite bewitched by Pinter's personality from my earliest meeting. Harold was married to Vivien Merchant at this time. They gave a party once for the *Butley* cast in their beautiful house in Regent's Park. It was most elegantly decorated, absolutely no clutter. But what I remember most about the decor was a pair of very pointed, black, high-heeled shoes with mud on the heels, placed on one side of the mantlepiece. They almost seemed to speak to you, and arrested everyone's attention, but no one dared to ask about their significance. The carpets were rolled back and we all danced until the small hours. Vivien did not appear that night as she was filming the next day, but Harold made sure we all had a good time. I will talk about working with him later, for I was fortunate enough to do so many times. He is one of the most loyal people I know. He protects his friends fiercely, and I have often been touched by his kindness.

Life with George was fun. We went out a great deal, and a little sparkle had been introduced into David's and my life. We spent many weekends at George's parents' house in Kent. They were very welcoming. All his sisters and his brother congregated there, and we were made to feel part of a family, a new and comforting feeling for us both.

Little did I know that I was about to be offered a job that really was to change the shape of my career. Max Stafford-Clark, the director of the Royal Court Theatre, Sloane Square, asked me to play the part of Ann in David Hare's *Slag*. I accepted and started out on the most extraordinary journey.

CHAPTER 13

SLAG TURNED OUT TO BE ONE OF THE MOST ENJOYABLE engagements of my theatre life. It was the start of my long and close friendship with David Hare. There are very few friends that, in a dire emergency, you feel you could call up at four in the morning. David Hare is one of those few. I hasten to add that I have never burdened a friend with such a demand, but, when you live alone, it is an enormous comfort to know that they are there.

Slag had been performed very successfully at the Hampstead Theatre. Now it was being put on at the Royal Court Theatre with an entirely new cast – Lynn Redgrave, Barbara Ferris and myself. Max Stafford-Clark was to direct. I felt that at last I had left the commercial West End, and joined the real theatre of imagination and adventure.

Slag is a satire set in a girls' boarding school, where the anarchic Joanne expounds her revolutionary, feminist views to the very feminine Elise, and the rather masculine and traditionalist headmistress Ann. Lynn was to play Joanne, Barbara was to be Elise, and I was to play Ann.

The play is divided into six scenes, set in four different locations, three in the common room, one on the edge of a cricket pitch, another in the bathroom, and one in a bedroom. The scenes are so original, and bursting with wit and irony. The play has, as David says in his foreword, a dreamlike vitality. The dialogue is precise and unusual, requiring great breath control and concentration. All David's writing has its own rhythm. It is not easy to learn, because the phrasing is so often unexpected. This was his first full-length play. It was fascinating that he had dared to write so successfully about a secluded female establishment. He had of course drawn on his days at Lancing College.

Rehearsals were to take place at the Irish Club off Eaton Square, in rather a grand and dilapidated salon. David arrived at our first rehearsal looking about sixteen. We read through the play as is the usual custom, but thereafter things were entirely different. Max was the first director I had met who liked improvisations, and we started to improvise from that very first day. These exercises involve using your own invented dialogue in situations chosen by the director to help you discover more about your characters. When improvisations are controlled and conducted by someone as precise and focused as Max, they can be profoundly illuminating. Unfortunately they often have no prepared aim, and become an irritating waste of time.

Max, like the director Vivian Matalon, abhorred demonstration or 'embroidery' in performances. He said that whenever we speak in life there is always an action or intention behind the line. For example you might want to say to someone, 'I love you', but instead of simply wanting to inform them of your feeling, you might want to 'shame' them or 'humiliate' them, depending on the circumstances. Max's aim was to encourage us to discover as much as we possibly could about the characters and the scenes, and to give each thought its rightful depth and value. Through these improvisations we uncovered many subtleties. It was a most interesting and rewarding time. We delved into the text with a fine toothcomb, and early on in the rehearsals Max would ask us to say our lines preceded by the 'action'. For example, if the line was, 'I'm pretty tough. I'll go back up,' I would have to say, 'Ann reassures Joanne and Elise,' and then say the line. I used the word 'reassures' because in the scene I had just fallen off a roof. This sounds very complicated, but in fact it clarifies the text, and helps the lines to become part of your inner self. After a week or so, you drop saying the action, and feel free to 'live in the moment'. Some actors dislike this way of working, while others are devotees. To this day I always work on my actions when preparing a part. It helps you to explore in depth, and is a brilliant shortcut to the arduous task of learning lines. Of course it works better when everyone is working in the same way, because then the discoveries are shared. But even working alone with this method, I think a performance becomes fuller and more interesting.

In *Slag* there was a delicate scene in which Barbara and I had to kiss whilst an angry Lynn looked on in fury. The scene made us nervous, for in 1970 such explicitness was quite new. Out of nerves, Barbara and I often laughed, or 'corpsed' as it's called in the profession. This infuriated Lynn, who was a perfectionist, and she felt we were being 'unprofessional'. But it was truly fear that made us giggle, and the more we tried to control it, the less we succeeded.

Comedy is such a difficult task. It is far easier to make an audience cry than to make it laugh. On the First Night of *Slag*, I got a laugh in the first scene that brought the house down, but from that night on, I never got so much as a titter on the line. Comedy is delicate and elusive, and can never be striven for. The mood of each audience is different, and their humour and attention varies. No one has ever really analysed this successfully. It is one of the most interesting aspects of acting. Each night you ride uncharted waters. This is what makes it frightening, but on a good night when everything goes well, makes it thrilling.

One night Noel Coward came. He was going on to some event afterwards, and asked to see us in the interval. We met him in the front of house, dressed in our costumes, and he was fulsome in his praise, clearly loving the originality of the evening. He told David afterwards that he had written five brilliant scenes and one bad one, that being the final scene. The following day he rang me up and said that David had simply not found an ending to his play, always the hardest part according to Noel. But his encouragement had been warming. He always nurtured new talent when he saw it.

Lynn, Barbara and I became close friends during the production. We have not seen each other much since, which is often the way in actors' lives. You become extremely intimate for a while, and then afterwards because of other demands and family life, you drift apart. This makes me so grateful that David and I managed to develop our friendship. But during the run of the play, we three girls were like sisters, in and out of each other's dressing rooms all the time, seemingly inseparable, comforting and supporting each other, and laughing till we cried. David reminded me not long ago of a backstage story that he found one of the oddest of his life. I was visiting Barbara in her dressing room. She was topless, and asked me if I thought her breasts were very small. Unbeknown to us, David had entered the room and overheard this question. His face was a study in astonishment. Barbara, with no embarrassment, and completely unfazed, neatly covered her breasts with a towel, and coolly said, 'Oh, hello David', which I think astonished him even more.

When I say that actors often drift apart after a run of a play, this does not mean that they forget the extraordinary closeness that they have shared. You meet again in different circumstances, and feel effortlessly at ease with each other as though you had never had time apart. I think most actors have this ability to carry on a friendship from where they left off. The terror and tensions that surround a First Night and a long run bind casts together in a unique way. I find this warming and reassuring. It touches me.

The run of *Slag* ended. I was sad because we had had so much fun, and I felt this time that I'd really learnt how to work in more depth, how to prepare for a part. The journeys to the heart of a play were from now on going to be more fulfilling, and hopefully would be richer and provide less opportunity for panic or the dreaded stage fright. I had more work to do, but I felt at least that I was heading in the right direction. Superficial rehearsal days were well and truly over. This sea change had started with Vivian Matalon, and had been deepened by Max.

But for now my evenings were free, and it was time for fun. George's first professional commitment in the theatre had been playing one of the schoolboys in Alan Bennett's *Forty Years On*. Alan and George had remained good friends. Every Saturday Alan came to supper with us and watched the football. He looked like a rather overgrown schoolboy himself, tweed-jacketed and slightly untidy with his heavy framed spectacles perched on his nose, but he had a crispness of tongue that astounded. He always brought his little notebook with him, and if anything amused him during the evening, he would jot it down. I found this quite unnerving at first. After a while I got used to it and felt a bit of a failure if I hadn't said anything entertaining enough for him to record. His wisdom and wit were so bracing that it was easy to forget that underneath he was the kindest and most caring of friends.

When David came back for the school holidays, George and I decided that the three of us should go to Cornwall. We had a great time rock climbing, swimming in a rather cold sea, but cheering ourselves afterwards with Cornish pasties and cream teas. A balance had entered my life. It was a time of unexpected calm. David and George got on so well, and that meant a lot to me. Our lives till then had been fractured. For a while my depression lifted.

Around this time my father came over to London to appear in a play called *I Never Sang For My Father*. I believe Father had adapted the play, and, when he arrived, he was excited and in a high state of tension. Vivian Matalon was to direct, so Father was in safe hands. Dan had been offered the part of the son, but had declined, fortunately causing no ill feeling. Dorothy was in attendance of course, but we did manage to see quite a bit of Father on this visit. Daniel at this time was living with Lydia, Duchess of Bedford, who was considerably older than him. I imagine Father must have been somewhat surprised to find his son and daughter residing with companions so vastly differing in age from themselves. But if he was surprised, he made no comment. Dorothy called George 'Mr Fenton' throughout the entire visit, which I found churlish and unfriendly. She was obviously making some point or other, but I rose above it.

On the First Night of Father's play, Daniel, George and I sat in the stalls feeling strangely nervous. It was a big ordeal for Father, as he had not appeared on the London stage for over forty years. He had gone to his old tailors, Messrs Lesley and Roberts, to make his suit for the play. They had made his first suit when he was at Balliol College in 1920, and the cutter Mr Robinson was still wielding his scissors. Father had asked him to cut the suit rather loosely, as he was playing a very old man. This had horrified Mr Robinson, almost as much as the price of the suit had horrified Father. In 1920 he had paid ten guineas.

At one point during the First Night, Father had had a most dramatic dry, which seemed to go on for minutes. We squirmed in our seats with anguish, unable to help in any way. The discomfort and embarrassment was far worse than if either of us had dried. But after the performance Father was elated and never mentioned the moment. He had taken it in his stride. It was to be the last time that Father appeared on stage, and I am happy to think that he really enjoyed the run.

Not long after I returned from Cornwall, my agent rang me to ask if I would go to see Alfred Hitchcock. He was planning a new film to be set in Covent Garden. No scripts were to be given out. It was simply an interview. I made my way to the very luxurious office in Piccadilly that he was using during his

London stay. Mr Hitchcock sat behind the most enormous desk I have ever seen. He was a short, very round man, as we know, and he was dwarfed physically by this gigantic piece of furniture. After two minutes in his presence, you realised that not even Mount Everest could diminish his personality, and his charm was equally formidable.

I had been told that I was being considered for the part of a secretary. No more specific details were given. I went dressed in suitable attire, but I decided not to look too severe. Instinct told me to not to appear the cliché secretary, but to add a little frivolity to my wardrobe. I was with Mr Hitchcock for an hour, which is an extremely long time for an interview. Fifteen minutes is quite normal. For the first forty-five minutes neither the script nor the plot was mentioned. First of all he told me all about how he liked to make his own batter pudding, requiring refrigeration for some hours. He told me his icebox in Los Angeles was the size of a small room. He obviously adored cooking.

I was quite beguiled by him, and was put completely at my ease. By the time he started talking about the script, the atmosphere was warm and friendly. He asked how tall I was. I said that I didn't know. It appeared that the part he was considering me for needed the actress to be quite short, as she had to end up in a potato truck.

A secretary in a potato truck, I pondered? Well, I thought, this was a Hitchcock film where anything can happen. I sat at the desk and silently took off my shoes. I think I did this in case he asked me to stand up. He went on talking about the character. It gradually became clear that he was thinking about me for the part of the cockney barmaid. The interview came to an end. No offer was made then, but I had the feeling that he was interested. I said goodbye and made my way to the door. As I was about to go out, I remembered that I'd left my shoes under the chair. There was no choice. I had to go back to get them. Explanations seemed unnecessary so I said nothing and

Hitch said nothing, but he was completely unfazed and no awkwardness lingered in the air.

If I was walking on air after I left him, I was in the stratosphere the following day when my agent rang to say that he wanted me to play the cockney barmaid. I was told I would have to accept the part without reading the script, and that the money would have to be agreed before anything could proceed. I accepted at once. To work with a legend was too good an opportunity to miss. A meeting was arranged with him for the next day. It was quite strange. At a certain moment I suggested that I would need someone to help me with the cockney accent. He said this would be impossible, as you couldn't embarrass anyone with such a request. He was a little behind the times, I think. But very soon he accepted my problem, and a lovely girl was found who was to be my coach, and also my stand-in for the lighting. This was really good news because it meant she would be around for all the rehearsals as well as the takes. She was called Sylvia and she had a heart of gold, and a very sharp ear.

At last I read the script. It was very violent in parts, but I still did not regret my decision. It was going to be an adventure. Hitchcock was financing the film with some of his own money. The budget was not generous, but frankly these are small concerns when the work is so engrossing. As long as there is enough for the bare necessities of life, I have always gone ahead and accepted poorly paid jobs, believing that money will come later.

The plot of *Frenzy*, as his film was called, was about a serial killer in Covent Garden. I was to play Babs the friendly barmaid of the Globe public house, who was in love with an ex-RAF pilot from World War Two, played by Jon Finch. Bernard Cribbins was the pub landlord, and Barry Foster was a Covent Garden vegetable dealer, who turns out to be the villain. This was meant to be a big shock to one and all, as he had been so warm and friendly to the whole community. Frankly it was rather a dated script and, as Hitch hadn't been in London for a long time, I don't think he was aware of how old-fashioned the dialogue really was. Eventually, through the script advisor, some changes were made. But all this required much tact. This is a quality Jon Finch lacked, and he and Hitch had great difficulties communicating.

Hitchcock was involved in every department. He wanted to see all my costumes, and insisted that my bust be padded. At this meeting he told me he had made a similar request to Grace Kelly, and then told me a rather risqué joke that ended, 'There's gold in them there hills.' I didn't understand this joke, but I think that it referred to Miss Kelly's décolletage. His humour was rather salacious and schoolboyish, and frequently I was not quite sure when to laugh. He would often start telling a joke just after the first assistant had alerted him everything was ready for a take. I think he hoped to calm the cast by doing this. It had the opposite effect on me. I was so nervous that I'd laugh too soon or too late, and ruin his punchline.

The myth that Hitch treated actors like cattle is completely false. He was extremely courteous to his players. He was ironic with us because that was his way. But he always had time for you, and you could ask him for guidance whenever you needed to. In one scene I had to make a phone call to my lover whilst I was working in the pub, and, after the rehearsal, I went up to Hitch and asked if it was all right. He said, 'Do you want everyone in the pub to hear you?'

'No,' I said.

'Then I suggest you speak a little more quietly,' he replied. This is how he guided you, with consummate irony. Alec McCowen, who played the police inspector in the film, received an equally ironic retort when he asked if Hitch liked the way he was playing a scene. 'Well it isn't the way I'd play it,' came the answer. Hitch then of course proceeded to tell him how he would play it himself. But this was all executed with warmth and humour, and there was never any bad feeling on the set.

At the time Hitch was in great pain as he'd had a bad fall just before leaving the States. Also his wife, Alma, had recently had a stroke, so together they were a frail pair. However he did not let these problems deter him, and arrived promptly on the set each day in his Rolls-Royce, dressed elegantly in a suit and tie. At lunch he always had a vodka, which made him a little sleepy in the afternoons. Once we were filming in a hotel on the Bayswater Road. Elsie Randolph was playing the receptionist. She did her speech, and instead of hearing Hitch say, 'Cut', there was a loud snore coming from his chair. The first assistant dealt with the moment brilliantly. He gently woke him and said, 'Would you like to go again, sir'? Calm was restored immediately, but Elsie said she had never before had such success in sending someone to sleep.

Hitchcock was of course a supreme technician. He had a miraculous eye. The camera operator on the film was Paul Osborne. He was amazed one day by Hitchcock's uncanny insight. I had exited from the pub on location in Covent Garden. They had discussed at length the point where Hitch wanted to frame the shot on my skirt. We did the take and Hitchcock, who had been sitting on the left side of the camera, turned to the operator and said, 'You were an inch out weren't you'? Yes, that was the case, but Paul told me afterwards that it was unbelievable that Hitch could have seen that from where he was sitting. Mr H was a genius.

We would always rehearse a set-up with the camera crew in the usual way, after which the actors would go and get dressed for the scene whilst the lighting was assembled, then, when we came back, we would rehearse for a long time until we were fully prepared. Just the same way that John Ford and Michael Powell worked. We did one take, and usually that was it. If Hitch was happy with that first take he never took another for insurance. He knew when he had what he wanted. There were no video screens for checking the shots as there are nowadays.

One day he asked me to come and see the rushes with him. I declined, saying that it would make me self-conscious. He accepted that, but insisted that I go and see some rushes that I was not in. I went with him during the lunch break. The Rolls-Royce met us outside the studio door and drove us thirty or forty feet to the editing chamber. Hitch walked nowhere.

The episode in the potato truck proved a problem. Hitch realised, once it was roughly cut together, that he needed extra shots to show Barry Foster remembering that my character, Babs, had grabbed his tiepin during her murder, which was not seen on screen. So overnight he himself storyboarded six or eight shots showing close ups of my horrified face, and the tiepin being ripped from Barry's throat. This was filmed during our last week, a brilliant, quick series of shots not originally scheduled.

In the film I had a scene in a hotel bedroom with Jon Finch, which involved me getting out of bed with no clothes on. Hitchcock never asked me to strip. A double had been organised without my knowledge. But when my father saw the film he assumed that the naked body was mine, and wrote me a furious letter, telling me that I had made a great mistake accepting a role in such a film. I took absolutely no notice of his diatribe. I felt his prudishness was out of date, and also that having participated so little in my upbringing, he had no right to tell me what to do at the age of thirty-five.

The film opened to very poor reviews, and I am sure Hitch must have been very depressed by them. He celebrated his seventy-third birthday during the shoot, and he must have known that he would not make many more films.

I went to the première with George, and afterwards I became very depressed. I had not enjoyed the film at all. It is always a difficult experience watching oneself, but in fact I did not embarrass myself as the barmaid. It was the film that had depressed me. I found it stilted and old-fashioned, and the violence disturbing. The Hitchcock magic had not been there. But years later, I saw the film on television, and liked it. The story fitted the small screen more happily, and perhaps by this time, it had become a period piece.

Hitch came to the première with Ingrid Bergman, who was première utterly delightful and courteous to us all. She had a special inner radiance and was as warm as toast. I met her once more, many years later, at a dinner party and found her one of the most simple and genuine people that I have ever encountered. She had a gaiety about her that was most infectious. I am sure Hitch was comforted by her when the reviews appeared the following day. I never saw him again after the première, but I hold many happy memories of my days with him.

But the happy time at home with George, David and I was about to come to an end. During the bad times in life it's good to remember to say to yourself, 'This too shall pass,' but equally you must remember to say it when things are going well. It helps one to relish the good times, and to find comfort from the fact that horrible times are not permanent. Confucius I believe was the originator of this adage, and many centuries later Abraham Lincoln quoted him. In my later years it has given me great solace.

So *Frenzy* was over, and only a few months later, David and I were on our own again. George had left us. It was an amicable parting. The age gap probably made it inevitable. Nevertheless, separating is always extremely painful, and I was heading for a very difficult period.

CHAPTER 14

WHEN I WAS QUITE YOUNG MY MOTHER TOLD ME A THEATRICAL anecdote that amused me then, but I think deep down frightened me. She told me about an old actor who was playing Friar Laurence in *Romeo and Juliet*. One night in a scene with Romeo, the old actor had completely forgotten what he should say next. After an interminable pause when no one spoke, the actor playing Romeo had improvised by saying, 'Hast nought to say Friar Laurence?' and the old thespian had simply replied, 'Nought.' The scene then came to an abrupt and unexpected end.

I also remember hearing about an actor who takes a prompt from the stage manager, in the wings, and says, 'Yes we know the line, but who says it?' This is how confused long runs and months of repetition can render you. For me, drying is the main source of fear. If someone had waved a magic wand over me and said, 'You will never dry in your life,' the most destructive part of my anxiety would have been eradicated. Controlled nerves, of course, are a vital part of a performance. I am suspicious of actors who say they haven't a nerve in their body. In my experience this usually means they are giving rather unfocused and dull performances. You have to live in the moment and be at concert pitch. This cannot be a nerveless experience.

The fear of drying is much worse than the actual dry. I have in fact forgotten my lines very seldom in my life, but on the occasions when I have, once you have dealt with the moment –

either by taking a prompt or managing to get out of it your-self, or by being helped by a fellow actor saying, 'You were going to tell me such and such, weren't you?' – the adrenalin flows so furiously through your veins that a special sort of concentration descends on you for the rest of the performance. Many actors dry a great deal and have no problem with it. They accept the moment as part of the journey. I have never been able to be so nonchalant about it.

As I have illustrated earlier, stage fright and all irrational fears are reduced enormously when you work with imaginative direc-tors. These directors give you so much to think about, and help you to delve so deeply into your part, that there is literally no time for panic. Drying only happens when you lose concentra-tion. There are many ways in which this can happen. Curiously, the restlessness of an audience seldom contributes to a loss of concentration. If someone is coughing or rustling sweet papers, it may be intensely annoying and disturbing, but these griev-ances tend to sharpen the resolve not to be thrown or be taken out of the world of the play. The lack of focus that brings about a dry is much more elusive. Forgetfulness during long runs is understandable, for the brain is rebelling against the endless repe-tition. But I have experienced a form of drying that is almost self-induced. It is like a little devil within one that says, 'I am not going to let you into this part of the play tonight.' There is no rational explanation for the little devil's presence other than an inner self-destructive force, over which you have no control. Over the years I have almost succeeded in freeing myself from this torment, which prevents any real enjoyment of being on stage. Sheila Hancock, who also suffered from stage fright, put me on to hypnotherapy, and I found this helped a great deal. Also I started to study the Alexander technique, which was a revelation. It gave me an incredible physical freedom, and increased my vocal range considerably. This may not seem a very direct way of dealing with the problem, but the more supple you are, the more power and control you have over your voice, and the more it frees the mind and enables you to focus and to feel less inhibited. Your imagination is unleashed. Pilates classes have also been an enormous help in freeing up the body, and greatly reducing tension. If your muscles are expertly stretched, you are given strength, and this sense of well-being sharpens concentration.

Anne Battye is a formidable teacher of the Alexander technique. Initially I only had fourteen lessons, and then the technique was in my hands. But I would go back to Anne at times of stress, or before a First Night. But on the whole, after I had acquired the technique, it became part of my daily life. I have found that in the course of seeking new methods to help me in my working journey, the best teachers let you go. They have a supreme confidence in themselves, and have no need to keep demonstrating their powers. To be self-assured and not self-satisfied is a major goal in life, but not always easy to achieve. The good teachers who have guided me, like Iris Warren (the voice coach who was of fantastic help early on in my career), Anne Battye and a few others, have shown me the importance of remaining open to criticism, but not to be thrown by it, to keep on with the learning process, and to remain individual and not to conform automatically. This means you can never become self-satisfied, and, hopefully, in the end you will develop a little self-assurance. I am still working at this.

There are many actors who would be baffled by the hurdles I have encountered. The whole process for them is natural and presents no problems other than the stressful demands of certain roles. These are born actors, and I envy them. They relish their talent and love to go on stage and share it with an audience. But I have to turn the tannoy off in my dressing room so as not to hear the jolly buzz of the incoming crowd. I once shared a dressing room on tour with Dame Judi Dench, and we had to invent a rule that the tannoy could be on for the quarter of an hour before she went on, otherwise it was silent. She needed the stimulus that the buzz of the audience gave her. Some nights she would say, 'Oh, I can't wait to go on tonight.' I have never said that in my life. But, that doesn't mean that when I'm on stage, magical things don't happen. They do. It's just before a performance that my nerves do not allow me to relish the prospect of the journey ahead.

There have been two nights in my life when I became so totally immersed in a part that the real world appeared to vanish for the duration of the performance. One time was when I played Ariadne Utterword in a production of *Heartbreak House*, and the other was when I played Goneril in *King Lear* at the National Theatre. I will discuss these evenings later, when I tell you about the engagements, both of which were absorbing experiences.

Acting has presented such difficulties for me that some may wonder why I didn't give up and join some other profession. I did often think of it, but always came back to the same conclusion that acting is a deep and rewarding profession, in spite of all the pitfalls.

Acting doesn't allow you to grow old in the accepted sense. Of course wrinkles appear, and bones may not be quite so supple, but if you are in a room full of actors in their later years, you will be conscious of an extraordinary youthful energy. It is invigorating to be with these people. Actors never give up. Their questing is eternal. This is both touching and brave. For most actors, the fear of being out of work continues to the end of their lives. Even if this may be a painful experience, it energises them. They keep in touch with what is going on, and cobwebs do not enshroud them.

One of the other great rewards of the profession is that it enables you to travel to parts of the world that you might never visit in the ordinary way. I am not the most intrepid of people, but, when work is involved, I become quite adventurous.

Soon after George Fenton disappeared from my life, I accepted the role of Lady Laura Standish in a twenty-six part television series to be filmed by the BBC of Trollope's Palliser novels. I was to be in nine episodes, and the location filming, prior to the studio recordings, took us to many of the most spectacular country houses in the British Isles. This was a perfect example of how spoilt the visiting actor can be. Portmeirion where we were filming in North Wales opened specially for us on a day when they were officially closed, and we were able to go round this amazing place unhindered by the usual crowds. The unique gardens and the fantastic buildings held such magic for us as we wandered about in our Victorian regalia. Sir Clough Williams-Ellis and his wife gave us tea in a private garden, all extremely informal. Sir Clough owned Portmeirion and had designed everything, incorporating many fragments of destroyed buildings into his fanciful design, which was loosely based on the seaside town of Portofino.

But it isn't always an aesthetic treat with tea parties. I was once meeting an American girlfriend at the Ritz Hotel in Madrid. She was flying in from New York, arriving late in the afternoon, and I had taken the night train from Malaga, and went straight to the hotel from the station. The concierge told me my room would be ready by ten o'clock. I filled in the reservation form, submitted my passport, and went to the dining room. When I had finished my breakfast I asked to go to my room. I was told there would be a delay, and would I mind waiting for an hour or so. I decided to go to the Prado, and lost myself for the rest of the morning utterly entranced by the treasures that hung on the overcrowded walls. The Goyas were mesmerising. I had only seen photographs of them before. They obsessed me; the little infantas in their massive dresses and ornate coiffeurs. I returned to the Ritz for a late lunch, hoping that my room would now be ready. Again I was told there would be a delay. So I went off for lunch, and another visit to the Prado. This time I became obsessed by the Breughels, which in the early sixties were hung very close together in a dark room far away from the main salons. After two hours or so, foot-weary and longing for a bath, I went back to reception. This time I was told that my room would not be ready that day, and that they had booked me into a hotel on the other side of the Plaza. I received no real explanation for the delays, and obediently I went to the new hotel in a very unsettled frame of mind. When my friend arrived later that evening all was explained. They had read my passport in which I had put as my profession, 'Actress'. Apparently not too long before Ava Gardner had stayed at the Ritz, and there had been a drama in her suite involving a matador of some renown. Since this episode, no actors had been allowed to stay there. Why they had not told me this I shall never know. They could have explained the situation the minute they saw my passport. Instead they kept me in the dark. I'd had a wonderful time in the Prado, hours of pleasure that I shall treasure always, but they had made me feel like a pariah. So this was the one instance when I discovered that being an actor was not to my advantage. I am sure that the Ritz has now changed that particular rule. I hope so, for it is usually fun to have artists around, because, on the whole, they are life-enhancers.

I worked on the Palliser series for over six months, and really enjoyed playing Lady Laura. What a full and rounded character Trollope created. Her desperate life is charted with such compassion and precision – doomed to marry the wrong man and to end her days virtually imprisoned by her cruel husband, Kennedy, while pining for Phinaeus Finn, her true soulmate.

When the engagement ended, I felt bereft. David was away at boarding school. A gloom descended on me that I couldn't shake off. I had no immediate prospect of work, but, even so, much of my depression was inexplicable, and this type of depression is the worst. Up until this point I had managed to avoid deep pessimism. Someone had once told me that optimism was a spiritual magnet. I still believe this to be true, for no one wants to be around indulgent negativity.

As in all times of trouble I turned to Daniel for help. We were very close at this time, and he was always able to lighten pain with his infectious sense of humour. On several occasions prior to this, he had suggested that I should go to an analyst. I had always refused, thinking that I could work through whatever was causing my distress on my own. Now Daniel became quite fierce with me, and I shall be eternally grateful for that. He said I was arrogant to think I could avoid analysis, and that no one other than a professional could help me now. He didn't let up. At first his vehemence had frightened me, but finally I succumbed and said I would go to an analyst if he found me a good one. He did, and on a sunny day in May I went up to a small box-like flat in Highgate and talked to Millicent Dewar. I stayed for an hour and a half on that first visit. She was assessing if I was strong enough to submit to the rigorous and painful process. I returned for another long session the next week, and finally it was decided that I would start my sessions in earnest the following week. For six years every Monday I went to Highgate. My sessions began at seven o'clock in the morning so that I could get to rehearsals, if I needed to, by nine thirty. I started going once a week, but, after a while, I went three times. In those days I paid £9 for an hour. A normal analytical session lasts for fifty minutes, but Dr Dewar took pity on me I think, and gave me the extra ten minutes because my journey was long, and I had to rise at five thirty in order to be there on time. Not everyone needs to be analysed, but for me it was an absolute lifesaver. Without it I would definitely have given up acting, and I am sure I would have been prescribed strong antidepressants and probably ended up in some clinic. Analysis is a long process and can be extremely painful at times, but, if you persevere, the benefit is worth every pound spent and every minute suffered. I avoided the clinic and the pills that veil your life, and am eternally grateful to Sigmund Freud.

Millicent Dewar was very good at her job, and I know how

lucky I was, for so many people go to a poor analyst at the beginning and then give up the struggle. I think the role of the analyst is more demanding than can ever be imagined. They nurse you through untold anguish and sometimes a session ends with the patient in despair. All they can say at that moment is that they will see you at your next session. Freudian-based analysis has very strict rules. The greeting is very formal, with the minimum of small talk, and likewise at the end of a session. The whole point is to remain as emotionally detached as possible. Many years later I was to play an analyst in a documentary film for the BBC, sponsored by the Child Psychotherapy Trust and directed by Ken Howard. I had a small boy as my patient, a small boy in turmoil because of a desperate situation at home. I longed to comfort him and forgive him for his misdemeanours. But Dr Dorothy Judd, who was advising us on the programme, explained that this would have been detrimental to the therapy. In that sense it was one of the hardest jobs I have ever had to do. I had to go against all instinct. Dorothy Judd and her husband, the historian Professor Denis Judd, have since become very close friends. It is through her that I have learnt of the enormous demands and strains that analysts suffer. To be called at any hour of the night by patients, to deal with their aggression and negative attitudes, is arduous in the extreme.

At the time of making the documentary I had long since finished my own sessions, but, looking back, I realised how patient and strong my analysts had been. The two things that I admired most about Dr Dewar were, firstly, the way in which she wound up a session, pulling together all the random threads that you had laid in a heap at her feet, and secondly, her interpretation of my dreams. I had always been bored by relating my dreams, or hearing other people describe theirs. The plots were always too convoluted, like demented, abstract films. However, Dr Dewar explained that dreams were a short cut into understanding the subconscious mind. When I told her my dreams, I understood what she meant. She was a brilliant interpreter, and would find things in the dreams that illuminated whole sections of your problems. She told me that in dreaming, you are the director and the producer and all the players. So frequently you are both the villain and the victim. How complex the subconscious is, and what invaluable clues lie hidden there, until unearthed by a master sleuth.

One of the many problems Dr Dewar helped me with was blasphemy. I have always been a person who swears quite easily. I am sure over the years I have shocked some people, but once Dr Dewar had said that it was probably quite helpful, for it released tensions that would otherwise have built up inside me, I relaxed, and felt less guilty.

During the first few months of analysis in 1974, I was offered the part of Ariadne Utterword in Shaw's *Heartbreak House*. It was supposed to be one of the opening productions on the Olivier stage at the new National Theatre on the South Bank, but the theatre was not ready in time, and so we opened at the Old Vic where the National was temporarily housed. John Schlesinger was going to direct the production, and the cast was quite stellar. Colin Blakely was to play Shotover, Eileen Atkins Hesione, and Kate Nelligan Ellie Dunn. We assembled for rehearsals and there was much tension in the air. John Schlesinger was in a very nervous state. I got to know him very well from this production, and loved him dearly, but he was an inveterate worrier. I myself was in a state of inner panic.

I had confided to Dr Dewar that perhaps it would be better not to do the play at all. But she had persuaded me that at all costs I should continue to work during my therapy. She said that if I gave up this commitment I would find it very hard to continue to act. Keep going, she urged me, and I am very glad that I did, for it turned out to be a very rewarding engagement. I was really quite sick at this time, although I did not fully realise this. Dr Dewar told me afterwards that I had been in a bad way.

Funnily enough I had not even asked her what school of analysts she belonged to. It was two years before I got round to asking what kind of therapy I was receiving. She was a member of the Institute, which is in fact Freudian-based, but by 1974 there had been much dialogue between all the different schools of analysis. The strict old-fashioned Freudian, who remained silent throughout the sessions, was no longer. With Dr Dewar there was a great exchange of ideas, and often the sessions could become quite lively. I am sure this was not the case when Sigmund had officiated.

Colin Blakely was the sunshine of our production. He was the warmest of people, and he drew us all together. His Shotover was a small white bear of a man, someone you wanted to cuddle and love, tender but amusingly irascible. His performance dominated the evening. He was quite young at the time and, in order to look the right age, he had to have a make-up done each evening that took nearly an hour and a half. His benevolence was heart-warming, and at times we all clung to him like drowning sailors to a raft. I was once sitting in his dressing room just before he had to go on for a scene, and as he was called on the tannoy, he rose from his chair and touched a photograph of his family, 'For luck,' he said. If he made a mistake during the performance, I asked him if it affected the rest of the evening. 'No,' he replied, 'I just cancel and go on.' An invaluable tip, because a mistake can colour a whole evening if you let it.

Patience Collier, who played the old nurse in the play, took me under her wing. She calmed me. John was unable to calm anyone, because he was so nervous himself. He was quite open about this. He knew what he wanted, but could not always help you to achieve it. He had great visual instinct, but he was not a teacher, he was far too impatient for that. I remember on the first day of the technical rehearsals, I went into the stalls to look at the set, which was a fabulous design by the late Michael Annals. John was sitting there huddled up in his seat, like a fretful

Buddha. He said to me in a really frightened little voice, 'Do you think it's going to be all right?' He didn't realise he was asking the most panicky person in the building. It was strangely calming to see someone so talented and successful needing so desperately to be comforted and reassured. We hugged each other and the technical rehearsal proceeded.

On the night of our first preview, I sat in my dressing room in a terrible state. I was not sure that I had the nerve to go on. Eileen Atkins came in, and I burst into tears. She was wonderfully sympathetic, and said afterwards that she knew I'd be all right, because whilst crying I had very carefully wiped my eyes with the point of a Kleenex, so as not to disturb my elaborate make-up, devised for me by Ken Lintott. I shall never forget Eileen's help that night. Actors often have that ability. They completely empathise with another's plight. It is a most life-affirming quality.

The first preview went extremely well. I got a laugh in my first scene that brought the house down. I was playing a diplomat's wife who was obviously deeply discontented underneath, but putting on a social face. I snapped out the line, 'I have been so happy,' and the audience almost applauded. This gave me a terrific boost. Colin said to me in the wings, 'Well they've got your character in one, haven't they?' and gave me a squeeze. The rest of the play went really well, and I felt I'd notched up a small victory over my fears. Each night was a battle, though. I had to take two calming pills to get through the performances. They were light pills, but still medication. I felt bad about this, but I couldn't have continued without them. By the end of the run I was able to go on pill-free, and this pleased me greatly.

Michael Annals had designed the most beautiful costumes. In the second act I had one of the sexiest dresses I have ever worn. It could be said that it almost acted for me, so seductively did it drape my figure. I received great reviews for my performance, which helped me to gain a little confidence, and I also won the Plays and Players Award for Best Supporting Actress.

It was during the run of *Heartbreak House* that I had an evening of magical concentration, when the outside world seemed to vanish and I was utterly immersed in the play. The audience were completely on my wavelength, and responded to every breath I took. I have seldom felt such empathy. It was unbelievably exciting, but what created this atmosphere, I shall never know. It almost felt like living in a dream. I visited no one's dressing room during that performance, but kept to myself, for once longing to go back on stage.

The show continued, and so did my analysis. It was during the run of *Heartbreak House* that I devised a way of working that helped me for evermore. I am sure many actors have devised similar methods, but each has to make it their own. I will try to explain.

Actors are always being asked how they learn their lines. I have always replied, 'With difficulty.' Some actors have photographic memories. They see the text on the page and that is the way they remember their lines. This technique is not for me. My aim is to get as far away as possible from seeing the text. I want to take the words as deeply into my mind as possible, to imagine them, if you like. So imagery has become my method. Each speech, in fact each sentence, has its own imagery. For example, if the line was, 'The Siamese cat sat on the Paisley rug,' I would picture the scene in my mind, filling out the whole room where the action was taking place, not just the room but the entire house. In life many people do this all the time, or at least those of us who think and talk in images. In life when I am speaking on the telephone, I imagine where the other person is sitting. I imagine the whole room where they are. In other words, my mind is able to picture the scene, without detracting from what I am saying. The same happens with my method in acting. You have a strong background of images from which the words and thoughts spring. This not only helps you to learn the text, but it helps you to remember it in depth. You also create for yourself the whole world and background of the character, from when they were very young. This way you have a huge album to pick from when choosing your images. It is like taking photographs with an emotional camera.

Irene Worth, one of the greatest actresses that I have had the privilege to get to know, worked in images. Irene was an extraordinary creature. She looked like an exotic bird, and dressed in vivid colours, keeping subtly abreast of fashion until the end of her life. She died in her mid eighties, but her face remained unlined, and her intense and curious eyes pierced your very soul. She was one of life's searchers, and shared her findings generously. I remember sitting in Peter Eyre's basement kitchen, and listening to Irene tell us how she worked on a certain speech, how she found the images to deepen her comprehension of the text. We were two actors soaking up the thoughts of a genius. She used to visit art galleries to find particular pictures to illuminate her roles. I recall that she spoke on this occasion of apricots, and we were salivating at the lusciousness of the world that she created before our eyes. To this day I see her bedecked in her Byzantine gold jewellery, encouraging us to probe ever further into a script. So many actors are in her debt. She was an exceptional person, and her encouragement and guidance meant a very great deal to me.

We did six weeks of *Heartbreak House* on tour. I had rather dreaded this, but it turned out to be great fun. Eileen and I became good friends. We both had enormous difficulty sleeping in hotels, and finding a quiet room became our joint mission. Insomnia has plagued me since I was a child, and strange beds and extraneous noise heighten the problem. We always arrived at the hotels in good time to change our rooms at least once before going to theatre for the Monday night performance. We were wary of lifts or maids' service rooms, and longed to be tucked away in quiet corners where no other guests would wake us up in the mornings. Of course this was not always possible, and once Eileen ended up next to a gentleman's loo that turned out to be quite busy in the night. She changed her room the next day. I was grateful to find in Eileen someone as fussy as I was. The good sleepers of this world are often extremely vexed by the neuroses and antics of the insomniacs. We used to go around shopping and sightseeing together during the day, and each night after the performance we would dine in one or the other's room. We laughed a lot, and the dread of being away from home was greatly eased.

I also became good friends with John Schlesinger. He was the most generous man, and entertained lavishly and frequently in his highly decorated house in Kensington. But the grandeur of the decor didn't prevent all his gatherings from being most cosy affairs. You instantly felt at home, even in the company of Kiri Te Kanawa, Michael Douglas and Melanie Griffiths. I met David Hockney at John's on one occasion. He was one of the most open people I have ever met. He shared his thoughts with you in an utterly endearing way. We spent only a brief time together but I felt I had known him for ages.

The most famous guests at John's feasts became relaxed very quickly and dropped all the trappings of stardom. This ability to welcome people and put them at their ease was one of John's greatest gifts. Everyone just loved being with him. He was so sympathetic and understanding of the fragility in his friends, and always had time to listen to your worries, and to share his own with you. He was completely unspoilt by all his success.

John gave a party once for Dustin Hoffman, and I sat next to him at dinner. He was very relaxed with a wicked sense of humour, and not at all the Hollywood star. At the end of the evening we emerged from the house together. Dustin asked me if I needed a lift, as his chauffeur-driven Rolls was waiting outside. I said, 'No thank you, I have my own car,' and pointed to my little green Mini. Quick as a flash he said, 'Don't worry, we can put it in the boot'.

The run of *Heartbreak House* came to an end after running in repertory at the Old Vic for nearly a year. So much had happened to me during that engagement. I was truly ensconced in analysis. I had made new friends, and I'd conquered the worst of stage terror. I'd won my first award, and I had moved house. I now owned a very small place in Fulham with a bijou garden. David was doing brilliantly at school. Things seemed to be on the mend. I felt more positive about life. I had no partner, but I was coping.

CHAPTER 15

ALL MY LIFE I HAVE LOVED WORKING ON THE RADIO. THE microphone has for me all the intimacy of the camera, and the two mediums of filming and recording have many similarities. Theatre demands vocal projection, and thus intimacy is harder to achieve. There is a sense of freedom at a microphone and before a camera, and the merest whisper can effortlessly convey your innermost thought. Live audiences show their anger or appreciation audibly and immediately. Their mood is inconstant, whereas the microphone and the camera are silent recorders, and therefore constant and non-judgemental, at least at the time of the performance.

I have always felt that radio is an extremely visual medium. When recording a radio play, you must bring the listener into the world of the action with the utmost subtlety and detail, and all you have at your disposal in this medium is your voice. This instrument must convey everything, the heartbeat of your character. The microphone picks up in an instant anything that is false. It is like a complicated lie detector. Over the years I have moved physically closer to the microphone, for in this way you can attain the greatest truth with the minimum effort, a good goal for most things in life. New technology has made all this possible of course. When I started working in radio in the mid fifties, we only had mono microphones (that is one-directional), stereo was being talked about as a plan for the future, but extraordinary effects were attained with non-stereo equipment, as a great deal of archive material at the BBC will demonstrate. I have heard a very early recording of Virginia Woolf that gives a glorious insight into her formidable character. The microphone even in its earliest days had infinite powers.

Originally radio plays were recorded live. This added much tension to the proceedings. I am grateful that by the time I started, they were on the whole pre-recorded. There is a famous story of a live transmission of *The White Devil* with John Gielgud, when accidentally he dropped his script during the performance. Unfazed, he continued making up lines in perfect Websterian verse, until the text was rescued for him from the floor. I can think of few actors who would have been able to cope so brilliantly.

My first radio play was in 1955. It was a production of Alain Fournier's *Le Grand Meaulnes*, the story of adolescent love and longing. Nigel Stock played Meaulnes and Donald McWhinnie, a gentle master of the medium, directed it. He looked like a tall sad camel with very strong, thick-framed glasses, a cigarette drooping permanently from his mouth, and in the lunch breaks, after his visit to the bar, he would usually be found at a piano in the studio, for he was a very accomplished jazz musician. *Le Grand Meaulnes* was pre-recorded, but in one long take with no breaks or edits. It felt very much as though we were going out live, and therefore an enormous amount of tension was created. But Donald knew exactly what he wanted. He gave notes precisely and deftly, rather like an artist putting final touches to a painting. He kept everyone calm and alert, whilst he himself remained almost detached from the proceedings. He was always at the helm, but sometimes it felt in an almost ghostlike way.

I have been fortunate to have met and worked with some of the great figures of radio. Reginald Smith was an enthusiast and an original, and his personality reigned supreme for many years at the BBC. I first met Reggie when he asked me to play in Georg Buchner's *Leonce and Lena*, a 'black' comedy, and as one critic wrote, 'A punk masterpiece'. He was quite the opposite of Donald McWhinnie. He conducted his productions with gusto, and set the studio alight with thoughts and directions. You came away from a day with Reggie feeling that your brain had been given an electric shock. He was married to the author Olivia Manning, and they were a powerful duo.

I was asked sometime later to play in the radio production of Olivia's *The Balkan Trilogy* with Jack Shepherd. This was one of the highlights of my life at the microphone. It was directed by the then Head of Drama at the BBC, John Tydeman. I owe so much to John, for he gave me some wonderful parts to play, and his friendship and support and encouragement have meant a very great deal to me. We met in rather unusual circumstances. One morning I was lying in my bath when the telephone rang. It was John Tydeman's secretary asking if I would come at once to Studio B10 at the BBC, and take over the role of Varya in Chekhov's *The Cherry Orchard*, as Eileen Atkins had been taken ill. I nearly fainted with fright. I had to confess there and then that I had never read the play. I was most ashamed at my ignorance, but I thought it better to be honest. I knew it would be full of Russian names that I would find difficult to pronounce, and I was terrified that I would hold up the recording. John Tydeman's secretary came back with the message to get in a taxi post-haste, which is exactly what I did.

We recorded the play over a period of four or five days, and nobody could have had a happier baptism into Chekhov's world than I did. Everybody welcomed me to the Russian orchard, and I can remember standing at the microphone next to Sinead Cusack who was playing Anya, and feeling her positively willing me through the scenes, and praying that I would not stumble on the patronymics. It was an exciting production, and John created, as always, a special atmosphere. Gwen Ffrançon-Davies was Madame Ranevskaya, shedding years and bringing infinite subtleties to her role. Gwen really had the ability to take you on the deepest journeys with her voice. I learnt so much from her. In spite of her appalling eyesight, Gwen could paint the spaces surrounding her with her voice, and draw you into the picture. People often talk of actors having a love affair with the camera, like Garbo and Monroe. There are also actors who have a love affair with the microphone, and Gwen was one of these.

After the production of *The Cherry Orchard*, I did a great many radio plays, and worked and made friends with several really good producers. I played parts that I would never have been considered for in visual mediums, and this enabled me to stretch my imagination. Age and beauty can be conveyed vocally, and to play characters so far away from your own physical type is a bracing challenge. I must thank those producers who took such risks with me: Cherry Cookson, Gordon House, Martin Jenkins, David Hitchinson, Richard Wortley and Marion Nancarrow are a few of the directors who have trusted me with wonderful roles. Each has given me invaluable guidance and exercised enormous patience. Gordon House once said to me when I was playing in Ibsen's *When We Dead Awaken*, 'Anna, I need more than the voice beautiful,' a note that I took very much to heart, and remember to this day with gratitude. The voice cannot carry the burden of the role alone.

Richard Wortley gave me one of the greatest challenges of my microphone life. He asked me to play Victoria in Ingmar Bergman's *A Matter of the Soul*, a powerful monologue of a woman's journey into madness and despair, full of intricate caprices and crescendos, making you feel that you are on an eternal evil switchback. I emerged from the studio feeling numb. Bergman probes deeply into the psyche of his characters, and you almost drown in the effort to take the listener to these dark forbidden places. The images he paints are from the world of Munch. Images are of course an absolutely vital part of radio performances, and painters frequently offer you an entrée to the different settings in which you find yourself.

A radio play takes between one and five days to record, depending on the length of the work. It is an intense time. You usually start with the read-through of the piece, and then immediately begin to rehearse-record. The clock is on the wall and there is no opportunity for playing around. Consequently I always do an enormous amount of preparation before going into the studio, as there is no time to 'discover' your character. Choices can be made during the recording, naturally, but the groundwork has to have been done. Nowadays it is quite common for a play to be recorded on location. With these outside broadcasts much of the atmosphere is given to you without you having to create it for yourself. I have recently done a double bill of an Edith Wharton short story called 'Roman Fever' with the late Sheila Gish, adapted for radio by Peter Eyre, and directed by Marion Nancarrow. We recorded this in Studio N41 at Bush House, as it was a World Service production. The second part of the double bill was Tennessee Williams' *Something Unspoken*, and this we recorded at Sheila's house. I think if I had to choose between the studio and the location recording, I would opt for the studio, because its less personal setting offers you a blank canvas upon which the imagination can play. Also it is easier to control the lighting, and I really like to work in extremely dimly lit studios. It helps me to focus my attention, and believe myself to be in other worlds. Some actors have found my darkened studios difficult to work in, and a compromise has had to be reached. Of course I can only ask for dim lights when I am playing a leading role, but when I record books, and I'm on my own, then I have a single lamp on the table focused on the text, and no other light in the studio at all. When notes are given, I'm quite difficult to find.

Recording books is the most tiring commitment of all. The preparation takes on average twenty hours. I mark my scripts heavily in black, and all the dialogue I highlight in bright colours, choosing a different tone for each character. This takes a great deal of time, and once this is completed, I like to read through the text at least two more times. I once had to read an Agatha Christie novel where there was a scene with twelve men and women at a dinner party. It was a mammoth task to find subtle voices for the whole group. I hate heavy accents and funny voices when recording a book, but sometimes I have had to resort to the odd lisp or vocal mannerism, simply for clarification.

Reading Jung Chang's *Wild Swans* was an enormous and rewarding challenge. There were so many Chinese names and places, and to pronounce them simply and believably, without distracting from the tense and dramatic narrative, presented quite a few headaches. Prior to the recording I went to visit Jung Chang and her husband, Jon Halliday. They were very helpful and patient with me, giving me most of the pronunciations phonetically. But of course that was only one hurdle. The story itself had to be delivered, and the harrowing tale recorded with simplicity and respect.

The highlight of my visit with Jung was when her mother appeared from the basement, a small figure, who spoke no English, but seemed to follow everything with her penetrating eyes. She had shown such courage and strength when battling against all the horrors in Jung's story, that it was hard to imagine how those tiny shoulders had borne it all. Quiet though she was at our meeting, you could still sense her formidable spirit and will.

The technical crews of broadcasting are the unsung heroes. When recording a play there are usually three in the team: the studio manager who controls the panel, assisted by someone on grams, and a third person on spot. Those on spot are in charge of all the effects in the studio, and without them we could not perform. They open all doors when necessary, and play a myriad of ghostlike roles for the production. Once I needed their help to bake a cake and do the washing-up, or rather to make it sound as though that was what I was doing. Their invention is prodigious and often in the mornings they are seen carrying lots of props brought painstakingly from their homes, kettles or wire netting or ping-pong balls, all to be put to imaginative use. They are an extremely dedicated group.

Those that work on grams are responsible for getting it all recorded, and they get on with things in their corner making little fuss. The studio manager on the panel is the wizard who can transport the scene from the Moon to Piccadilly Circus at the push of a button. They sit at a control board that nowadays looks like something out of Cape Canaveral, and deftly touch these magic knobs, and enable us to be convincing in all the preposterous settings that the plays demand. My admiration for these teams is boundless. It is similar, of course, in all the mediums. Stage crews and camera crews are the mainstays of the production, and their expertise and good humour have saved many a performance on sets and in theatres.

Many directors in all three mediums usually try to work with the same team again and again, so that everyone can talk in a kind of shorthand, as they know each other so well. This not only saves time, but also creates a kind of harmony and eases any unnecessary tension.

Broadcasting House, where I have worked mainly, is a mammoth organisation, but the warmth and good humour of the producers there prevent one from being daunted by the size of the corporation. The miles of corridors leading to the various studios have with time become navigable routes ending with friendly welcomes.

During the last three years leading up to the Millennium, I was asked to record *This Sceptred Isle*, Christopher Lee's history of Britain from the Roman occupation until the year 2000. It was the greatest gift anyone could be offered, the opportunity to learn so much, and at the same time be paid for it. My schooling had been sadly lacking, and now these intricate and illuminating scripts were going to fill in whole periods of our history hitherto unknown to me. In all, we recorded 310 fifteen-minute episodes over about three years. Pete Atkin, the producer, was a tower of strength, and guided me through the various mazes with infinite care and encouragement. There were of course other actors who read extracts during the episodes, but towards the end it was mainly me. I never felt threatened by the magnitude of the task, because Pete kept it all bubbling along and never made heavy weather of anything.

I wish I could say that I am now absolutely *au courant* with the whole of the history of our Sceptred Isle, but alas, though I retained much of what I read, the pressure was so great that many passages have slipped from my memory. However, certain characters have stuck in my mind, one of those being Emma of Normandy, who led one of the busiest lives imaginable. She married Aethelred and Cnut and was the mother of Edward the Confessor. She spent most of her time scheming for her own position and those of her children, and it seemed to me as though her life spanned more years than lesser mortals of her time. She was feisty and courageous, and on the whole behaved atrociously. I would love to have played her.

Our Isle has hosted such colourful characters, and been riven by such bloody battles, that during the recordings I marvelled at our resilience. I began to see whole stretches of countryside with new eyes. Many of the London streets bear the names of eighteenth- and nineteenth-century Ministers, and this has helped me to recall parliamentary activities in a unique way.

I was really sad when the series finally ended. It had become an integral part of my life. But it was not long before I was involved in another BBC project. I found myself working with Imelda Staunton in an Ivy Compton-Burnett play on radio, and during the recording, we decided that we would try to create a project for ourselves. We thought it would be interesting to be two women who find themselves unemployed after World War

Two, and start up a detective agency together. Imelda was amazing at bringing all the ideas together, working out our backgrounds and how we met. She was the real innovator of the series. Guy Meredith was engaged to write the scripts, and Cherry Cookson was the producer. It was strange, because I was the only person on the team who had been around during the war. It made me feel rather old. But I was able to provide a few details, one of which was that just after the war many train windows carried the advertisement, 'No Smoking Not Even Abdullah', Abdullah being a chic and popular brand at the time. It must have been a successful campaign, as I have remembered it for over sixty years.

I also told them about the two most popular tea rooms in London after the war, my favourite being Gunters off Park Lane, where the delicious walnut cake was a rare treat after rationing. Searcy and Tansley in Sloane Street was another restaurant I was taken to by Nanny when I behaved well. The waitresses dressed in black with white collars and starched white aprons. Everyone there seemed to speak in whispers.

Imelda was exciting to work with. She is a perfectionist, asks all the right questions, and really investigates a storyline. We were also extremely lucky to have some really good actors join us for the episodes. Bill Paterson became a regular member of the detective agency, bringing all his skills to make our world believable. I came up with the title for the series, *Daunt and Dervish*. It's rewarding when ideas develop and get commissioned in this way, and this time it was made possible because Imelda's imagination infected everyone.

Radio has taught me so much. In some ways it has been my university. I have read books and narrated programmes that have opened up new worlds for me and broadened my horizons. Somehow when you read something at the microphone, you travel to the places you talk of, and experience these journeys more deeply than if you simply read the texts by yourself at home. I have made many friends in the radio world, and at times in my life when I have been lonely and depressed, the thought of doing a radio play has lifted my spirits, for there is always conviviality around the microphone, and you feel part of a group and wanted again.

In my very early radio days, a director once told me to play to one person sitting in an armchair at home. He said that should be your focus. I have never forgotten his advice. It has always pleased me greatly, therefore, that I have received quite a few fan letters from quite a few armchairs, and they have given me untold pleasure over the years.

CHAPTER 16

IN 1976 I WAS ENSCONCED IN MY LITTLE TERRACED HOUSE IN Fulham. It had a pretty garden, with an active fig tree and a giant toad, but the sun had a battle to reach it, as a neighbour's huge plane tree shrouded it for a good part of the day. It was my first time living alone in a house. Having your own front door onto the street, not shielded or surrounded by other tenants in a block of flats, was daunting. I lived there for five years, and there wasn't a night when I climbed the small flight of stairs to my bedroom that I didn't feel a bit apprehensive, often double-checking that I'd locked and bolted the front door. Houses need people more than flats. Even though I only had two floors and a basement, it felt echoey and lacked warmth and laughter, and somehow felt unlived in.

David was around in the holidays, but he was now nearly seventeen and starting to lead a more independent life. Within a year or two of my moving to Fulham, he went to live in a small self-contained flat above his father's house in Notting Hill. This gave him much more freedom, at times I thought too much. Looking back, I think his exodus from my house was too precipitate, but a single working mother in London has difficult decisions to make, and I freely admit that I did make some wrong choices.

When you are constantly offered work in the acting profession, and that work demands a great deal of study and attention, it is difficult to achieve an ordered, comforting home life. I know that I deprived David of that solace. On the other hand I had to earn a living, and acting was what I'd chosen to do. It meant I was often absent, rehearsing in the daytime, at a theatre in the evenings, or away filming, and in this way the happy family photograph is not easy to capture. As I've said, when he was younger I did try and refuse work if it conflicted with the school holidays, but now David wanted to go off with his friends for his holidays, and not have Mum tagging along. So at this stage I often accepted work when he was back from school. We muddled through it all somehow, and managed to stay close midst tears and laughter, and I think he always knew that I was there for him when it really mattered.

Once I'd moved to Fulham I started to be offered a great deal of work in theatre, television and radio. I had little chance to sing the actor's song, 'Will I Ever Work Again?' That would come later, but for now I was flying from one medium to the other, going to my analyst three times a week at seven in the morning, and then on to rehearsals or recordings. So it was a busy patch for me and gave me little time to ponder, although from time to time, even with all this activity, I had to fight depressions. Analysis was helping greatly, but until you find the root cause of these dark demons, they taunt you at the oddest moments. Anxiety can hit you hard, so you feel you're on a switchback. Sometimes I thought analysis was taking too long and the rewards were too small. I confronted Dr Dewar with this, and she quoted one of her past patients as saying, 'It's like walking through a field of manure to pick a daisy,' and I must say it did sometimes feel like that. But of course once you get to the daisy, it is worth it, and the manure turns into a navigable field. Deep down I longed for romance, companionship and comfort; but I was in no way ready for these riches. What Noel Coward had said to me in Switzerland, about an actor being bound to suffer in love, was becoming clearer to me. I was certainly not in a fit state to give myself to someone, or to see that someone clearly, despite this being my permanent desire. I was too fractured, and the pieces had to be put back together and healed before anything positive could take root. My analyst had a hard task ahead. My daisy was still far away.

However, my work was interesting and didn't allow me to wallow in my loneliness too much. Charles Wood had written a play about the fall of Singapore called *Jingo*, which Richard Eyre was to direct. Michael Williams, John Standing and Peter Jefferies were to be my fellow players. I was to be Gwendolen, a marvellously flighty character, married to Michael Williams, but fairly unfettered by the small band of gold. There was a scene in which Peter Jefferies, the commanding officer, in full regimental regalia, begged to spank my bottom with a hairbrush, after we had returned from some banquet. The scene was both hilarious and deeply moving, his pain, pleasure and guilt interwoven, as I perched on my arms and knees in embarrassment. I loved *Jingo*. It was by no means a perfect piece, and Charles worked on it all the time we were rehearsing. He is a perfectionist and a writer with the lightest of touches, a very emotional man, and I feel that we let him down. He wanted to be at all the rehearsals, and, of course, should have been, but John Standing found this inhibiting. He is a fine instinctive actor, but I think he found the author's presence distracting, and he was fearful of the cerebral input. He should not have worried, for Charles' sensitivity to actors is prodigious. I personally think it is vital that authors be involved. After all, it's a journey of discovery to be shared by everyone, and the author's eyes and ears can solve many a problem. Richard Eyre found himself in an awkward position, for I know he would have liked Charles to have been with us each day. Richard has a fierce intelligence and is a romantic, which is an interesting combination. He directs in great detail, and is quite a taskmaster, but by the opening night he makes sure you really know what you are doing, and you feel absolutely grounded in your role. Unfortunately on the opening night at the Aldwych Theatre, John Gunter's evocative set of Raffles Hotel got stuck, and the curtain was twenty minutes late going up. As I started the proceedings with a witty, pithy monologue alone and centre stage, this was quite a strain. I felt like a greyhound held reluctantly in its trap. The technical difficulty was ironed out, and the show began.

I was still battling with stage fright and, although my work process had gathered depth, my nerves still jangled merrily each night before this initial explanation of the intricate adventures of Gwendolen. Once the monologue was over, I enjoyed the piece, and relished the sexiness and ease with which my character glided through her troubles, conquering all those around her. But the monologue was a lesson for me in how to play with an audience and enable them to relax into the narrative. This is what the great comedians do, but it was new to me. You cannot let them see your nerves or fear for it makes an audience tense, and then they won't listen. Each night that monologue was a journey, and each night I learnt something fresh. There were times when I wanted the courage to say, 'Please can I start again?' The mood you took on with you coloured everything, very much like the mood with which you enter a party. Sometimes people flock to your side, and at other times you're left standing alone. With the monologue, I found that I had to make friends with the audience in an instant. Charles Wood had given me a tremendous challenge. He also gave me an epilogue, but that was easier, because by then the audience had been nourished by the evening, and their attention was fully engaged. It was a most rewarding learning experience. Charles had caught the desperation of these people at this dangerous time with humour and pathos. Alas, audiences didn't flock to see it, and we closed after a short run. Sadly I don't think that it has ever been revived.

★   ★   ★

During the five years that I lived in Fulham, I did some interesting television films. One of these was a four-part serial of Thomas Hardy's novel *The Mayor of Casterbridge*, adapted by Dennis Potter. It was to star Alan Bates as Michael Henchard, and David Giles was to direct. I was to play Lucetta Templeman, the lady from Jersey, a very juicy role. She captivates Henchard, ditches him, falls into the arms of Donald Farfrae and is punished cruelly for her follies. It was all to be filmed on location in Dorset, around Corfe and Swanage. What freedom that gave us. When writing about radio, I said I preferred the studio to the outside broadcasts, but with the camera and filming, it is the opposite. Filming on location adds so much to a story; the real settings liberate your spirits.

Janet Maw was to play Elisabeth, and Jack Galloway the dashing Donald Farfrae. We rehearsed in London before packing our bags and heading for Swanage. Alan was very much the leader of our band. His generosity embraced us all, and we followed him everywhere.

During the last days of London rehearsals, Elvis Presley died. This shocked the world. It shocked Alan profoundly. He left for the West Country with every song that Elvis had ever recorded carefully packed in his luggage. We all sat and listened to these tapes, either in his car during the lunch breaks, or at his rented cottage, where we frequently gathered, and where Alan treated us to delicious vegetarian meals. He was a wonderful cook, and could make even the rather monotonous mung bean into a tasty dish. He was in the vanguard of healthy eating, because in the late seventies few people were aware of their diets in the way they are today.

How generous he was, not only as a person, but as an actor. He was always concerned that you were happy in a scene, and each take was a spontaneous experience. He thought it afresh every time, and led his fellow players to do the same. Once we had a very long scene together walking up a steep and winding path. It was an intense emotional take, full of subtleties and swings of mood. It was shot on steady cam, which is when the camera is strapped to the cameraman's back and he leads the way sighting the actors in his viewfinder as they follow him. Nowadays this is fairly common practice, but in the late seventies it was rare in drama productions. The steady cam was also extremely heavy and, as our scene took place on a steep incline, this added to the burden. Alan and I had to keep to fairly rigid marks, and the take lasted for about six minutes. We did the shot three or four times, so it was a pretty demanding experience for all concerned, physically exhausting for the cameraman, and emotionally gruelling for the players. Alan made it all pleasurable though, not letting nerves get in the way. I find nerves when filming useful and not negative as they can be for me in the theatre. There is of course the safety net that you can have another take if disaster strikes, so this frees the imagination.

Alan's kindly ironic humour was a mainstay throughout. He did from time to time let you glimpse his vulnerable side. He was a strong mix of self-assurance and doubt, but assurance almost always triumphed.

Off the set I have such happy memories of all of us walking along the Dorset coast, being taken by Alan for delicious meals at the Sea Cow in Weymouth, laughing a lot, and playing Elvis till we knew most of the songs by heart. Not a day went by without Alan paying a small tribute to The King. Elvis really was his God. Personally I think Elvis would have been pleased.

I now started going to the improvisation classes of the writer and director Peter Gill. These were jolly gatherings held at Riverside Studios in Hammersmith. Peter is a very sensitive man who loves to be surrounded by his close friends, many of whom are actors. The classes he held in the late seventies were attended by those in search of something, all wanting to come to grips with nerves, or to stretch themselves in some way. Sometimes it seemed to me that we were only playing games, fun games though they were, and getting to know each other well. One day we did an exercise that involved taking off your shoes and putting them in a pile in the middle of the floor; then each person had to choose a pair from the pile and parade around in them. I had just bought a pair of expensive sandals from Pied à Terre, and was rather upset when Paul Kember, a good actor, but with rather large feet, selected my shoes for his parade. The shoes never fitted me as well again, and I often wondered what we had all gained from this endeavour, other than much mirth. But clearly Peter had his own hidden agenda. Sometimes we worked on texts, and this was much more rewarding, as Peter really understands words. He helped us to unravel complicated Shakespearean verses in a clear and profound way, teaching us phrasing by penetrating questioning. I once read that George Bernard Shaw said that if you were concerned with making sense of one of the speeches in his plays, 'Go for the verb.' It helped immeasurably when I played in *Heartbreak House*, and I think in all instances it is a good guide.

Working on Shakespeare's texts with Peter Gill reinforced this view. The verb illuminates the often complicated hidden meaning and provides a way in. During these sessions it was reassuring to learn that others often battled with nerves when performing. A shared problem lessens its intensity.

Around this time I learned that there was to be a television production of Daphne du Maurier's *Rebecca* starring Jeremy Brett as Max de Winter. It was to be adapted by Hugh Whitemore in four parts, and directed by Simon Langton. I had seen Hitchcock's film, and thought to myself that I would love to play the enigmatic and cruel Mrs Danvers. Even though Jeremy was the lead, my desire to play this part was not weakened. Simon Langton thought it a tremendous idea and gave me his full backing, but the producer was against it, saying that I was too young. The age had never entered my mind. With clever make-up and a good wig, age presents no problem in my eyes. It is the essence of the character that everything hinges upon, and I thought that I could convincingly portray this evil force.

I had seen many French films where women played lesbians in a most subtle way, and this is how I wanted to play Mrs Danvers. I felt that she had been in love with the first Mrs de Winter. Maybe this was only in her subconscious, but Rebecca's beauty and her talents had certainly enthralled her. I wanted to shun what Daphne du Maurier had written about her wardrobe in the book, the old-fashioned, long Victorian dress sweeping the corridors of Manderly; I wanted to wear a slinky, mid-calf black silk dress, and move about the house like a vicious snake. The way that Mrs Danvers described Mrs de Winter's possessions, the nightgown laid lovingly on the bed in a room unchanged from the day she died, the hairbrush which she picked up to taunt the second Mrs de Winter: these actions suggested to me a hidden sexual agenda, only alluded to, but nonetheless clear indications of passion unspent. I conveyed all these ideas to Simon, and he heartily approved them. The stumbling block was still the producer who wanted an older, weightier actress. Finally, not too long before the production started, the producer gave way and I became Mrs Danvers, one of my favourite roles to this day.

It was a strange engagement, and working with Jeremy was not easy. During rehearsals, unbeknown to me, he had given David a motorbike, something that I had always been against. I was utterly furious. We could not have a vehement row, as it would have upset everyone and created tension where it was not needed. So I decided to ignore Jeremy and not speak to him, except in the most formal way, and of course when we had to rehearse our scene together in the play. It was an odd experience, but my side of the argument was reinforced when, a few weeks after getting the bike, David had an accident and injured his leg, not badly, but enough to make Jeremy understand that his gift had been a foolish one. We never spoke of this episode during the production or afterwards, but a few months later the bike was abandoned, and peace was restored without a bloody war having taken place. In fact when the show was first shown on television, Jeremy wrote me a most complimentary letter about my performance, which I found very touching.

I loved playing Mrs Danvers, and loved playing with Joanna David, who was the perfect second Mrs de Winter. Our scenes together were pure joy. We were both nervous of the demands of our roles, but we used these nerves constructively and creatively. The three months it took to complete the filming rolled by most pleasantly, and one of the nicest outcomes of the engagement was my lasting friendship with Joanna.

Not long after completing *Rebecca*, I was to work with the great Katharine Hepburn, an experience that I shall never forget. Miss Hepburn had agreed to play the part of the teacher Miss Moffat in a television film of Emlyn Williams' *The Corn is Green*, a semi-autobiographical tale of his early years in Wales, and how he came to go up to university, an event that entirely changed his life. His teacher in real life was Miss Cook, who had seen Emlyn's potential. She encouraged him to work extra hours, and to sit the exams for Oxford. I once met her. She was a warm and earthy lady, full of compassion, common sense and insight, which shone through even in her later years. Emlyn always felt he owed her everything.

Katharine Hepburn had a formidable presence as the world knows. She was forthright in all she did and all she said, and phenomenally wilful. She had been involved in the adaptation of the script from the early stages, and by the time she arrived in London to cast and set up the production, she knew every word of her role, and kept strict control over the entire project. Her old friend George Cukor was her choice of director, which was not surprising, considering their past track record. By this time, though, George was very stiff in his limbs. He bent forward as he walked, and I think was in considerable pain, which made him extremely short-tempered. Kate and he joked and goaded each other in a way that only the closest friends can. He always wanted to do another take, no matter how good the last one had been. Kate would ask why, and he would shout back that he wanted one anyway. It was like a double act. Instead of saying 'action' before each take, George shouted 'camera', which someone told me was because he had originally worked in silent films.

I was to play Miss Ronberry, a flirtatious spinster in the village. Looking back, it amazes and saddens me that I so misjudged my performance. I elected to play her with a light voice, which during the filming became higher and higher, until it was almost unbearable. My wig too was a disaster. I had asked for a lightly curled blonde wig, feminine and pretty to behold, but I ended up with something that made me look more like Harpo Marx on a bad hair day. Why George allowed me to sport such a wig, and use such a voice, I will never know. I think he was tired at the time, and had his heart in California. He was old to embark on such a journey, setting off to Wales and staying in the beautiful countryside around Betws-y-Coed in a rented cottage. He seemed to be a little removed from the proceedings, and any notes he did give were delivered in a peppery tone.

Kate had mapped out her performance, as I've said, long before shooting began. She spoke as she always spoke, but by now the magical tremor in her voice was more pronounced. I was hypnotised by her. She was utterly focused at all times, and completely absorbed by her work. She could prompt anyone if they forgot a line, and her energy was golden. It was a delight to work with her. She was generous and perceptive, and gave as much when she fed lines off camera to another actor, as when the take was her own close-up. This is warming and always boosts morale on set. She was known affectionately as the 'Diva'.

The main part of George, the character based on Emlyn, was played by a young Welsh actor called Ian Saynor, a good-looking, slender chap. Personally I think the role demanded a rougher pit pony, but I suspect Hollywood rules prevailed when casting took place.

We filmed from Monday to Friday, but Saturdays and Sundays were time for play, and each Saturday Kate took a few of us out on picnics in the Welsh hills. I can see her now in frayed beige slacks and one of Spencer Tracy's old, slightly stained shirts, sitting under an umbrella to protect her fragile skin. She had a cancerous condition that meant she had no lines, but her skin was thin like tissue paper and, without make-up, slightly blotchy. At the weekends she was absolutely au naturel. She found that the water from the Welsh hills was most soothing and refreshing for her face, and at the end of the shoot she had a great deal put in bottles and shipped to the States.

Kate and her companion Phyllis prepared the most delicious meals for our picnics; everything was succulent and fresh, wrapped in greaseproof paper. Her energy was like a tonic, no hill or pathway daunted her, and her curiosity was prodigious. They were days that I shall always remember. She was very much a spirit of the present, and did not keep harking back to the past, as some major stars are prone to do. Practicality seemed to be her password. Superlatives were not in her vocabulary, but you felt that if a battle needed to be fought, she would be the victor. Despite these rather mannish traits, she was extremely romantic and feminine. She was nature's eternal heroine.

Our cameraman was taken ill during the filming, and the famous cinematographer Jack Cardiff came to the rescue for a few days. He, of course, had been in charge of the camera on *The African Queen*, so he was only too ready to help Kate out of any difficulties.

Quite a few years later, I was asked to do a commercial to be filmed on the Tana Delta in Kenya. The promotion was for Buxton Spring Water, and the scene was to be a forty-second version of a scene from *The African Queen*, the scene when Hepburn throws all of Bogart's liquor into the river. Alun Armstrong played Bogart, and the late Harold Innocent was the vicar, originally played by Robert Morley. We were all dressed to look exactly like the original cast, and who was to photograph the shoot? Jack Cardiff, whom I'd last seen in Betws-y-Coed helping out Kate Hepburn for those few days on *The Corn is Green*. It seemed that something was coming full circle, or that fate was dealing preordained cards.

There is an odd little postscript to this tale. I was invited to be on Russell Harty's radio programme, *Start the Week*, and when I was asked what I'd been doing, I explained about the forty-second remake of *The African Queen*. When Sir John Wolf, who had co-produced the original film with Sam Speigel, heard the programme, which went out live, all hell broke loose. The advertising company had not cleared the rights, and consequently had to pay out a handsome sum in recompense. I never felt very guilty about what I'd said, because nobody had warned me not to talk about it, and anyway the advertisement was being aired nightly on television, so trouble would have arisen eventually without my help. The commercial company never blamed me, and dealt with the whole situation most charmingly. But it was an odd coda to the whole event.

The days spent in Africa shooting the advertisement were not without drama. Jack Cardiff fell into the Tana Delta, but recovered quickly and showed true grit and courage. I read Kate's diaries about shooting *The African Queen*, and after my few days in Kenya, my admiration for her soared. Churchill called Africa 'the Devil's Paradise'. How right he was. We all became ill, and the conditions were extremely difficult. I was grateful it was only four days and not many months. Whisky had apparently saved

Bogart and John Huston, but Kate had been very ill during the shoot and took several months to recover fully. I envied her stamina and fortitude.

I shall always consider myself most fortunate to have met her and worked with her. She was one of life's 'specials'.

CHAPTER 17

IN 1979 WHEN DAVID HAD MOVED OUT OF THE LITTLE FULHAM house, I began to feel really lonely. Loneliness is very different from solitude. The latter is bearable (sometimes even pleasurable), the former is not, and so I began to look around for a flat in the Notting Hill area as it was close to where David lived in the studio flat above his father's house. The search took a long time, and I left it to the estate agents, and went on working.

I was asked to appear in Samuel Beckett's *Play* at the Royal Court Theatre, as part of a Beckett triple bill. Here I rekindled my friendship with the delightful Donald McWhinnie of my early radio days, for he was an old friend of Beckett, and was to direct our piece.

For those who don't know the play, it involves three actors, two women and one man, W1, W2 and M. These three characters are found in urns up to their necks, with their faces covered in oatmeal to denote decay. They talk at a rate of knots, each one speaking only when a harsh white light is shone on to their face. The entire text is gone through twice, and the whole exercise takes twenty minutes. They were the most terrifying twenty minutes of my life. I wanted to stretch myself. Now that I'm older, and I hope wiser, I only do things if I'm going to enjoy them. Penelope Wilton and Ronald Pickup played W2 and M, and I was W1. I think I can safely say that they were both as petrified as I was. In fact my analyst told me that if the run had been longer, it was likely that I would have had a breakdown.

In order to keep our balance in the urns, iron bars were fixed inside. These really helped, and provided a much-needed lifeline. I found that conducting myself vigorously with one hand when I spoke enabled me to speak faster, and still retain clarity.

The text was a puzzle with only the faintest clues. W1 and W2 had clearly both been married to the man at different times, and it seems that they were all in some sort of purgatory, eternally regurgitating their stories. Many friends came to the production, all with their personal views on what the play meant to them. But for me it remained mysterious, rather like flying blind. Later, after the run had finished, Donald said it was an ordinary domestic triangle, and it always struck me as strange that he had not said this during the rehearsals. Maybe he felt that it would not have been helpful.

Apart from the terror, what I remember most about the commitment was when Beckett himself came to a late run-through, two or three days before the opening. We had been told that we could not ask him any questions ourselves. He walked into the rehearsal room one morning, a tall eagle with piercing pale blue eyes, accompanied by Barbara Bray, the translator of those of his works originally written in French. We were told that he was immensely shy. I always think that shy people are rather self-involved and confident, for when they walk into a room they assume that everyone will be looking at them. The less shy assume they will need to attract someone's attention.

Anyway, we ran through the play at the speed Donald had dictated, and in the uninflected robot voices that Beckett had indicated in his printed text. At the end of the run, we found out that we had failed on both scores. He wanted it at twice the speed, with even less expression. It seemed the impossible had to be achieved. We worked very hard to deliver what Beckett required. He never wrote or acknowledged the performance, so all we could do was hope. It is perfectly possible that he never came to see the play with an audience; after all we were not performing in a World Première.

It was a painful time, and overwhelming relief followed the last night of the run. 'Never again,' I said to myself. I kept my word, for I have never been in another Beckett piece.

I finally found a flat in Holland Park with a little studio above it, which was convenient, as it provided a bolthole for David, who had to leave his father's flat when Jeremy moved to Clapham. So all that worked out well, and I remained in Holland Park for the next ten years, when my life took another momentous turn.

Shortly before moving from Fulham, I did a television play by John Osborne called, *You're Not Watching Me Mummy*. It was about an actress in her dressing room after the performance of a long-running play. The first half was a witty duologue between the actress and her camp male dresser, played by Peter Sallis. The second half was the invasion of friends and acquaintances, ending in chaos. The actress was of course based on Jill Bennett. It was a somewhat vicious portrait, and although it was many years since their marriage had ended, the anger still raged in Osborne's breast. How sad that he couldn't just let it all go. To hark on about the past in this public way seemed graceless, and not worthy of his enormous talent. The dialogue in the first half, though, was brittle and brilliant, and enormous fun to play.

Many years earlier I had turned down a part in John's *Hotel in Amsterdam*. But he forgave me and was understanding, and over the years he invited me to his delightful Sunday parties in Kent, where he entertained lavishly with his wife, Helen. Before we started rehearsals for the television, John took me out to lunch. He was a courteous man, and he had the most beautiful speaking voice, mellifluous and sexy. He always wore a bright kerchief round his neck in the actor laddie style, and sartorial taste seemed not to be uppermost in his mind. By this time his love of champagne was treating his features unkindly, but the old charm was still light and beguiling, and felt genuine.

We had quite a rocky journey over the recording, because Yorkshire Television kept having technician's strikes. It took three attempts to complete the show. This was distressing, for each time you had to rev yourself up and get back in the mood. Suzanne Bertish, who played the author of the play within the play, was a tower of strength and support, and another good friendship was founded.

I was in America when the show went out on television, and when I returned I found that neighbours had taken in an enormous bouquet of flowers from John. The flowers of course had wilted, but the delightful card and bright blue ribbon remained and gave much pleasure. His manners were rare and touching.

The reason that I'd travelled to America was to try to obtain a green card, so that I would be able to work on both sides of the Atlantic. I needed my father to sign some papers, because my official reason for wanting to be in the States was to be near my ageing father. Firstly I went to New York to see a lawyer, and then travelled on to Los Angeles, where Father now lived in Beverly Hills. Jeremy invited me to stay with him at his house in the Hollywood Hills, where he was now living. I accepted, because I found the prospect of being alone in LA daunting, as I don't drive outside the UK. (I once nearly killed myself and Christopher Hampton and his wife, Laura in Corfu, where we were on holiday, by going for the brake on my wrong side to avoid a collision with a charabanc on a hairpin bend. Christopher grabbed the brake for me and saved us, but I vowed never to drive abroad again, thus probably saving many lives.) In Los Angeles life without a car is difficult. To buy a box of Kleenex there involves a ten-minute car ride, and I think the journey between the Hollywood Hills and Beverly Hills would have defeated me. But by accepting Jeremy's hospitality, I put myself in an extremely awkward situation, and looking back, I see that I made a serious mistake. He was really quite sick at this time, and during this visit he was extravagantly, and embarrassingly, generous. This was one of the symptoms of his manic depression. He hardly slept, and could not be still, and his restlessness was disturbing.

I only saw my father twice during my stay. His house in North Beverly Drive was quite small, and, as in Connecticut, decorated in dark greens and reds. All his memorabilia had travelled with him, and was now fitted into this much smaller space. I was shocked by his frailty. He'd had a successful hip operation some years earlier, and now urgently needed the second hip to be dealt with, but Dorothy had refused to let him have this operation. She clearly had her own perverse reasons for this, but meanwhile poor Father was forced to use a walking frame, and could no longer exercise or play a round of golf, which had been his passion.

On my first visit to his house, I went alone. I was invited for tea. I wanted to explain the green-card situation quietly to him. Dorothy was present, so vast quantities of tension hung in the air. He was slow to understand what I required and, egged on by Dorothy, slightly suspicious. After a while, though, his reluctance to sign subsided. Obviously at some point Dorothy had given her silent approval.

The signing was to take place at the Polo Lounge at the Beverly Hills Hotel. Jeremy was also to be present, which was a nightmare for me, as you could never be sure what he'd say, and his attention-seeking was now paramount. Father arrived with his walking frame and took a long and painful time to reach the table. Dorothy was her usual acid self, smiling malevolently at everybody, Jeremy showed off, Father stammered appallingly, and I wanted to run into the Pacific Ocean. Finally the ordeal was over, and we went our separate ways. The papers had been signed, and I would now have a green card; a green card but no real tenderness, no loving embrace to melt away the protective armour that had built up over the years. Dorothy of course had prevented that. She had kept guard and seen that

Father and I were never alone together. This was the last time that I saw him.

Soon after this lunch, I left California and said goodbye to Jeremy, who had driven me to the airport wearing a Mickey Mouse hat. The visit had left me in a disturbed state. Both these men, key players in my life, if seldom seen, had behaved in ways that left me feeling bereft. My father was not the rock that deep down I must have always craved, and Jeremy had reinforced my knowledge that I had once been married to an extremely troubled man who was by now beyond the help of friends. He needed serious medical care, and I was the last person who could offer that advice. I arrived back at my little house in Fulham, grateful for the peace and quiet.

An odd little postscript to this tale is that, after I was issued with my much-desired green card, I never worked in the States again.

Shortly after my return to England, I moved into my new flat in Holland Park, where I was to stay for the next ten years. My funds were somewhat stretched at this time, so I had to live with the previous owners' decoration, very modern fitments and rather busy carpeting throughout. It had a beautiful high-ceilinged large reception room, with a tiny kitchen, one-and-a-half bedrooms, and a bathroom and little studio above. The tiny kitchen never bothered me, as cooking is not one of my fortes. My brother Daniel once came to dinner with me, and the next day sent me a copy of Constance Spry's cookery book. Alas, his generous gift never really bore fruit, and only the simplest of repasts are within my range. The decor of the flat was rather like a hotel, comfortable but impersonal. By the time my coffers were in a healthier state, I had accepted my surroundings and didn't make any changes. I'd simply moved on to other priorities. Moving is such an upheaval. Someone once said to me that where you live is the inkwell of your life. I believe this to be true. It is where you gather strength, and rest from all external stresses. As I spend a lot of time in my home, the imperatives for me are to have as much light as possible, to be in as quiet a position as London allows, and to see a tree from at least one of the windows.

With the move to Holland Park, there were other changes in the air. My analyst, Millicent Dewar, had decided to retire to Edinburgh. She told me that she had three kinds of patient: those that she knew had completed their therapy, those that she knew had not, and those she was not sure about. I fell into the last category. I was left on my own for three months. At the end of that period I rang and said that I now knew I hadn't completed my analysis, and asked her if she could find me someone else. It took her a long time to contact me, but finally she arranged for me to see Eric Rayner. It was a new experience going to a male analyst, and the transition was not easy. During my sessions with Dr Dewar I had sat opposite her, at difficult moments staring at her Persian carpet, each pattern eventually becoming an old friend. At Eric Rayner's I lay down on a couch and stared at a bookcase, and ultimately found this easier and more liberating. Changing analysts is traumatic, and really means starting again, albeit with some insight.

I went to Eric Rayner for six years, three times a week. I knew when the end was nigh, because I began to think that I knew more about myself than he did, and became a little bored. So it was decided in 1986 that I should end my therapy. I was now to be my own analyst. The night of my last session, I had a very strange but revealing dream. I was flying a small plane all alone over the Alps. I think this illustrates perfectly my anxiety, and the courage that I would now need.

In 1972 my friend Angela Huth had written her second successful novel, *Virginia Fly is Drowning*. Angie always says that we had known each other when we were two, thus making her my very oldest friend. Her novel was about a woman who imagines herself 'raped, in her mind, at least twice a week'. But what made her special was that at the age of thirty-one she was not ashamed to admit that in reality she was still a virgin. This she declared on television, when interviewed about her private life. It was an original and charming story, told with Angie's acute perceptions and unfailing eye for detail. In 1980 she adapted the story for television, and I was asked to play Virginia. I think at the time I was a little old for the role, but with a brilliant make-up artist, this obstacle was removed.

This is the engagement where I met Richard Wilson, and thus began another very important friendship in my life. Richard was to play the professor of music, who eventually becomes Virginia's husband. Richard is not only a famous and talented actor, but he is also one of the subtlest directors. He has never directed me professionally, but I have worked privately with him on count-less roles, and value his judgement enormously. In *Virginia Fly*, he guided me, and I much enjoyed our scenes together, for Richard was wonderfully free and kept the scenes fresh and spontaneous right up to the taping. He is a brilliant improviser, and believes that one must always remain open. This prevents parrot repetition, and makes a performance truly alive. He taught me to trust myself more, and to know that a flick of a thought suffices, and nothing should be signalled. For example, you have a scene where you walk into a room and find someone there you were not expecting. The actor of course knows that the person will be there, but the challenge is to convey the surprise with the minimum effort, and the maximum spontaneity. I had such a scene in our television adaptation, where Virginia un-expectedly found the professor in her flat, and Richard helped me to react with the subtlety required – thinking of other things prior to opening the door, so that your mind is in another space and therefore more likely to be taken off guard. As a director he is an excellent fine tuner, a minimalist. He is also the most generous friend.

I had had no formal training as an actress, neither drama

school nor time in a repertory company. My lessons had all been learnt in the heart of the West End, in front of critical audiences. When instinct failed me, I had nothing to fall back on, and developed bad habits. Therefore I always craved the guidance and wisdom of others for reassurance. Richard gave me much-needed confidence.

Soon after finishing *Virginia Fly*, I found myself back at the Royal Court Theatre, Sloane Square, and this engagement was to be a tremendous learning experience. Thomas Kilroy, the Irish playwright, had adapted Chekhov's *The Seagull*, and set the play in rural Galway in the latter part of the nineteenth century. The Russian intelligentsia became the absentee land-lords and the privileged artists of the Anglo-Celtic twilight, and the local dissatisfactions and unrest in both rural areas were not dissimilar. The play breathed happily in its new setting. The characters assumed new names: the actress, Arkadina, became Isobel, the writer, Trigorin became Aston, Nina became Lily, and so on. Constantin was able to retain his name, but without the patronymic.

Max Stafford-Clark was the director, and so once again I relished the prospect of his detailed approach to a play. Alan Rickman was to be Aston, and here I met not only a new friend, but also a performer with profound concentration and insight. I knew from the start that the journey would be intense.

Max had gathered together a great group of actors. Harriet Walter was our Nina, and Anton Lesser was Constantin. The director, Stuart Burge, who had run the Royal Court so success-fully for many years, returned to the stage to play Arkadina's brother, Peter. Stuart was in his seventies and I don't think he had acted since he was a very young man, so his task was quite daunting, but he was in safe hands with Max, who gives his casts so much to think about that there is no place for panic.

Our rehearsals lasted five weeks, unlike the nine months that Stanislavski would have given his troupe. The first week we read through the play many times, and talked about all aspects of life in the latter part of the nineteenth century, each actor being given the task of researching in depth the background of their particular character. I went off to the library to gather as many books that I could find on the theatre of the 1880s and 90s. Isobel was an actress whose career was on the wane. She no longer played in the great city playhouses and spent her time touring. I tried to glean what this would have been like at that time, what discomforts were endured, or what pleasures were to be enjoyed. At the end of the first week, those of us who were able were asked to give a talk to the rest of the cast on their discoveries. I decided to be brave and prepared my speech. It was the first time that I had done anything like this, and it was an interesting experience. My audience were attentive and appreciative, but I fear I rattled through it and allowed them no time to savour the material. Public speakers, like actors, need to take the time to paint the pictures.

The second week of rehearsals were devoted to examining each scene with a microscope, and Max was still investigating the actions behind each verb, as we had done in *Slag*. In the days of my baptism in the West End theatre, the directors worked out the moves in the first few days of rehearsals, but Max left that till much later on, when the text was fully understood and the relationships were beginning to develop. By this time the actors knew where they wanted to be in a scene.

One interesting improvisation he gave us involved the whole cast, and concerned status. The highest status was given the number ten, the lowest, one. You then had to walk into the room according to the number that Max called out. Eventually you had to choose the correct status for your character. Isobel, in most scenes, was a ten, but occasionally she dropped to a seven or a six, like when she was insecure and pleading with Aston. The status exercise allowed each character to establish themselves in the household so that when Jack, the labourer, came on with our luggage, he had a specific role to play, and greeted us all with a different subtext, warm with some and diffident with others. Detailed work like this enriches a text, and takes an audience to the heart of a play.

The famous scene in Act Three when Isobel uses all her old worn-out wiles to persuade Aston to leave with her, after he has confessed his love of Lily, presented Alan and me with an exciting challenge. At the end of the five weeks we ended up playing the scene rolling on the floor, all the usual corseted decorum of the period blown away – and nerves and emotions laid bare. I dribbled all over him as tears and rage poured out. It turned into an ugly scene, played as though we were on an unmade bed rather than in the drawing room of the house, where anyone could have entered in an instant. It was thrilling to play each night. On stage Alan lives in the moment, and I always felt there was danger in the air, an element of the unexpected. Since our production, both he and I have read of other Arkadinas and Trigorins fighting on the floor, but we feel confident that we were the pioneers who took the scene from the vertical to the horizontal.

Max didn't begin to run through the play until nearly the fourth week of rehearsals. The performer who made most progress during a run was awarded 'the yellow jersey', as in cycling. I have never been more thrilled than when I was given this accolade. I felt that at last I had left the old West End and joined legitimate democratic theatre.

One aspect of democratic theatre that didn't initially appeal to me, though, was the fact that we had to share dressing rooms. Since *The Reluctant Debutante*, I had always been fortunate enough to have a room to myself. At the Court I asked if it would be possible for me to have a broom cupboard, in order not to have to be with someone else. No was the answer, and so I shared with Harriet Walter, and I have never enjoyed myself more. We got on so well together, became friends for life, respected each other's need for occasional silence, and laughed until we cried. I shall always treasure our dressing-room conversations, peppered with Harriet's wit and insight, and her delightful sense of the ludicrous. For once I longed to get to the theatre.

On the morning of the First Night, I rang Max up and asked him to give me a note to take my mind off the ordeal ahead. I didn't want my usual nerves to impede the freedom that I was experiencing. He gave me something to think about, and I went on that night ready to enjoy myself for once, a rare and good feeling.

The work didn't stop with the First Night. During the twelve-week run, we all went on trying out new ideas, and keeping the journey fresh. Max came quite often and gave us notes, and there was a feeling of work in progress, which is the best, because nothing gets too set.

The run ended, and we all went our separate ways, but this time I knew that Alan and Harriet and I would be in constant touch, and indeed to this day we have been.

My roll of work continued, and I now found myself high up in the Swiss Alps at Pontresina, where Fred Zinnemann was filming *Five Days One Summer* with Sean Connery. It was a strange tale of an affair between a man and his wife's niece. Betsey Brantley played the niece, and Lambert Wilson their young mountain guide, with whom she eventually falls in love. Sheila Reid and I were to play two sisters staying in the hotel. They were not mountaineers, but enjoyed cycling on a tandem over the rocky mountain paths. They were amusing cameo roles and I had envisaged no problems when accepting my part, relishing the thought of working with Zinnemann and Connery and spending two weeks of early summer in a luxury hotel in Pontresina. Little did Sheila and I know how arduous a task riding a tandem is. The terrain was extremely uneven, and at times precipitous. The person who sat behind had the greatest difficulty, for they were entirely at the mercy of the leader, and to keep your balance in this position was quite tricky. I shall always be grateful to Sheila that she let me lead.

Zinnemann was most charming and courteous, and spoke to everyone in the quietest tones. He had difficulty communicating with Betsey, though, and a few days after I arrived he asked me if I would like to help her with her scenes. I accepted the challenge at once, and much enjoyed the sessions. She was delightful to work with, and appeared appreciative, although I'll never know how beneficial our meetings were, because soon after I left Pontresina I heard that a professional acting coach was brought in for Betsey. However, to show his appreciation, Fred gave me a beautiful gold pendant, which was a touching memento.

Sean Connery was kind and considerate to work with, and never behaved like the big Hollywood star. He always asked if we were happy with a set-up, and seemed to care for other people's needs, which I found most refreshing. He was also great fun to be with, and captivated us with his twinkling eyes and mischievous sense of humour. He made Sheila and me feel most welcome, and took us out to tasty dinners in local restaurants. The Swiss air is intoxicating, and the scenery breathtaking, and it sometimes felt that we were on holiday rather than working. I returned to London ready for anything.

That autumn I started a job that would require all the strength and patience that I could muster. In Switzerland I had been really pampered. At the National Theatre in November 1981, I found myself working with the coldest man that I have ever met.

CHAPTER 18

EDWARD BOND HAD WRITTEN A NEW PLAY CALLED *SUMMER* THAT he was to direct at the Cottesloe theatre, opening in January 1982. I was summoned one stormy evening in November to meet him. The room was warm, I remember. Edward remained seated when I entered, sporting steel-framed spectacles, the skin on his face flushed and as smooth as a peach, no lines of mirth or laughter having left their imprint. He asked if I was interested in playing evil characters. When I answered in the affirmative, he seemed genuinely pleased and intrigued. Three days later I was recalled to read a scene with Yvonne Bryceland who was already cast to play Marthe. The character that I was being considered for was Xenia. The play was set in an Eastern European country, and centred around the meeting of these two women, whose pasts were inextricably bound up with the German occupation of the area during World War Two. Xenia's family had entertained German officers in the house where Marthe had been a servant. When she was taken hostage and condemned to be shot, only Xenia's intervention had saved her life. Forty years later when Xenia returns for her usual summer visit, she learns that Marthe is dying from an incurable disease. This news provokes a reappraisal of past events, and presents the two actresses with highly charged scenes. After reading with Yvonne, Edward offered me the role of Xenia. He had thought that I might be too young to play a sixty-year-old, but again wigs and make-up came to my rescue and we embarked on eight weeks of intensive and agonising rehearsals.

The first week was quite friendly. Edward arrived on the third morning with a poem that he had written for me. The poem did not seem particularly relevant to the play, but I was touched, and thought that it was a good omen. How wrong I was. The second week tensions started to mount. Edward saw Xenia as pure evil, and Marthe as the victim. He wanted me to play her like the wicked witch from the privileged upper classes, with fire streaming from my nostrils, showing no subtleties or nuances. I began to argue with him, for I felt his political beliefs were getting in the way of his directing. Everything was too black and white. I protested that there were more colours on the emotional palette than he was allowing me to use. Xenia was extremely egocentric and demanding, but there were many facets to her character that he forbade me to explore. As the rehearsals progressed the tensions rose. I must add that the other members of the cast had no such problems with Edward. Everything that Yvonne did was praised, and the two young actors who played my daughter and Marthe's son found the rehearsals far less painful than I did.

After one particular run-through on the Cottesloe stage, Edward lambasted me in front of the other actors, and I could take it no more. I stormed off the stage and went to my dressing room. I had never done anything like this before or since, but I really wanted to leave the production and let Edward find someone else to play his dragon, if that was how he wanted it played. My instincts were against every note he gave me, and I was in despair. Gillian Diamond, who was the casting director at the National during this period, came to find me and sat with me until I had calmed down. I was literally sobbing and shaking with fear and rage. She was most sympathetic. Apart from Edward's dissatisfaction with my performance, I thought he was cold towards me, and I told her of the pain this caused me. Actors need warmth and encouragement when they embark on a journey, and the ice of Edward's gaze was inhibiting and frightening. We were ten days away from the first preview, so something had to be done to ease the situation. Gillian arranged a meeting between Edward and myself for that evening.

I can't remember the details of our discussion, but I know that I told him that his coldness frightened me, and that he understood this, and agreed that he lacked warmth. I remember we talked about my relationship with my own father, which I found difficult. I really did not want to reveal anything of my private life to someone who seemed to me so austere and unsympathetic, but I felt obliged to follow his lead in the conversation, if it would help resolve the deadlock that we had reached. I left the meeting feeling numb. I knew that I could not quit the production at this late stage, and we had to arrive at some tenuous peace. There was another flare-up three days later. This time I threw my car keys at his feet as I stormed off the stage. My rage was out of control. Another uncomfortable peace was reached, and we started the previews.

The play was enormously difficult to perform. The scenes were complex and full of long speeches, which needed detailed work to bring them to life. Edward had not helped us with his strict approach. It was as though he had held on to his play, and not released it to the players. I think it is difficult for authors to direct their own work. They are often unable to stand back and appraise the whole. David Hare is an exception to this rule, but I think Edward proved the point. He was not ready to be surprised.

After five previews, we opened to mixed reviews. I now looked forward to being able to breathe more freely in the play when Edward would not be around all the time. I tried to mellow my performance and added softer touches to portray a fuller character. But every so often a note would arrive from Edward admonishing me for the changes. It was a taxing run, and I never felt at home in the part.

I heard an amusing anecdote from someone who had been at the first preview. After the performance, Edward was talking in the foyer with his agent Peggy Ramsay, who was also the carer and nurturer of a large proportion of literary London. Peggy was overheard saying, 'Edward, I don't think you should direct your plays any more.' To which Edward replied, 'Well then, who should direct them?' And Peggy had replied, 'Anybody.'

I cannot vouch for the truth of this tale, but I have to confess that at the time it much amused me. Peggy's wit and outspokenness were legendary, and only she would have presumed to talk to Edward in this way.

Summer came to an end, but there were two small postscripts to relate. The first came as an enormous surprise. I received a nomination for Best Actress from the Society of West End Theatre Managers for my performance as Xenia. I did not win, but the nomination gave me a great boost, having suffered such pain to get through the ordeal. The second postscript was, I thought, Edward's revenge. When the paperback of the play was published, the photograph of only three actors appeared on the front cover. My character had been omitted.

To clear my head and fill my lungs with sea air, Richard Wilson and I planned to go on holiday together to Crete. When you live alone, casting a holiday can sometimes be as difficult as casting *King Lear*. So I was delighted that Richard was free at this time, and willing. We booked into a comfortable hotel in the north eastern part of the island where we each had chalets overlooking the bay. Everything was a little run down, but this rather added to its charm. After a few days Alan Rickman and his partner, Rima Horton, joined us. This was a delightful surprise. They stayed in a nearby pension. The three of them went off most days on trips by bus. I was very unadventurous, and apart from swimming, I just lay under a parasol on the beach and read countless books. The temperature reached 110 degrees some days, and the beaches, where Richard and Alan and Rima went, were too hot to walk on. One day, though, Richard hired a car and we went on a grand tour of the area. Richard had only just passed his driving test, so we all had to keep fairly quiet so that he could concentrate. He is now an accomplished driver, and the owner of the most powerful and stunning cars that I have ever seen, but that summer in Crete he was cautious, and Rima and I sat in the back gazing at the sun-baked landscape, refraining from conversation. All went well until a hornet flew in one of the rear windows. Rima and I screamed out to stop the car at once, and Richard quite rightly screamed back that this was impossible. Eventually we came to a lay-by and the intruder was dealt with. Fortunately nobody had been stung.

Alan is very clever at finding out-of-the-way places of interest, and we stopped at several small churches off the beaten track, and wandered around picturesque villages buying the odd memento, breathing in the pine-scented air, and laughing the while. We lunched on a beach where the fish was caught before our eyes, and we drank a lot of retsina, which I used to adore. It is the perfect drink for a hot climate. But it doesn't travel well.

The holiday was a great success, and everyone remained good friends. I was sad when we had to come home. The two weeks had flown by, and we all felt refreshed and ready to tackle the work that awaited us.

I had agreed to go back to the National, where Peter Hall was directing *The Importance of Being Earnest*, with Judi Dench as Lady Bracknell. I was to be Miss Prism, Nigel Havers and Martin Jarvis were to be Algernon and Jack, and Paul Rogers Canon Chasuble. We were also going to be in *Other Places*, a triple bill of Pinter plays – his new work *A Kind of Alaska*, together with *Victoria Station* and *Family Voices*, all to be directed by Peter Hall.

Margaret Rutherford had played Miss Prism so uniquely in

Anthony Asquith's film of the play that I felt daunted by the prospect of tackling the part. I asked Alan Rickman if he would talk about the character with me. He agreed, and one afternoon we walked around Holland Park, and he gave me some brilliant ideas. First of all he said that anyone who could mislay a baby and deposit a manuscript in the pram in its stead was supremely absent-minded, and probably not just on this particular occasion, but frequently. We decided that this forgetful trait could be shown in the way that I dressed, frayed skirts, buttons mislaid, and safety pins to the rescue. The hair should also be distracted, unable to stay in its proper place, with strands poking out in different directions. Gradually a truthful portrait emerged, not just for effect, but grounded in reality. I was so grateful to Alan, for he headed me in a safe direction and I relished the rehearsals and the run. Peter Hall left Paul and me much to our own devices, but after we started previewing, he gave us quite brilliant notes. I have never enjoyed a First Night more in my life. We did a matinée in the afternoon, and in the evening I felt really prepared. The audience were a delight, and laughed almost continuously. I was very thrilled to receive the Best Supporting Actress award from the Society of West End Theatre Managers for my performance. It was the same year that I had been nominated for the Bond play. The joy of playing Miss Prism helped heal the wounds of *Summer*.

The Pinter plays were fascinating to work on, and he attended most of the rehearsals. He had written *A Kind of Alaska* after reading Oliver Sacks' *Awakenings*. This book is a fascinating document, relating the case histories of some twenty patients who suffered from a bizarre disease that spread throughout the world from 1916 to 1927. Many of the people who survived the disease were left as living statues, imprisoned in endless sleep. Fifty years later, in 1969, it was discovered that the drug L-DOPA had a dramatic effect on these people, many of whom experienced a sudden 'awakening'. Judi was to play the part of Deborah, who awakens after twenty-nine years of imprisoned sleep. She is still trapped in the past, and talks as a sixteen year-old, gradually realising what has happened. Most of these patients could not accept the present and retreated back into their comatose states. This is what one imagines happens to Deborah. After talking to the doctor, played by Paul Rogers, and to her sister, played by me, she sums up the facts that she now knows of the present, and says with poignant dignity, that 'she has the matter in perspective'. She has closed the door on her family.

It was remarkable to see Judi at work on this role. She had not read *Awakenings*, but I lent her my copy, which she kept for two or three days. Her instinct is amazing; she seems to breathe in a part by osmosis. All her movements were taken from the photographs in the book, haunting images of people who had not moved a muscle for nearly fifty years. Judi conveyed this state with delicate brilliance. Many years later, I played the part of Deborah on radio for the World Service, with Harold playing the doctor. There was not one inflection of Judi's that I did not remember. She had made the part uniquely her own. It was a fascinating experience acting with Harold. He is a great exponent of his own work, and also one of the best speakers of poetry. His readings of the work of Pablo Neruda are particularly fine.

I found the part of the sister an enormous challenge. I think Harold really wanted a big-bosomed maternal woman in the role. They tried padding me, but if your arms and legs are thin, its difficult not to appear like a pear walking on matchsticks. The text was so precise and perfect that some nights I felt it completely slip from my fragile grasp. It was like skating on the thinnest ice.

We played *Importance* in repertory for nearly a year, and during that time we toured for six weeks. This was interesting, for the audience reactions differed greatly from the quick sophisticated London houses. I had found this when we had toured *Heartbreak*

House. Provincial audiences are hugely appreciative, but their humour is different, and on the whole broader. We played the vast theatres of the North, like Manchester and Liverpool, and I am afraid that I lost the subtleties of my performance. Wilde demands the lightest of touches, and when you have to project to over two thousand people, it is difficult not to resort to belting it out. Towards the end of the run at the National, one of my friends came to a performance and gave me a great many notes. I had started to chant my part, and had stopped listening. With their help I was hopefully able to retrieve the spontaneity that I had at the outset.

Judi was a delightful touring companion. We used to walk from the theatre to our hotel each night, where supper would be waiting for us in one of our rooms. One night Judi said, 'If you could make a wish for the person of your dreams to be waiting in the hotel for you tonight, whom would you choose?' I thought briefly, and decided that the time had come for me to wish for someone suitable for my age. So I replied, 'The Pope.' Judi laughed until she cried. We both had to cling on to a lamp post to stop ourselves from falling over. Tears were streaming down our faces. I adore her sense of humour. It is quick as a flash, and never unkind. Touring is quite demanding and disruptive to your life, but with someone like Judi, the effort disappears and fun pops out at every corner. Her dressing room was filled each night with adoring fans. How she found the energy to cope with those demands was amazing. When we were in Nottingham, one of her fans who worked at the Boots factory outside the city invited Judi and me to visit the laboratories. This was a fascinating experience. We went in the early morning and, having donned white overalls, hats and hairnets, we spent three hours touring around all the departments, looking at enormous vats where the products are mixed and watching the conveyor belts where all the brightly coloured liquid soaps are bottled. The aroma in these halls is extremely powerful, but the staff said that they got used to it. Both Judi and I, however, were grateful for a stroll in the fresh air afterwards. The Boots team were a very jolly group, and they ladened us with enough gifts on our departure to keep us clean and fresh for a year.

We did not tour with Pinter's *Other Places*. One night after a performance of the plays at the National, Harold took us all to Le Caprice to have dinner with Oliver Sacks. What an interesting man. He speaks very rapidly, so that it is not always easy to catch the subtleties of his thoughts. I wish that I could have spent more time with him, for there were many questions that I would like to have asked him that dinner-party conversation prohibits. My stepfather Bill had developed Parkinson's disease towards the end of his life. During the great influenza pandemic in 1919, the virus had struck him, and one of his specialists had thought that this might have caused the Parkinsonism. He died eventually from pneumonia in 1973. For the last three years of his life he had been unable to speak coherently, and could not walk properly, but shuffled everywhere. It had been very sad to see this intelligent and active man become imprisoned in his own body. His death was a release from the difficulties and pains he had endured. They did administer the drug L-DOPA a year or so before he died, but the change in him was not great. I longed to ask Oliver Sacks more about this condition. He was a big bear of a man, sporting a beard at this time. Physically you could cast him as the cuddly uncle, but after the hour or so that we all spent together that evening, he seemed too neurotic for such a role, and presented a far more complex character. I regret that I have never had the chance to meet him again.

When work becomes a learning process, the journey is most rewarding. My next engagement took me into the world of art. I was asked to play the painter Gwen John in a film about her life. *A Journey Into the Shadows* was to be directed by Anna

Benson-Gyles, who set about our research most diligently and made the whole process exciting and fun.

I had often been told that I looked very like Gwen John, and I do see the similarity myself. I also think that Daniel looked a little like Gwen's brother, Augustus, but not everyone agrees about this. Anna B-G did want him to play the wild brother in the film, but he declined. I was relieved, because as I have already explained, it is very difficult acting with your family, and there were always tensions in the air when Dan was around. The journey ahead was difficult enough without having to cope with that.

First of all I had to learn to paint. I hate it when you see actors impersonating artists, and looking as though it is the first time that they have picked up a brush. I myself am quite hopeless at painting. I can't even draw matchstick people. My son David is an expert draughtsman, and I think he must have inherited this gift from his father's side of the family. Anna B-G arranged for me to have painting classes. I went to see Boney Le Touzel, the actress Sylvestra Le Touzel's father. Boney was utterly charming. He was a brilliant copier of any painter that took his fancy, and happily adopted Gwen John's style. We started to copy a small painting entitled *Green Leaves in a White Jug*. I learnt how to use a palette, and how to apply the paint to the canvas. After a few sessions, Anna B-G planned that we should visit the artist Mary Taubman, who was a great authority on Gwen, and who was to be the official artistic consultant on the film. We set off for Bath and spent an enthralling day in Mary's studio. She had been commissioned to paint a copy of *A Corner of the Artist's Room in Paris*, which I was going to be seen working on. The painting is a gentle reproduction of her attic quarters, depicting a small table with a vase of primroses and a wicker chair, a parasol resting on one arm. Gwen's palette was very particular, for she had studied with Whistler, and this painting was a perfect example of the subtle tones she used. Mary's copy was very fine, and enabled Anna B-G to shoot quite close when we were in the studio. Gwen's other paintings on the set were to be duplicates of the originals created by a special photographic process, and to which Mary would add texture if the camera came in close.

Mary moved around her studio with great delicacy, and all her gestures were accurate and deftly executed. She taught me how to correct perspective, and all the finer details that an artist employs to attain perfection, for there was no greater perfectionist than Gwen. At the end of our day in Bath, I began to feel more confident. The world of oils and turpentine, brushes and easels, was not so alien as I had anticipated. Mary was going to be on the set whenever I was seen at work, so I knew that she would not let me do anything that would appear amateurish.

We also visited the Tate in London and the National Gallery of Wales in Cardiff, where we were taken to see the sketches and watercolours and paintings of Gwen that were not on display in the galleries. Her output was phenomenal. What a consummate draughtsman she was. Her work conveys deep emotion effortlessly, but to achieve this perfection she suffered inordinately.

One day Anna B-G arranged a visit to an old lady in Kensington who had met Gwen John in her studio at Meudon. This was really helpful, for she remembered that Gwen moved like lightning, and spoke rapidly, but very softly. Gradually I was able to form a picture in my mind of this delicate and elusive character, who had lived all of her adult life alone in France, away from family and friends. Rodin was the love of her life, and when he rejected her, she fell apart, turning her face to the wall to die. She was saved by her friend Ursula Tyrwhitt, who gently nursed her back to life. Gwen was a complex mixture of frailty and strength. To capture her spirit sometimes felt a little like chasing a rainbow. Eventually I had to commit to my performance. The research had been engrossing and diverting, but now the mountain had to be climbed.

Gwen's obsession with Rodin was to be central to our film. I therefore had to prepare myself for the sequence when she posed as his muse in the nude, standing with her right foot on a high rock, her head bowed, and her mouth open. Gwen was used to taking her clothes off, and revelled in her nudity. I had never been required to strip in a film, and the idea filled me with dread. However, this was a hurdle that had to be overcome. On the day when the sequence was to be filmed, I stood in my pose wearing a Japanese kimono, which I planned to abandon at the very last minute. The cameraman, Colin Waldeck, came up to me and whispered in my ear, 'Have you been sunbathing lately?' I thought he was making polite conversation in order to put me at my ease. But this was not the reason. He genuinely wanted to know in case I had a bikini mark. The scene started and I did not faint as I had feared; all proceeded calmly and was not nearly so frightening an ordeal as I had anticipated. The emotional part of the scene proved far more difficult, but Anna B-G was extremely patient and eventually the sequence was completed. On my birthday I had to do another scene, where Gwen ran into the sea leaving all her clothes in a neat pile on the beach. The nudity by now presented no problem, but the freezing English Channel was extremely unwelcoming.

We took five weeks to complete the film, and the schedule was gruelling, as there wasn't a day when I was not needed. Gwen's despair and torments demanded enormous emotional resources to portray them truthfully. She lived on a knife-edge, her work and her cats providing her main solace. She became more and more withdrawn as her life progressed, and died alone in Dieppe, where she had gone to try to get to England. The whereabouts of her grave is unknown.

This tragic tale touched the hearts of many when the film was shown, and we received ecstatic reviews. Two days after the screening, I received through the post a watercolour of me as Gwen, sporting her well-worn grey hat and coat, with her long, thin pale face, painted by Hugh Casson, the President of the Royal Academy. Underneath were inscribed the words, 'Thank you for last night's wonderful performance.' I am eternally grateful that the Royal Mail did not damage the portrait, and I treasure it to this day.

Anna B-G had steered her emotional cargo into port safely, and to mark the event she gave me Proust's *A la recherche du temps perdu*, in three volumes, a gift that was to provide months of untold pleasure. I also received the award for Best Actress in a television movie at the Locarno Film Festival. I know that there is really no 'Best' when it comes to acting, but awards do give one a welcome boost, and although they resemble school prizes, they make all the preparation and hard work seem worthwhile.

Ten days before we finished filming, Daniel called me from Los Angeles to tell me that our father was in hospital with pneumonia. Anna B-G had generously offered to let me fly out to be with him. I knew how utterly disruptive this would be to the schedule, and that the budget was tight. I decided therefore to remain in London and complete the film. The story behind this decision was complex, and had caused me much pain.

CHAPTER 19

IN 1981 MY STEPMOTHER, DOROTHY, DIED. SHE HAD BEEN bedridden for the last year of her life, and her death was a release from suffering. I had hoped that after her demise, Father would want all of his children to visit him. I received no invitation. A young girl in her early twenties, Wendy, had been employed to take care of him, as he was now so lame that he could not walk without aid and needed constant supervision. About three months before I started the Gwen John film, Father had rung me to say that he wanted me to talk to my new sister. This statement surprised me, until he explained that he planned to adopt Wendy, and that he wanted me to welcome her into the family. My mind was in a whirl. I could not take in the full consequences of his request, and so I blindly obeyed his wishes and muttered a few clichés to Wendy, fervently hoping that I would never have to speak to her again. After I put down the telephone, I let the hurt and anger rage through me. Here was a man who had never fulfilled his duties as my father. A man I had had to share with my 'wicked' stepmother, a man who I had only seen infrequently, and now I was being asked to share him with an unknown girl, who had become the centre of his life and the apple of his eye, a role that I had never been permitted to play. It took a long time for me to come to terms with this news. I had lost all respect for him, and saw him as a selfish figure, a man who was only concerned with his personal comforts, and who really had no time for other people unless they could be of use to him. This was a brutal summing up of his character, and I knew that I would have to force myself to understand his point of view, and therefore mitigate my pain.

Time plays a great part when such dramatic events occur in life. I thought of Father's childhood, and remembered that he had lost his mother when he was very young. Having a detached and cold father himself, he must have learnt to swathe himself in protective armour. He had not seen much warmth in his formative years. Tenderness and cuddles had been alien to him. When he left my mother he had probably had to cut off all the natural feelings for his children, because otherwise the pain and guilt would have been too great for him to bear. These were some of the thoughts that went through my mind whilst I attempted to understand his behaviour over the adoption of Wendy. What hurt the most was that the conversation had been conducted with Wendy in the room. He had not given me the chance to talk to him privately. He had never said, 'I hope you won't be hurt, but this is the situation.' It was taken for granted that I would accept the news with the joyous response that he had anticipated. This I did find hard to forgive. However, I had to understand that now he was being well taken care of, and that he was happy. This was an important consideration.

The adoption never became final. Three days after Dan had rung to say that Father was in hospital with pneumonia, he died. As I have said, I had not flown out to be with him, as Anna B–G had so kindly offered. I was not very well myself at this time, and due to go into hospital for a hysterectomy as soon as the filming was completed. I had put off this operation for nearly a year because of work, and now I was in a lot of pain. I do not think I would have been up to the long flight, nor the emotional situation that would have greeted me. Daniel and my half-brother Geoffrey were with him, so Father did have immediate family round his bedside. The thought of meeting

Wendy was a deterrent, I have to admit, but had no other family member been there, I would have overcome this problem. So I stayed in England. It was on a Saturday morning that I received the news of his death, and it happened to be our rest day from filming. Soon after I put the telephone down, dry-eyed, but in a daze, I went out shopping. I returned in the early afternoon, and closed the front door to my flat, sat down and started to sob uncontrollably for an hour. David came in at one point and tried to comfort me, but the tears continued to pour out of me. I was sobbing for all the loss I felt, for all the love I felt for him, which I had never been able to express. I saw Father during this period of anguish as the victim, for he too had never been able to express his true feelings for me. I had always seen him as the man who played my father, in some ways untouchable. As a child I had never been able to sit on his knee. He had never read me a bedtime story. The awkwardness that hung in the air when I was with him had been an awkwardness for him too. We were locked into this painful situation together, and now there was no chance for us to change the pattern. His death made me feel as though a carpet had been swept from under my feet. I experienced a sense of desolation that was unrealistic, for he had hardly played a great part in my life, and yet the grief I experienced was profound, for I owed my very existence to him.

Daniel and Geoffrey had sorted out all Father's possessions, keeping for themselves the odd memento. In order that I should not feel left out, they found some jewellery in Father's bedside table that they thought I might like to have. Everyone was surprised to find this jewellery in his room, and we all wondered how it had arrived there, and to whom it had originally belonged. Naturally no explanation was forthcoming. There was a pearl necklace that I have to confess I thought was costume jewellery, and another necklace of different coloured stones, set prettily with hanging pendants. I am not a wearer of jewellery myself, so I decided to find out the value of the two necklaces, and took them to an auction house. I was amazed to discover that they were both quite valuable pieces. And I decided that, as I would never wear them, I would rather have something that I would use all the time to remind me of Father, so I sold them and bought myself an expensive holdall, reminiscent of the kind used in the thirties. This exquisite piece of luggage goes with me everywhere, and reminds me of my father's elegance.

Guilt and regret do no one any good. I don't blame Father for anything. He did what he did in his life, and I have accepted that. I might wish things had turned out differently, but those wishes will change nothing, and so I try to remember the positives. He did make us laugh on the occasions when we were alone with him, and a sense of humour is a precious gift. He also had great style and, when I think of him, this elegant, smiling man is what I see.

We finished filming *Journey Into the Shadows*, and two days later I went into hospital to have my operation. They kept me in for two weeks, as I had no one to care for me when I went home. Friends came to see me each day, which kept my spirits up, and Richard Wilson and I planned another holiday together where I could convalesce, and he could enjoy the sun and swimming. We booked into a grand hotel outside Palermo in Sicily, where it said in the brochure that the elite of European royalty had stayed. We arrived at night, and found that our rooms were right over the dance floor. There was no chance of sleep until the small hours. When we awoke, we were both horrified to find that the garden, much vaunted in the publicity, was in fact miniscule. And the view from our rooms was mainly of a busy port, where major reconstruction work was taking place. The noise during the morning was unbearable. Richard and I were both Londoners craving a rural break. We had been led to believe we would be in acres of luscious secluded greenery. The garden, such as it was, comprised a few palm trees and the odd plant, all dominated by the bulldozers busily beavering away in the port.

We decided to try and book into another hotel in a more rural setting on the other side of the island. No luck. Everything was full as it was the height of the season. Next we asked to change our rooms to a quieter part of the hotel. Here we were luckier. I was moved at once to an enormous room that was quiet as a tomb, but rather dark. This I could tolerate, for at least it assured a good night's sleep. The following day Richard was given a beautiful sunny room with a balcony, where we spent many hours sipping the local wine, and pretending that the view was gentler and more peaceful.

On the third day Alan Rickman arrived, and cheered us up no end. He was staying in extremely noisy lodgings, so he came and spent his days with us, finding the noise of our port quieter than the incessant Palermo traffic. He often stayed on to dinner, for the food in the hotel was superb. We assumed this must be the only reason that foreign heads of Europe had deigned to stay there.

I cannot say that we all returned refreshed, as we had done after our Cretan trip, but we had laughed a lot and shared the hazards of travel with good humour. I had not been strong enough to do any sightseeing, but Richard and Alan were as intrepid as ever, and each evening told me of their expeditions to churches and museums and neighbouring villages.

A hysterectomy operation is not easy to recover from, and the convalescence requires mental as well as physical healing. On my return to London I still felt frail, but when I was asked to do two days on Julian Mitchell's film of his stage play, *Another Country*, I accepted at once. Sometimes work can help revive your spirits more powerfully than a holiday.

Another Country is set in an English public school, and centres on the romances of the young Guy Bennett (based on Guy

Burgess), and his involvement with a Marxist student, which eventually leads to his becoming one of the most notorious spies in English history. The two days that I spent on that film were like a tonic. Marek Kaniewska was the director. I had worked with Marek before on a couple of television plays, and I loved his spriteful manner, and his wild Polish humour. He always knew precisely what he wanted from his actors, and helped them to achieve his goals with wit and patience, often rewarding them with a delicious dinner cooked by him. I shall always regret that we lost him to Hollywood.

My two scenes in the film were with the delightful Rupert Everett who played Bennett. I was to be his selfish right-wing mother. In the original play she was an off-stage character, but in the film Julian had written two witty scenes set at her second wedding, where Rupert acted as the best man, he looking elegant in his morning suit, and me draped in baby pink chiffon. Everyone treated me as though I was a piece of Dresden china. I wish I could have been with them all for months. Rupert is not only one of the most generous and thoughtful people I know, but he is also hilarious. He kept me in stitches of laughter from morn till night.

For the next year or so I worked on television and radio, but there were long periods between engagements when I had time to enjoy myself, to meet friends, and to read many books. Reading has always been an important part of my life, but when you are working on a part it is difficult to immerse yourself in a book. At such times I distract myself with light literature. But the year following my operation, I did manage to read an enormous amount. There were weekends when I saw no one. Apart from sleeping and eating, and the occasional walk in Holland Park, I read until I was so tired that the book fell from my hands. I often set myself goals. For example, at one time I devoted myself to Russian literature, devouring the works of Turgenev, Dostoyevsky, Tolstoy and Lermentov. Later I was to be introduced to other

Russian writers by my husband, but for now I was content with the well-known literary giants.

My four literary advisers were, as I have mentioned already, Peter Eyre, David Hare, Howard Schuman and Christopher Hampton. They guided me towards interesting books, and discussed them with me too, which added greatly to my pleasure and understanding. It was like being at the most charming university. Their tastes are very different, and therefore my library became extremely eclectic. David is a discoverer of out-of-the-way biographies and American writers, Christopher encouraged the classics, Howard reads the very latest books, and his analysis doubles your delight. But Peter has probably had the most influence on my library. He has encouraged me to read a great deal of European literature, and only recently gave me Stefan Zweig's autobiography, *The World of Yesterday*, which is certainly on my list of top ten favourite reads. It was Peter who told me about Anita Brookner, which was to have interesting ramifications. But for the time being I had set myself the task of reading the whole of Proust.

Like many other people, I had started Proust, but abandoned the project after 'Swann's Way'. Now that Anna B-G had given me the work in three volumes, the task seemed less daunting. I cancelled nearly all weekend engagements, and for nine months settled down to the magical journey. Sometimes I felt it was like putting on a snorkel, as I dived into endless pages with no full stops, relishing the characters and observations of this extraordinary genius.

Towards the end of 1984, there was really very little work coming my way, and I had started to sing the actor's song, 'Will I Ever Work Again?' This is a genuine refrain, for rejection is very much part of an actor's luggage. You go up for a part and are turned down in favour of someone else, or you get the part, and are then told by the critics that you are no good in it. You have to be strong enough for all this not to shatter your confidence, for frequently your inner self feels bruised, and this is where your agent plays a vital role. A lot of actors, when they are going through a bad patch, think that changing their agent will make everything all right. This is a fallacy. Sometimes there are just not the parts around that you are right for, and you have to be patient and wait. A good agent at such times will be able to keep you in an optimistic frame of mind, for a good agent is also a good psychologist. I have only changed agents three times in fifty years. I always did so when I felt that we had come to the end of mutual advancement, and I always ended the relationships as amicably as possible. An agent is your umbilical cord to the profession, for they know what is happening long in advance of the general public, and they know when it is suitable to put you forward for a job. You have to trust in their judgement completely.

In 1990 I joined the agency of Markham and Froggatt, which is one of the most respected agencies in the country. Pippa Markham, Stephanie Randall and Alex Irwin care for a list of very sought-after actors, and they care for them twenty-four hours a day. Nothing ever seems too much trouble for them. I feel that I am a member of a family, and utterly protected from all hazards. They have a magnificent team who always lift your spirits when you talk with them. The finance department is run by Bill Higgins, who has enormous patience and the greatest skills for chasing up outstanding cheques. He would keep the World Bank in good order.

Each actor has different needs and neuroses, and Pippa, Stephanie and Alex know how to deal with these specific individual requirements. They are excellent psychologists, and when they have the hateful task of telling you that a part has gone to someone else, they convey the tidings directly, but in such a way that you still feel hopeful about the future. This is an art. They also work extraordinary hours, for after the regular office hours, they usually go to see a client in a play, and then during the night they are often called from Los Angeles about a deal or an availability, which means that they frequently work a fifteen-hour shift. On top of that they have to read at least fifty scripts a week. So anyone who thinks that an agent just sits back and rakes in the percentage are wrong, for they toil on our behalf more than most people would believe possible. They need as much love and gratitude as their clients, and when we do land a magnificent role, their pride and sense of achievement is rightly as great as ours. Since joining Markham and Froggatt I really do fret less about my next job, for I know that this unique group of people are working round the clock on our behalf, and that if there is something out there that I would be right for, they will be on to it before the ink is dry. I am very lucky to be a member of their family.

CHAPTER 20

THE NOVELS OF ANITA BROOKNER CAPTIVATED ME. PETER EYRE had told me to read *A Start in Life*, her first novel, and I immediately read her next two, *Providence* and *Look at Me*. Peter had said he thought her heroines would be good parts for me. I agreed, for they were single women, rather contained and independent. The only problem was that I was too old, for they were in their late twenties and I had reached my forties. How to solve this dilemma?

The television producer Sue Birtwhistle and I had often talked about finding a project that we could work on together. I now told her to get the Brookner novels, and if she was as excited as I was, to meet up and make plans. We went to the cinema one evening shortly after, and during the ensuing dinner, we decided that Sue should write to Anita, and find out if she was interested in writing an original screenplay for us, with a slightly older heroine. The reply came back promptly. She was not interested in writing for television, but she had just completed a novel with an older heroine, and would be delighted for me to play the part if we wanted to buy the rights. She said she was a fan of mine since seeing the Gwen John film. Sue and I were thrilled. As a rule nothing in this profession goes so smoothly. There are usually enormous delays and discussions and nail biting. This time everything was ticking like clockwork. The novel was still in proof form, and we read it avidly. It was called *Hotel du Lac*.

The main character was Edith Hope, another perfect Brookner heroine, private, successful, independent, and having an affair with a married man. But like a great many of Anita's heroines, she had friends who were always meddling in her private life, and wanting to pair her off with unsuitable men. She finds herself somewhat unwillingly engaged to a gentleman and, as she is arriving at the registry office, she decides to defy everybody, and tells the chauffeur to drive on. To escape the wrath and admonishments of all her friends, she goes to stay at the Hotel du Lac in Switzerland. There are countless Hotel du Lacs to be found in that country, but Anita chose the one in Vevey, which ironically I knew very well, as it was only a few minutes drive from my mother's apartment at La Tour de Peilz.

Sue and I immediately decided to put in an offer and buy the rights. We were successful, and only a few weeks after the deal was completed, *Hotel du Lac* was shortlisted for the Booker prize. Several other producers subsequently wanted to get hold of the rights. They were too late. By the time the book won the famous literary prize, we were already immersed in pre-production. It was the most exciting time.

We chose Giles Foster to direct, and he and Sue soon set off to find suitable locations. I was very involved with the casting, and we were all thrilled when Denholm Elliot agreed to play the mysterious Mr Neville, the Devil's advocate, who she meets at the hotel, and who proposes to her, and from whom she fortunately escapes at the end. I had known Denholm since I was about ten years old. He used to come to Mother's parties, both in New York and London. When I was nineteen, and still living with Mother and Bill in Highgate, Denholm had taken me out to dinner one evening, and had kissed me. This had delighted me, for I had always had a great crush on him. Our dalliance was chaste and short. In the early seventies, I had acted with Denholm in the television film of Ibsen's *The Doll's House*, starring Claire Bloom. This was when I had met Christopher

Alfred Hitchcock directing me and Jon Finch in *Frenzy*

Denholm Elliot and me filming *Hotel du Lac* in Witznau in Switzerland

Taken during His Royal Highness the Duke of Edinburgh's visit to my uncle Vincent Massey's home in Port Hope, Canada

Daniel, my half-brother Geoffrey, David, Father and me

Me as Ariadne Utterword
in *Heartbreak House*

Me as Queen Elizabeth in
Schiller's *Mary Stuart*

Me as Miss Prism in *The Importance of Being
Earnest*, with Martin Jarvis as John Worthing
and Judi Dench as Lady Bracknell

Katharine Hepburn as Miss Moffat and me as
Miss Ronberry in *The Corn is Green*

Me as Mrs Danvers in *Rebecca*

Me as Gwen John in
The Journey Into the Shadows

Me filming the Buxton Mineral
Water ad in the Tana Delta

My son David, fishing

David teaching my grandson, Dan, to fish

Me and Uri on
our wedding day

And David and Maddie
on their wedding day

My grandson Dan

And my grand–
daughter Iris

Uri and me soon after we were married

Hampton, for he had adapted the screenplay. Everything seemed to be turning full circle, for we now asked Christopher if he would write the screenplay of *Hotel du Lac*. Anita had not wanted to adapt it herself, and was so far perfectly happy with all our ideas.

Sue and I had by this time met Anita. She had generously taken us both out to lunch on my birthday at a restaurant round the corner from where she lives. She had even ordered me a small and delicious cake. I was most touched. We had had a drink at her flat before the lunch. The flat was incredibly neat, light and welcoming. I felt that I had met the first person who rivalled me for order. Anita also dressed immaculately, and her hair was impeccably coiffed. The only thing that surprised me was that she smoked incessantly. This seemed strangely out of character.

It had been a real treat to meet this formidable writer, for not only were her stories beautifully crafted, but they were also written in the finest prose. She is a supreme stylist, and I think without rivals in her field. She said she was going to leave us alone while we filmed, and that she looked forward to the first screening. How trusting she was.

Everything was progressing rapidly. The casting was complete, the locations had been confirmed, and we were very pleased with Christopher's script. I now put aside my producer's hat, and concentrated on my role. After a week of rehearsals in London, we all flew to Zurich, and then went by car to Witznau on Lake Lucerne. The Park Hotel was providing accommodation for the cast and crew. I was given the most luxurious room in the turret, with windows on three sides, and remarkable views of the lake and mountains. I did feel like a fairy-tale princess. Would I have to let down my hair, so that the prince could climb up my tresses and reach my apartments? The schedule was unfortunately too busy to permit any dalliances with princes or paupers. Make-up calls and shooting started each day at six a.m., and I never had a day off. I revelled in the discipline, and looked forward to the quiet mornings when Demelza Rogers, my brilliant make-up artist, and I would creep along the empty hotel corridors, preparing for the many scenes to be shot that day.

Denholm was extraordinary to work with, and he gave me some wonderfully useful tips, which I have remembered to this day. When filming scenes at dinner tables he said, 'Never eat anything during the take, for you will have to keep matching the mouthfuls in other takes and close-ups, and this will limit your freedom.' How right he was. I just toyed with my food as he did, and nobody ever commented on the fact that neither of us swallowed so much as a morsel.

Denholm knew his lines perfectly for his close-ups and for the master shot, but when it came to my close-ups, I noticed that he read his lines from the script. He explained that without the camera being on him, his concentration would have wandered, and he would give me wrong cues, which he figured would be more off-putting than seeing him read the text. I saw his point and soon got used to this method and enjoyed playing our scenes together very much. He was such a subtle actor and conveyed a host of thoughts with the merest flick of his eye. He also taught me that just before a take, when the camera crew and the director are talking through the shot, it is essential for the actor to switch off and not to get distracted or involved in this chatter, for it breaks valuable concentration. I have always thought it was generous of Denholm to pass on these tips. Some masters prefer keeping these secrets to themselves.

We spent three weeks in Witznau, and on returning to London, we filmed for a further five days. Then the film was complete. It was under a year since Sue and I had had our dinner together to discuss a project, and *Hotel du Lac* was already in the can, ready to be screened the following spring. I think everyone agreed that this was a small miracle.

We received wonderful reviews when it was shown one Sunday on BBC2, and for a while I walked on air. Anita wrote me saying that she liked it very much, but that she had found the hotel rather grander than she had imagined. A few months later it was repeated on BBC1, and she wrote me again, this time to say that she now found the setting perfect, and was very pleased with everything.

I now felt confident enough to invite Anita to dinner. She accepted, and an evening was arranged. I had invited Peter Eyre, who had pointed me toward Anita, Sue Birtwistle and Richard Eyre (who is Sue's husband and not related to Peter). Anita arrived early looking chic and spritely. She talks extremely fast, and in the most elegant phrases. I had prepared all the food in advance as I wanted to be free to administer to everyone's needs. My prowess in the kitchen is lamentable, as I have already said, and I didn't want to disappear for any length of time, thus drawing attention to my limitations.

Everyone sat down at the dining table, and I handed round the prawn and watercress salad, seasoned with a honey and mustard dressing, whereupon Anita exclaimed that if she so much as touched a prawn, she would die. Inside, I myself died. What to do? Elizabeth David or Jamie Oliver would immediately whip up an omelette, and the evening would proceed as though nothing had happened. This was not possible chez moi, as I found boiling an egg an ordeal. So poor Anita nibbled crispbread and waited for the next course, which was to be chicken Marengo, a dish that I had taken hours to prepare. I have to confess that the evening was a disaster. The guest of honour left before we'd all finished the pudding. I felt a complete failure and decided that acting was a great deal easier than entertaining. I am afraid that I still feel this way.

However, the following spring I once more walked on air when I won the television Best Actress award at BAFTA for my performance as Edith Hope. This provided a much-needed boost, for it was soon after I finished filming *Hotel du Lac* that Dan stopped speaking to me. The portcullis had been brought down again, but this time for good. He said he was on a journey to find himself and could not see me during this quest. No amount of pleading would change his mind. Other members of the family were too frightened to intercede on my behalf for fear of incurring his wrath. He had not spoken to Mother for two years. He said that she had not shown him love as a child and was a monster. I found it strange that he had waited fifty-one years to discover this. In the past he had always defended her if I was critical of her behaviour, but I kept these thoughts to myself and remained excluded from all his family gatherings for the next twelve years. This did cause me unbearable pain.

I ran into Dan only twice during this time, on both occasions by accident. I found this strange, considering that we were in the same profession, and that the London theatrical scene is quite small. Once was at the BBC, where we were both doing radio plays, and the other time was at a reception for the Arts Council. He barely spoke to me on either occasion, and a coldness hovered around him that was frightening. I could not understand how he managed to keep up this wall of indifference. To sever all feelings in this way seemed unreal.

My comforting adage, 'This too shall pass', ceased to help, for the passing was taking too long. I decided that I had to get on with my life and not become obsessed by Dan's behaviour. So I threw myself into work, and went back to the National Theatre. Coral Browne always said that when you lived alone, 'Acting was something to do in the evenings.' She was right. For most of the following year, I had something to occupy my evenings. I was going to play Goneril in David Hare's production of *King Lear* starring Anthony Hopkins.

I had first met Anthony in 1969 when I played the cameo role of his wife in *The Looking-Glass War*. In those days he was most unhappy and troubled, but when I met him at rehearsals for *Lear*, he was bouncing with energy, health and enthusiasm. The year before he had made an enormous hit as the oily newspaper proprietor in David's *Pravda* at the National, and now he was back there again to play the doughty old king.

It was the first time that I had played Shakespeare on stage, and I found the prospect daunting. When you are studying a language and you begin to dream in the tongue, you know that it has taken root. I never learnt to dream in verse. It is a great sadness to me not to have this proficiency. I can of course speak verse, but it does not come naturally to me. There were nights in *Lear* when I felt completely at sea. I dried one night in an early scene with Regan and I panicked because I was unable to give even an approximation of my thoughts. Suzanne Bertish, who played Regan, is a brilliant speaker of verse and each night I envied her dextrous negotiation of the text. Anthony Hopkins was also at home in Shakespeare's world, but he was undisciplined, and when David was not there during the run, he altered his performance, and some nights ran amok. He was a bullish Lear, and revelled in the physicality of the old man, but sometimes missed out on his spiritual side. To sustain a part of that magnitude is a mammoth task.

One evening during the rehearsals, Anthony and his then wife, Jenny, had invited me to dinner in their elegant Belgravia house. The conversation was almost entirely about Lear, but at some point Anthony had played the piano, and I had not known what a brilliant pianist he is. His playing is passionate and subtle, but with the lightest touch. He took us into another world, and I am sure he finds great solace in his music.

Michael Bryant was playing Gloucester. He was a formidable actor who had spent many years at the National, and was the only performer I know who was completely at home on the Olivier stage. He understood how to deal with all the hazards of that vast space. On the first preview Suzanne Bertish overheard Michael saying to Anthony in the wings, 'Nerves are vanity.' Suzanne related this to me as we were leaving the theatre that night. I put down my bag, took out a pen and pencil, and wrote this adage down. 'Brilliant,' I said. Then as I was writing I stopped and looked up at her and said, 'Yes, but fear is fucking human.'

We played *Lear* in repertory for a year. I never came off stage feeling satisfied with my performance, but there was one night near the end of the run when magic descended on my shoulders and I went through the evening totally absorbed. The enormity of the Olivier stage no longer frightened me. I was in Lear's world, and nothing disturbed my focus. The audience were like mice when I spoke, the verse tripped of my tongue, and my imagination flew. The complexities of Goneril's relationship with her father became clear for the first time. My performance was filled with nuances hitherto unexplored. It was one of the most exciting nights that I ever spent on stage. The next night I was eager to repeat this haunting experience. Alas it was not to be. The magic never touched me again. As Ralph Richardson once said, 'Sometimes it's there, and sometimes it's not.' I shall never forget that night, though, and it did give me the courage to go on experimenting, but I shall always feel that I let David down. If you are not at home in Shakespeare's language, you cannot be free to scale the heights and treasures that he lays at your feet.

For my fiftieth birthday, I decided to give a party for all my friends who had supported me so warmly during my troubled times, and who had kept me going and lifted my spirits and made me laugh. I hired Leighton House in Holland Park, and bade everyone to come and celebrate with a light dinner and drinks. Peter Eyre had sent me an enormous cake that was not unveiled until the guests started to arrive. It was in the shape of the front page of the *Independent* newspaper, iced in white with black script. At first I did not take in the details, but when I did, I realised that Peter had carefully and wittily chosen each headline: 'Washing machine disaster, Kitchen flooded', 'Boiler broken, No central Heating', 'Holiday hotel nowhere near the sea as promised', and so on and so on. I laughed and rejoiced at such an original and thoughtful gift. But later that night as I lay in bed mulling over the jollities of the evening, I began to think what a burden I had been on my friends, how much I leant on them, and depended on their comfort. The dramatic reactions to events that I thrust at them must sometimes have been irksome. I now saw that their patience was magnificent. I had to learn lessons from this cake, and start keeping my problems to myself. We had laughed over my domestic upheavals, and all my disasters were related very humorously, but enough was enough, I thought. From now on, try to keep your cool, girl. I fear I have not always succeeded, for even now if a light bulb bursts I panic. Nevertheless, the cake had made me dwell upon the importance of my friends. My mother had moved to Switzerland in 1959; my father was dead, and had never greatly featured in my life; Daniel was not now speaking to me; and my analysis had ended. My friends had thus become my family, and I depended deeply on their support and their belief in me.

My ruminations over the cake led to deeper probing. In what other ways had I annoyed my friends, apart from my domestic dramas? I am fanatically tidy. My mind is like a demented centipede, and ordered surroundings help to calm my spirit. I find clutter distracting. I try not to inflict these demands on anyone, but someone once came to my flat in Holland Park and said that my neatness made him want to throw tomato ketchup all over the walls. I was sorry to hear that, but I hope this desire was more his problem than mine. My scripts are chaotic, I write all over them in different colours, and sometimes fail to decipher my notes. This is really my only area of mayhem. It is probably an important safety valve. My cupboards are extraordinarily tidy. I could locate the smallest handkerchief in seconds. I was once interviewed on the radio about my wardrobe. The interviewer came to my house and, microphone in hand, inspected my clothes. She was surprised to find that all my cardigans were wrapped, as she thought, in plastic. I corrected her. 'In cellophane,' I said. Judi

Dench rang me that evening still laughing from my retort. I hoard nothing. If I buy something new, I throw out the garment that it is replacing. The words 'That'll come in useful' are anathema to me. I like few possessions, and thereby have fewer choices to make each day.

I drew this portrait of myself and thought what an eccentric person I must present to the world. But there is only so much you can do to change yourself. It takes a dramatic event to alter the patterns that have taken root.

Soon after my birthday, I went to stay with my mother in Switzerland. She was now quite frail, and we spent a quiet weekend together, and I really enjoyed her company. She was gentler than in the past, and deeply puzzled and distressed by Dan's behaviour toward her. All her gifts and letters to him had been returned unopened.

She was still the generous hostess, caring for your every comfort. We played cards together, and kept the conversation as light as possible. She was now eighty-four, and determined to end her days in her apartment, fiercely independent as always. I said goodbye to her feeling sad that she did not live nearer to me, so that I could care for her more as she grew weaker.

When I got back to London, I thought, 'Anna, this is it.' I told myself that I must enjoy where I was at, that I had a wonderful son, good work to do, warm and supportive friends, a nice flat, and enough money to live comfortably. I must stop being dissatisfied with my lot, and stop looking for Mr Right. I was very, very fortunate, and if he didn't appear, there was still much to be grateful for. In this calm frame of mind, on 10 August 1988 I set off to a dinner party at a friend's house.

CHAPTER 21

IN THE SIXTIES THERE WAS A CHILDREN'S TELEVISION PROGRAMME called *Jackanory* where actors read stories for a quarter of an hour each evening from an autocue. I so enjoyed watching the programme that I wrote to Joy Whitby, the producer, asking if I could read a story for her. She agreed, and I read five tales over a week. I had the greatest fun, and Joy and I became close friends ever since. She went on to be Head of Children's Programmes at Yorkshire Television, and now runs her own company, Grasshopper Films. Over the years Joy has been wonderfully supportive. She is a great hostess, and gives dinner parties where you meet the most interesting people from a wide range of professions. Joy is much travelled and she makes friends wherever she goes. She is a social magnet.

On 10 August 1988 she invited me to one of her dinner parties. It was a hot, sultry evening, and I was not in a very convivial mood, feeling rather tired. On arriving at Joy's my spirits rose. She has the ability to cheer those around her. We all congregated on the top floor of her Kensington house for champagne and canapés. Joy left at some point to deal with dinner and I was chatting away in a group of interesting people when the last guest arrived. He was given a glass of champagne by Joy's son, Max, and was left alone, so I beckoned him over to join our circle. He was an elegant grey-haired gentleman in a pale blue shirt and jeans. His blue eyes twinkled, and I instantly warmed to him. He told us that he had spent the day in Sheffield inspecting a magnet, for he was a metallurgist, a professor of mineral technology who worked at Imperial College. How interesting, I thought, to learn of another world, and how entertainingly he spoke about his subject. I have always loved meeting people outside the acting profession. The world of theatre can become quite claustrophobic at times. As we descended the stairs to dinner, I kept my fingers crossed that I would be seated next to this fascinating man, whose name was Uri Andres. My wish was granted for I sat on his left, and spent the whole evening talking to him, disregarding the social convention of speaking equally to the people on either side of you. The mathematician who sat on my left at one point commented on this lapse on my part. I apologised profusely, but that evening I was in a small inner whirl.

Uri is an original. I saw that at once. He is Russian, a Muscovite, and he speaks with the most beguiling accent. I learnt that he had emigrated to Israel in 1973, and that he had left the Technical University of Haifa in 1976 and joined Imperial College, where he was now working on the separation of minerals in an alternating magnetic field. He even managed to fascinate on this complex subject, as far removed as could be from my profession, which my mother used to call, 'The mad world of powder and paint.'

Uri and I were the last guests to leave that night. Joy suggested that I give Uri a lift home, as he had no car and had walked there that evening (I subsequently learnt that he walked everywhere). I was delighted to oblige, and when we said goodnight we exchanged telephone numbers, but as neither of us had a pen, we had to memorise them by heart. I repeated his number to myself until I reached home.

I was about to go to Manchester to play Miss Pross in a television film of *A Tale of Two Cities*, and I wanted to make contact with Uri before I left, for I knew that he too was going away. He had planned to visit his family in Moscow, and to go to St Petersburg, which was then still called Leningrad. The 11th of August was my birthday. I spent the day with David, and thought it a little too precipitate to ring Uri. But by the 12th, I decided to take the plunge. I thought that I was now fifty-one, and old enough to break the convention of waiting for the gentleman to be the first to call. I rang and left a message on his machine. Within ten minutes he called me back, and we arranged for him to come to dinner at my house on the 15th.

He arrived with exquisite flowers, and caviar and crab meat, great Russian delicacies. We went for a gentle walk after dinner, and planned to meet again three weeks later when he and I both returned from our trips. Whatever happened, I knew that I had met a great friend.

I told no one about Uri. He was my special secret, and I waited eagerly for his telephone call when he was back from Russia. He rang me on September the 3rd, and we met on the 4th for a long walk in Richmond Park and a light supper. And Reader, on November the 22nd he married me. I have never been so sure about anything before, and we are still together after seventeen years. Uri is the love of my life. Like all couples we have worked at our marriage, but I can truthfully say that everything changed when we got wed. Calm took the place of angst, uncertainty and pain. Like me, Uri had lived alone for fifteen years. I think we both feel that we are very, very lucky to have found each other. Life is absolutely bearable on your own. It is unbearable with the wrong companion, but it is so much richer with the right partner.

From the day we met on August the 10th until November the 22nd, the sun shone every day, literally. It was the most glorious autumn that I can remember. We were married in the morning at Chelsea Registry Office, and afterwards Peter Eyre generously gave us a wedding breakfast at the River Café. David came, and Dan and Penelope's beautiful golden-haired daughter, Alice. Anna B-G took photographs, and Richard Wilson filmed it all. It was a joyous day. Even Dan sent a gift of a magnum of champagne and an embroidered cushion with a simple card attached. No other communication from him. I was both touched and puzzled by his thought. I felt that if he wished me happiness, why could he not break the dreadful silence that he insisted upon? I did not dare ring him to ask this question. But absolutely nothing could mar the joy of our day. As we left the restaurant late in the afternoon, having feasted upon rare culinary delights, the sun was still glowing low in the sky. We returned home and went for a long walk, chatting over the pleasures of the celebrations.

Uri and I have such fun together. He has an unusual sense of humour, and combines Russian introspection with Jewish intelligence, an interesting mix. He has made me delve, where once I tended to skim over things. I have never met a more prolific reader, or a more brilliant scavenger of new books and authors. He never ceases to surprise me, and he has never ever bored me. We do have different views on things, I have to admit, and politically we are quite far apart, but that is to be expected, for we come from such vastly different backgrounds. But we have fiery and interesting debates, and he accepts no facile statements from me, and keeps me on my cerebral toes.

In the twenties Uri's father had worked in military intelligence in Trotsky's Ministry of War, leaving the army after Trotsky's expulsion from the Party and the State. He then became a journalist, and continued his writing in Hebrew, publishing several books clandestinely in Israel. In 1948 he was sentenced to fifteen years in a concentration camp in Kazakhstan for his Zionism. He was allowed no visitors, although Uri went all the way there to try and see him, only to be brutally turned away. In January 1953 his father was recalled to a prison in Moscow, where his interrogation started again. His mother was now given permission to visit her husband. This was considered a bad sign, as it usually meant that the prisoner was going to be shot. In

March 1953 Stalin died. Uri's father was now sent back to serve twenty-five years in the same concentration camp in Kazakhstan. In 1956 he was released and he returned to his family, exonerated. Thousands of political prisoners were similarly released after Khrushchev had delivered his speech against Stalin. The strains of these years though took their toll on Uri's mother. She died only three years after her husband's return.

Uri himself had been imprisoned for being a member of a secret student debating society. Life in Moscow had been tremendously difficult and harsh, and Uri told me countless tales of the courage and stamina of the people in his world. The comfort of my own childhood made stark contrast to the difficulties that Uri had had to endure.

When I went to Moscow and Leningrad soon after we were married, I was very touched by the warmth and generosity of his friends. In 1988 'perestroika' and 'glasnost' were words we were only beginning to hear. There were still great shortages, and people queued for hours for tins of food. Fresh fruit and vegetables were almost impossible to find in winter. But when we were invited to his friends' houses, feasts were laid on the table, vodka and wine flowed, and their rations had all been given to us. I have never been made to feel so welcome anywhere before. We stayed with Uri's daughter, Olga, in Moscow. She now lives with her family in California. His elder daughter Victoria also lives in the States with her family in New Jersey. Only Uri's sister, Tamara has stayed on in Moscow.

One day we had lunch with a very old school friend of Uri's called Susannah. The lunch went on a long time, and we drank the most delicious cranberry vodka. I had no idea how strong it was until we went out into the freezing snowy night, and I suddenly felt I was going to fall over. We went to Lubimov's Taganka Theatre that night, and saw his production of *Boris Godunov*, which sadly failed to impress us.

Uri showed me all the places where he had lived in Moscow,

often in communal flats where the families shared the kitchen, bathroom and loo. At one stage he lived in Granovsky Street which overlooked an enclave where members of the government lived in very grand apartments, generals and ministers and Party bosses, including Madame Furtzeva, and Molotov. There was a food distribution depot just opposite, and Uri used to see smoked salmon and caviar being taken to these elite neighbours, delights rarely available or affordable for the general public. These food packets were distributed almost free of charge. When these illustrious members encountered the public, they lowered their eyes in shame.

As a child Uri had lived in the district of Arbat, where the intelligentsia of Moscow congregated. I went there with him. It had a charming atmosphere, lighter than the rest of the city. We also visited the Pushkin Museum and saw the great Pasternak paintings, his portrait of Ahkmatova dominating the stairwell. This is the father of the writer Boris Pasternak.

But the greatest treats were the visits to his friends, for this is where I got a true feel of Moscow life. I loved listening to their talk. This way I learnt what a beautiful mellifluous voice Uri had. I have not, alas, learnt the language, but my pleasure in hearing it spoken has never abated.

On this trip he took me to Leningrad by overnight train. Before the railroad was constructed, Tzar Nicholas had drawn a straight line between the two great cities, holding his ruler down with his thumb, and when the line went round his thumb on the drawing, they omitted to correct this on the plan, so the rail track curves to this day, outlining the thumb print of the last ruler of the Romanovs. Uri managed to get permission for me to sleep in the guard's little cabin on the train. He had to share a compartment with two women.

Leningrad, or St Petersburg as it is now renamed, I found very beautiful. The pale pastel-painted buildings still evoke the period of late eighteenth-century Russia, and of course the Hermitage, majestic, but the scene of such brutality, dominates the whole city. We were there in January, and the mornings were like a grey blurred painting. There was no feeling of light until the early afternoon. We visited the Summer Palace outside the city, and the museum of Pavlosk beyond, and I felt that I was walking through the pages of a short story by Pushkin. Uri left me one morning in the Russian Museum of Art, and I could have stayed there for a week. What painters thrived there in the nineteenth century, artists of whom I had never heard. The treasures in the Hermitage are legendary, and we spent a couple of mornings there, but you really need a whole year.

It had been a deeply fascinating trip, but I must confess that we were both pleased to come home. Life there in 1988 was hard, and the climate is unyielding and demands great energy. We also longed for fresh salads and fruit. But the trip was an experience that I shall never forget. We said our sad farewells to Olga and her daughter Tanya, and hoped that they would soon be able to visit us in London.

Uri once read an interview with Joseph Brodsky, the great Russian poet. He was at the time living in the States, and he was asked how he felt about his emigration, and Brodsky had replied, 'Moving to a new country is simply a continuation of space.' I admire those who uproot themselves so calmly. I think when Uri arrived in England, life had not been easy for him, and there were times when he was very lonely. We are not the most welcoming nation. Soon after we were married he went away for a few days, and when he returned I went to the airport to meet his plane. He told me afterwards that he felt for the first time that he was really coming home. I have always tried to meet his planes since that day.

For the first two years of our marriage we stayed on in my flat in Holland Park, but in 1990 we sold both our places and moved to a house. We needed more space, for we had been used to living alone, and even if you spend ninety per cent of the time in the same room, it is good to know that you have a private bolt-hole to which you can disappear. The freedom this gives is one of life's luxuries.

Soon after our wedding, Anthony Clare asked me to be his guest on his radio programme, *In the Psychiatrist's Chair*. I agreed, for I had been a fully paid-up member of the singles club for a long time, and I wanted others to know that surprises were often round the corner when least expected, and quite late in life. I had no idea how difficult I would find being on the programme. Anthony asked me a question about my early life and I decided to answer it as fully as I could, but halfway through I completely lost my thread. I had to stop and ask him to remind me what the original question was. This happened a couple of times. I was utterly thrown. I thought that I had been through twelve years of analysis, and yet I was defeated by these simple questions. I very nearly suggested that I abandon the whole venture, but Anthony now brilliantly changed tack, and asked me about something that had occurred later in my life. I felt more at ease, and the interview took off. We recorded for about two hours, and the edited version lasted for forty minutes, so mercifully all my false starts were left on the cutting-room floor. I received a lot of letters after the programme was aired. There were, it seems, quite a few listeners who took comfort from the unexpected turn that my life had taken.

I relished the calm that Uri and I enjoyed, and learnt with pleasant surprise that domesticity need not kill romance or passion, which is the constant fear of some people. I tried to keep my dramatic reactions to daily hazards in chains. I now saw how disruptive they can be, and how unnecessary, but habits of a lifetime are difficult to change at the wave of a wand. I shall probably have to work at this till the end of my days.

Right from the beginning, our life took on a quiet rhythm. We enjoy our evenings watching DVDs or something good on television. We entertain very little because of my lack of culinary confidence, but close friends do come and brave my recipes, and we go with great pleasure to their houses.

Uri is a true inventor, and at the moment he is working on two of the biggest projects of his life. Some days when I am free, he decides to set aside his drawings of complicated and fascinating electrical machinery, and we read for a whole day. We share our library, and Uri's contributions have greatly enriched our bookshelves. He has introduced me to the brilliant and controversial Knut Hamsun, Ivan Bunin, Bulgakov, Joseph Roth, Thomas Mann, and many, many more authors whose works I did not know. When we travel we need an extra suitcase for our holiday reading.

We have both continued to work since our marriage, and it is comforting to know that at the end of each day, we both have a loving partner there to help iron out a problem, or rejoice at a triumph. I owe Uri so much, but most of all I thank him for showing me how joyful life can be, for shielding me from unnecessary pains, and for rekindling hope. He is my knight in shining armour.

CHAPTER 22

MARRIED LIFE WAS FUN AND BUSY. ONE DAY THE EVERYMAN Cinema in Hampstead asked if I would choose a film to be screened on a Sunday afternoon. They were asking several people from the world of cinema to do this, and to make a small speech before the screening. I decided to ask them to show *East of Eden*. I had only seen this film once on a very small television screen, and I wanted to see it again, and with an audience. Father had hated working with James Dean, as I think is well documented. Kazan had used their dislike of each other to good effect while filming. Dean was a method actor, and Father was very old-school. On one occasion Dean had to enter a scene out of breath, barely able to speak. Father had been aggravated at being forced to wait on set for twenty minutes, while Dean ran until he felt fully prepared for the take. Father would have thought you could 'act' the panting required. He had not moved with the times. There was another day when Dean added profanities to the text in order to further rile Father. Unfortunately this ploy misfired, for Father, who was extremely prudish, had walked off the set and refused to leave his caravan until Dean apologised. How long the apology took to arrive I never found out. In fact Father spoke little of the filming, although it was one of his greatest successes.

When I saw the film again at the Everyman, I was dis-appointed. I found Father very self-indulgent and sentimental, and I also thought Dean was unbelievably mannered, itching and mumbling, and failing to emulate his mentor, the great Marlon Brando, who had taken the 'method' to new heights. The performance that shone out for me was Jo Van Fleet as the mother who kept a brothel. I thought she was subtle, strong, truthful, and most moving. We know that films cannot alter, but our perceptions of them can, and I am sure the mood that I was in that Sunday afternoon had something to do with my disappointment about the way my father had behaved, and I left the cinema saddened that I was not able to rejoice at his portrayal. The problem I am sure was mine, and concerned the complex feelings that I still harboured about our relationship.

David was now doing very well. He had his own flat in Notting Hill, lots of good friends, and was busy as a successful illustrator and graphic designer. I was so pleased to see him flourishing. I think he too was glad to know that his mother was no longer lonely, but content at last, and really enjoying life. Parents always worry about their offspring, but equally, sensitive children are concerned for them.

Uri and I now took a holiday on Martha's Vineyard. My great friends Kate Whitney and her partner Frank Thomas had generously lent us one of their houses on the Vineyard, the old schoolhouse at Oak Bluff, decorated perfectly in early nineteenth-century American style. Kate and Frank were staying on the island for the first few days of our holiday, and they introduced us to the many delights to be found there. Frank is a unique person. It is always warming when close friends find their ideal soulmate. He was President of the Ford Foundation at this time, but has since retired from that post, although he still works hard on many important projects. He headed the 11 September Fund, a private charity, which assisted victims of that tragedy to rebuild their lives and communities. He was also greatly involved in the transition to democracy in South Africa, and continues to support the new Supreme Court there. His wisdom is sought after from all corners of the globe.

On our first evening Frank and Kate took us to eat clams at dusk by the seashore, and after viewing a magical sunset we went to dine on lobsters caught that day. The Vineyard has a special feel about it, gentle vistas and balmy air, and after a few days Uri and I felt refreshed and soothed. We didn't have a car, but we happily walked everywhere, which all the Americans found strange. Kate and Frank left us with a good knowledge of how to find interesting places, and there were buses if the distances were too far. In London we were used to a very quiet social life, but on the Vineyard we were soon going out every night. Carly Simon was responsible for this. She invited us to dinner on our third night, and from that evening our social activities snowballed.

I had met Carly in 1987 at a dinner party given by Edna O'Brien. She had just married the writer and poet Jim Hart, and was in London on honeymoon. Jim was not there that evening, but expected to join her the following day. Carly has the widest, warmest smile that I have ever seen, and she glows with blonde beauty. I found this major pop star utterly delightful, vulnerable and open. She talked touchingly of her struggle with stage fright, and told how she found singing in the open air eased her problems. I gave her a lift back to her hotel that night, and we planned to meet up in a few days. She rang me soon after to say that she had been given four tickets to a Michael Jackson concert at Wembley, and would I come along and bring a friend. I had never seen him perform, so this was going to be a real treat. I took my son David with me, as I thought he would appreciate the evening more than anyone I knew.

We all met at Michael Jackson's hotel at four in the afternoon, and were taken by bus to Wembley, where we stood in a queue to meet the renowned performer. Everyone filed past him quite quickly, except when it came to Carly. He asked her about

one of her songs, and seemed genuinely pleased to chat to her.
I sped by him, with only a second to shake his hand. He had
the limpest wrist I've ever held. It felt like brushing past a
butterfly.

We were then taken to seats on a raised dais in the middle
of the crowd. This had been specially built for VIPs, but it left
me feeling marooned in a very dangerous spot. The sheer energy
of the fans was daunting, and at the end of each number several
of the spectators fainted and had to be carried out on stretchers.
I am sure this is quite normal pop concert procedure, but I found
it upsetting, and I longed for the quieter numbers when fewer
people swooned. For the last number we were allowed to stand
in the wings and watch him perform. This was thrilling, and you
got a real feel of the vastness of the arena, and the nerve, energy
and concentration that is demanded of performers at Wembley,
or indeed in any of these enormous pop venues.

Michael Jackson's dancing had enthralled us. The effortless
delicacy of his movements seemed almost spiritual, and I now
realised that a firm handshake would have been impossible from
such a gossamer-like being. During the final moments of the
concert a double took Jackson's place, and by the time the
applause began, Michael was on his way to his hotel, safe from
the highly charged crowds. I must say that I was quite pleased
when our bus had also made a speedy getaway. Nevertheless it
had been a fascinating experience.

So that is how I got to know Carly, and how we came to be
entertained by her at her beautiful house on the Vineyard. Her
house is set romantically in a wood. It is full of subtle colours,
many cushions adorn the most inviting sofas, and the lighting is
low-key and flattering. She showed me every nook and cranny
with pride. She had designed everything; you saw no hand of
an interior decorator. It was far too personal for that. At dinner
I sat next to the author William Styron, and I found him
extremely sympathetic. I had not read any of his books, but I

had seen the film of *Sophie's Choice*. However, he didn't talk about his work, but spoke extensively about his horrendous depression and how he had shared this state with Philip Roth. They were both now free from their agonies, it seemed, and had been of great comfort to each other. Afterwards everyone had asked me how I found Mr Styron, and were amazed when I said that he had charmed me. Apparently he is renowned for his surly manner and lack of dinner-party chatter. That evening he confounded his critics.

Our Vineyard social life continued. We swam each morning in the rather chilly ocean, ate muffins and scallops, visited all the beauty spots and returned to London, where life seemed strangely quiet after the nightlife on the island.

For the first few years after we got married I did quite a bit of theatre. I much enjoyed playing in Doug Lucie's *Grace* at the Hampstead Theatre Club, directed by Mike Bradwell. He made us probe deeply into our characters, and the rehearsal process was a good experience. The play was about a group of American religious fanatics who wanted to buy a stately home, and the efforts of the owner to fight off this so-called 'invasion'. It was a witty and finely observed piece, and I loved the intimacy of the old Hampstead Theatre. It allowed for really minimal playing, and the audiences were ultra-bright and responsive.

I also played the wonderful Jewish mother in a revival of Neil Simon's *Broadway Bound* at Greenwich Theatre, which I found an enormous challenge, but on some nights I did feel that I'd achieved the journey to Brooklyn, smothering all my Englishness. I loved doing the Brooklyn accent. It is made for comedy, and Simon's play is a joy to perform. I even got to ballroom dance.

In 1994 Harold Pinter wrote *Moonlight* which was to open at the Almeida Theatre, starring Ian Holm. David Leveaux was going to direct, Douglas Hodge and Michael Sheen were to play his sons, Claire Skinner his daughter, and I was to be his wife. I was excited at the thought of working with Ian Holm. He had been away from the stage for many years, having suffered from severe stage fright, and this was to be his comeback. To play Pinter you need to be a detective, for a great deal at first appears to be left unsaid. I knew that Ian was a master sleuth when it came to Harold's work. I shall never forget his performance in *The Homecoming*.

The rehearsals were fascinating. Ian's character spends the entire ninety minutes of the play in bed, in the final throes of a fatal illness. He is estranged from his sons and we presume that the daughter has died, and that her presence is ghostly, although this is not specifically stated. His patient wife sits by his bedside embroidering, in her own world, tolerating the vituperations of her husband. Ian knew his lines from day one, and I have never seen an actor so prepared. He really could have opened at once, yet each day he brought new ideas and he and David Leveaux discussed those to hold on to, or those to eschew. Ian's imagination was boundless, and his freedom extraordinary. He showed no sign of nerves at rehearsals, and was generous and marvellously helpful to all of us. He did tell me when we were talking together once during a break that he found acting easy. He said this as though he were rather ashamed of the fact. I was filled with envy, and yet when he came to perform, he had to fight his demons like so many of us, for he was terrified that his mind would go blank and that he would lose his concentration, for this is what had happened to him when he played *The Iceman Cometh*, since when he had only appeared once on stage. I found it most strange that demons should strike at an actor who was so free and inventive, and seemingly so in control of what he did. But the mind is a fragile mechanism, and even the most confident cannot entirely master it.

To fill in the background of the family life, Claire Skinner, Michael Sheen and I went out to lunch together, so that we could talk a little about the characters' childhood, and fill in some of the details that are not in the play, hoping to give more depth to our performances. I found this very helpful. Pinter's text is brilliantly lean, but as a performer, you need to fill out the past, in order to enrich the present.

Harold came to some rehearsals, and once when we asked him what a particular phrase meant, he replied, 'It means what it says.' This was not said at all aggressively, but simply as a statement of fact. When he is directing himself, he is a master at simplifying problems, and preventing all fret.

I adored playing *Moonlight*. Once the opening night at the Almeida was over, we all settled into the play, and Ian made each performance a new and exciting journey. I have seldom met an actor with such sensitive antennae. He had conquered his stage fright, a tremendous feat, as every newspaper had interviewed him about it. No one's fears had ever been so heralded. I think the first preview audience were amazed that he managed to force himself on stage at all. The play was a great success, we transferred to the Comedy Theatre for a short run, Ian was given many awards and the whole experience was a delight.

During the run at the Almeida, I received a telephone call one morning telling me that my mother had died. I had spoken to her only the night before at the convent hospital in Vevey where she had been for the last two months, recovering from a fall. David and I had seen her earlier in the year; we had found her very frail and feared that she would soon be too weak to stay alone in her flat, something that she was absolutely determined to do. She dreaded the thought of going into an old people's home. It was strange, but the day she died was the day that she was to be moved into one. A room had been prepared for her with pieces of her furniture and some of her favourite possessions, in order that she would feel more comfortable and be less disturbed. On the telephone when I had talked with her the night before at the hospital, she was gentle and said she loved it when I called her. She was more lucid than she had been for some time. There were days when I rang and she found it difficult to recognise my voice. I thought she had a slight cold, but I said nothing, knowing that she was in safe hands. During the night, pneumonia developed and she died, they assured me, in no pain. How does one know that? I wished fervently that I had been with her to hold her hand and give her a little warmth and comfort. But I was in a play in London, and therefore she died alone in the country where she had lived for the last thirty-six years.

I felt deeply sad. My mother and I had not had an easy relationship, but she had had an enormous influence on my life, and wilful and selfish though she was at times, she was a generous spirit who had enhanced many people's lives. She was certainly not the monster that Dan painted.

The reason that Mother and Bill had gone to live in Switzerland was partly financial, but mainly because of a great disappointment that Mum had suffered in 1959. She had been playing in *Five Finger Exercise* by Anthony Shaffer, directed by John Gielgud, and had received wonderful reviews for her performance. When she learned that the other four actors were to go to Broadway with the production and that she had been excluded, her heart was broken and her confidence shattered. She never recovered from this blow and she never performed on stage again. Soon after this, the decision was taken to move abroad. She felt that the profession had rejected her, and she could no longer bear to live in London. They loved Lake Geneva, and the hypnotic Dents du Midi now became the backdrop to their lives.

There was no one who could make me laugh as Mother could. Her quick turn of phrase and dry observations were her calling card. She used to say that laughter had retrieved her from many difficult situations, and I can believe this. There are so many of her sayings that I use to this day. Whenever she was offered a dreadful part in a play, she used to say, 'I'd rather sell lampshades at Peter Jones.' I smile to myself even now as I stroll through that department, for she might have rather enjoyed herself there. She once ran a decorating business on the King's Road, and for a while it was quite a success. It was an emporium of brightly coloured chintz.

I once asked her not to be so ironic with me, for I sometimes found it quite painful. She said she didn't know what irony meant, and I think that this was genuine. Her irony was innate, and she had no control over it, and so many of her friends were masters of the art. She certainly never deliberately set out to hurt people, and she herself was frightened of slings and arrows coming her way.

She was the most wonderful grandmother, and David often went to stay with her in Switzerland, where she really put herself out to give him fun-filled times. She spoke to him as an adult, and disapproved of any kind of baby talk. She said she liked some children and not others, just as she felt about grown-ups.

David and I went over to La Tour de Peilz soon after her death to sort out her belongings. She never threw anything away, so it proved to be a mammoth task. All the letters that we had written her from childhood were kept, and memorabilia from her early life. There was a silver cigarette box inscribed in Noel Coward's own writing, saying, 'To Darling Plannie, With Fondest Love, Noel'. It was the fashion in the thirties to inscribe all gifts, and to monogram handbags and luggage. Mother had powder compacts, encrusted with jewels, inscribed lovingly in Father's handwriting.

It is a painful process going through someone's personal treasures, but one of the things that saddened me most was the state of her cupboards. She had supposedly been well taken care of by a relay of helpers and cleaners, but I found that no one had bothered to clean behind the cupboard doors. As she had hardly gone out for the last two years and her clothes had lain unused, spiders and small insects had nested in their folds. I know how shocked she would have been, for she was the most fastidious of people.

She had left instructions in her will that when David and I came over to sort out her things we were to be given enough money to buy ourselves sumptuous meals. So we went to the best restaurants and toasted her at each feast. This I know would have pleased her greatly, for to see everyone having a good time was one of her true delights. Champagne Charlie's daughter never changed.

She never understood why Daniel had stopped speaking to her. This caused her great pain and was the main reason for the depression that she suffered toward the end of her life. David had told Daniel that she was very ill and not likely to live for very long, but not even this had melted his heart. For twelve years she had endured his silence.

It was Uri who had helped ease the tensions between Mother and me. He instantly understood the situation without having met her. The respect of a mother was of paramount importance to Uri, and he led me to respect Mother, to appreciate her good qualities, and to be less critical of her irksome ways. I am eternally grateful to him, for in the last years of her life we were able to make up for some of the earlier stormier times.

Uri and I went over to visit Mother a year or so before she died. She gave us a little Russian lacquer ring box to commemorate our marriage. She was very frail at the time, and I am afraid there were too many trips to the drinks cabinet, and she was not at her best. This great and warm hostess was no longer ablaze with welcome and wit. Her spirit was dimmed. He had to believe me when I told him tales of her past *fêtes champêtres*, how charmingly she had entertained her guests and how at home they were always made to feel.

When I remember Mother now, I can see that she was full of fear, a very wilful and often unyielding person, but that she had really enjoyed her life to the hilt. She had travelled extensively, and got her own way most of the time. Bill had doted on her and indulged all her whims, but he had also sheltered her from many of life's harsh realities. I shall always believe that my father was the main love of her life, and that she adored Bill, but was not in love with him. She never said this, and it is only a feeling that I had. She once told me how she had seen my father descend a flight of steps at the Odeon Leicester Square, and how her heart had leapt at his grace and elegance. She related this tale with a gentleness that was unusual for her, and I saw a glimpse of a tenderness that was seldom shown.

I shall always regret that I was not closer to her in her lifetime. This was every bit as much my fault as hers. She really tried her best to be a good mother, and if she failed, it was not intentional. I still miss her, and her capacity to give pleasure to her family and friends remains unrivalled. She ran a small salon wherever she went, and those who flocked to it cherished her. Whenever I see a champagne bottle opened, I think of Mum, and I always will. She is, I'm sure, enjoying several glasses with the feathered choir.

CHAPTER 23

THE NINETIES WERE A BUSY TIME FOR US. URI WAS AT IMPERIAL College, and had interesting research projects that involved much travel. My work kept me mainly in London. I had two engagements that were learning experiences, which I always find rewarding. I did a film called *Déjà Vu* for the American director Henry Jaglom which was almost entirely improvised. We were given the story outline, and some suggestions for proposed scenes, but there was no dialogue written down. What an exciting challenge, I thought. The plot was a love story between a man and a woman who meet, as though by fate, in the house of mutual friends in London. Noel Harrison and I played the owners of that house, and Jaglom's wife, Victoria Hoyt, and Stephen Dillane played the lovers. The journey of each scene was discussed, and then the cameraman started to put it on film. It was an enormous challenge for him, because he never knew who was going to speak next. I absolutely adored the freedom this way of working provided. One day in the canteen bus over lunch, Henry overheard a conversation that I was having with Noel Harrison about our favourite sweets in childhood. Immediately after lunch, Henry put us into bed on the set, and we recreated the scene from the bus. It actually remained in the final cut, which pleased me, because improvising this way means an enormous amount of footage ends up on the cutting-room floor.

Vanessa Redgrave was also in the film. We played sisters-in-law, and had a scene together when we were discussing what to do with her mother. Vanessa wanted her to come and live with Noel and me, and I was determined to prevent this. That was the brief we were given before the camera rolled. At the end of the take the entire crew applauded us. I have never enjoyed improvising so much. Vanessa is brilliant at creating a real world around her, and the scene really took off. But alas, when I saw the film only a tiny part of the scene remained.

The cutting room plays a great part in filming. I learnt this to my cost when I appeared in *The Importance of Being Earnest*, directed by Oliver Parker and starring Judi Dench. Olly was a delight to work with. He had also done the adaptation, and it was a really witty script, full of new insights and little twists. He directed the whole piece with zest and speed, and when I saw the first screening for a few people, I sat enchanted. The music was racy and fun, and the whole rhythm of the film seemed perfect. A few weeks later I went to a cast and crew screening, and left concealing tears. The Hollywood studio had insisted on certain cuts, and Miss Prism and Canon Chasuble, played by Tom Wilkinson, were victims of the scissors. I cared more for Olly than myself. His film had lost the lovely pace it had, and some of the cuts were so brutal that the storyline suffered. Olly kindly rang me later to say that some of the Canon's and my scenes had been reinstated, but I had lost heart, and I have to confess that I never saw the final version.

My other learning experience on film was when I was asked to play a blind woman in Khaled Al Haggar's *Room to Rent*. I had always thought that Al Pacino's performance in *Scent of a Woman* was the most convincing 'blind' acting that I had seen. I studied his performance with great care, and realised that he was always seemingly looking at the mouth of the person he was talking to. I tried to do this myself, but the cameraman kept changing my eye line and demanding to see my 'blind' eyes, and therefore my efforts were in vain. When I saw the film, I wish that I had gone with my instinct, but the shoot was short, and there was no time for major discussions of this sort. I hope that one day I get the chance to play another unsighted person.

Among the more illustrious invitations that I received in the nineties was one to attend a luncheon party at Buckingham Palace given by the Queen and Prince Philip. It was a small gathering, and on entering the Palace we were shown the seating plan, which I tried to memorise. We had drinks in a splendid red and gold chamber, dominated by a stunning portrait of George III. The Queen and Prince Philip arrived with several dogs in tow. Her Majesty was dressed in a blue print dress with her handbag, as always, on her arm, her hair as carefully dressed as on all occasions, but what struck one was the translucence of her skin, completely flawless. In repose her face is rather dour, but when she smiled, she lit up the room, and her laugh is infectious. She much enjoys a good joke. They attend hundreds of these occasions a year, and it was amazing to see how fresh and interested they both were in all the guests. The conversation flowed. At one point the Queen asked me what I was doing, and I replied that I was recording a book on cassette. She beamed, and asked if it was for the blind. I felt rather ashamed when I had to confess that it was for a commercial company.

Luncheon was announced and we all went to the dining room, which was another splendid chamber overlooking the gardens. I walked to the far end of the room thinking that I would find my place as I had seen it on the seating plan. Alas, I had read the plan upside down, and to my great embarrassment, I had to run round the table to the other end, where I duly found my correct place. Everyone thankfully greeted my faux pas with humour, and I was not sent to the Tower.

I noticed that by Her Majesty's place was a small gold hook, upon which she hung her handbag. What a nifty idea this seemed.

At least it kept it off the floor and out of the way of the dogs, who had accompanied us to the dining room.

The food was quite superb. I was too nervous to remember all the delicacies that we were given, but I recall the main dish was venison from Sandringham, most succulently prepared (although whenever I eat venison I have to force myself not to think of Bambi). After luncheon we returned to the first chamber for delicious coffee, and then their Royal Highnesses bade us farewell, and we all went our merry ways. I really had thought that it would be a tense occasion, and was so pleased to find it relaxed and good fun. We had been made to feel most welcome.

The nineties were a strange decade for Uri and me. We had domestic peace and happiness at home, but throughout that period sadness stalked us. In 1993 my mother died, and two years later Jeremy suffered a massive and fatal heart attack. He had been fighting ill health and mental battles for the last years of his life, but even so his death came as a shock to us all. I was telephoned early one morning, and went immediately to tell David in person. He was devoted to his father, and had been a wonderful support to him throughout his troubles. I often wished that I could have shared some of the burden with him, but I was the last person in the world who could take on that role. No son could have done more for their father than David did, and he was completely shattered by the news. We immediately had to go about the business of death certificates and the funeral arrangements, which in some ways was a help, because it diverted David and allowed him time to gather his strength, for grieving is an exhausting process.

The funeral was a moving occasion, and all Jeremy's close friends came, and one realised what a loved person he was. People had found comfort and warmth in his company, even though at times he behaved most strangely, for his manic depression was so severe that there were periods when he went completely out of control. But throughout all his troubles not one friend had deserted him. This must illustrate the magnetic qualities that he possessed. I shall never forget his insight, the way he had seen instantly that I needed to leave home in order to gain some independence all those years ago when we had just met. But all these uncanny perceptions were mixed with restlessness. He was so often driven, and inhabited a world of fantasy in order not to have to face his earthly demons. Until the last ten years of his life I had seen him at the odd family event, and we had always managed to remain on friendly terms, which we both felt was important for David, but in the later years I found his delusions harder to accept and I stepped into the background. However, when I married Uri, he had been genuinely delighted, and sent us the most beautiful bottles of bath essence from Penhaligon's, and insisted on giving us a box to see his quite brilliant performance as Sherlock Holmes at Wyndhams Theatre, with champagne served at the interval. That sums up Jeremy perfectly – generous, warm, larger than life and often quite crazy. A light went out in many people's lives when he died, for he was one of life's true originals. It took David a very long time to recover. His sense of loss was deep.

But the unexpected is often round the corner, and David was about to surprise us all.

David had shown me a short piece he had written one day, about a man suffering a nervous breakdown. I had thought it arresting, and was impressed by the originality of his perceptions. He said he hoped to put it into a book, and after that had hardly spoken on the subject. Then quite suddenly it seemed to me the book was written, and within a very short space of time it was published. *The Big Kiss* by David Huggins was a big hit. 'Cool and hot – a novelist of power and wit and genuine artistry. Hooray,' wrote Stephen Fry, and many other critics shared his views. No mum has ever been so proud. I really do think it is a good book, full of scorching wit and original observations, a psychological thriller that leaves you anxiously turning the page for the next revelation, words and imagery jumping out at you at such a lively pace, and he had achieved all this with no fuss, just quietly writing away, until he was ready to present it to the world. His very oldest friend, Clare Conville, had encouraged him to write, as had Jon Riley, the editor. David and Clare were born two months apart, and her mother and I had often walked in the park with our offspring. Clare and Jon had told him that he should put some of his sparkling humour into a book, and this is exactly what he'd done. The only thing that saddened me was that Mother and Jeremy were not around to revel in David's success. I know that they would have been so proud of him.

The other good news is that it was not just a one-off wonder, for over the next few years he produced two more successes, *Luxury Amnesia* and *Me, Me, Me.* The latter is a witty broadside at the theatrical memoir, set in Los Angeles in the house of an ageing film star surrounded by members of his family, who are not a million miles away from some of the characters nestling in the pages of this very book. I look forward to many more hours of pleasure from his pen, and I know that he will make me laugh, for his sense of humour is always at the ready, even at the darkest moments. David's debut as a novelist was definitely the highlight of the nineties for me, and he cheered us all when we needed to be warmed.

CHAPTER 24

ONE OF THE MOST ENJOYABLE ENGAGEMENTS THAT CAME MY WAY in the nineties was offered to me by my good friend David Hare. He was to direct an episode of *Young Indiana Jones*, to be filmed in Prague. So I was to visit a city previously unknown to me, to work with David again, and to be remunerated for both these pleasures. I felt most spoilt.

I was to be in Prague for three weeks. Uri planned to join me for the second week when I had some days off, and we would be able to sightsee together.

The episode of *Young Indy* that we were filming was set at the Paris Peace Conference of 1919. I was to play Gertrude Bell, the famous mountaineer and explorer of the Middle East, a marvellous example of the doughty British ladies of the late nineteenth century whose courage and daring continuously astounded the more delicate flowers who stayed at home. Gertrude Bell was a participant of the British delegation, along with Arnold Toynbee, who was to be played by Michael Maloney. He was the most delightful sightseeing companion until Uri arrived, protecting me from the many pickpockets who haunted the underground stations.

Prague is a magical city offering the visitor untold treasures – the gentle pastel colours of many of its buildings, the Charles Bridge, which we crossed a hundred times, and the small cobbled streets through which we wandered trying to find restaurants

233

that suited our diets, for Michael and I were rather fussy eaters, me particularly so, and Prague at that time was not able to provide much fresh fruit and vegetables as it does today. Nicole Farhi, who was soon to marry David, joined us one weekend. She has since become a close friend, and it was good to see David and her so happy together. She is not only a great dress designer, but she is a sculptress of enormous imagination and strength. It is hard to believe that her tiny delicate hands can produce such powerful pieces. The great Eduardo Paolozzi was her mentor, and he had taught her how to sculpt in wax, how to melt it and build a piece of work. She was a terrific sightseeing companion, and took Michael and me to museums and galleries that we had not yet found. Her intrepidity rivalled that of Gertrude Bell.

When Uri arrived, we went off by ourselves, walking every-where. We visited the Jewish Museum, one of the most moving experiences that I can remember, the drawings of the children of Auschwitz adorning the walls, showing their courage and hope, and behind the museum the old Jewish cemetery.

I wish we could have stayed longer in Prague. The filming went well, and was fun, for David had gathered together a wonderful group of actors. We all said our goodbyes, and I hoped that one day I would return there. My wish was granted, for several years later I went back to Prague to play a small part in Jan Sverak's film *Dark Blue World* about the young Polish pilots in Britain in World War Two. Prague's beauty remained intact, but I found that there were many more tourists, and that you sometimes had to queue to cross the streets.

The sadnesses that pursued Uri and me during this decade, alas, persisted.

Soon after we were married, Uri's daughter and granddaughter, Olga and Tanya, came to visit us in London. At that time they were still living in Moscow, and it was touching to see Tanya's delight at all the shop windows filled with goodies that she had never seen in Moscow. Even the supermarkets entranced her, but what was remarkable about this six-year-old was that she never asked for anything like most young children do. She was content to gaze and relish what she saw without begging for this and that. She was the most beautiful little creature, with long blonde hair and piercing blue Slavic eyes. Wherever we went she won everyone's heart. She once came with me to a studio where I was to do a voice-over, and so that she wouldn't be bored whilst I was recording I gave her a tube of sweets, and instead of keeping them all for herself, she handed them round to everyone in the reception area. This is what made Tanya so unique. She had a sensitivity about her that was most unusual for a child. She saw the beauty in a sunset, and flowers in gardens, with a delight that amazed me, and she shared all her experiences with those around her. At this stage of her life she did not speak English, so all her pleasures were conveyed in Russian, and through her intense feelings.

When she was seven, she and Olga emigrated to San Diego, California. Here Tanya shone at the schools she went to, and captivated all who came in contact with her. She won a scholarship to the best private school only a short time after her arrival there. She came to stay with us again, this time on her own, and she gave us untold pleasure. She still asked for nothing, and was a delight to have around. Her intelligence was shining, and her curiosity knew no bounds. We were very sad when the day came for her to return to the States, which is not always the case when guests come to stay. Alas we only saw her once more on a brief visit to California. In 1997 she took her life, and this vibrant spirit left her family in a state of profound shock, from which they will never really recover. The pains and doubts that she must have suffered she kept to herself, but the difficulties that she must have foreseen proved too much for her to bear. She will be missed and thought of forever. One of her teachers after her death wrote a book of poems about her, a glowing memorial to this sprightly creature. Olga now has another little daughter, Katya, who has done much to heal the wounds, but nothing will ever diminish Tanya's memory, for she had the power to lift the spirits of all around her, and that is rare in someone so young.

Interspersed with these tragic events, life and work went on. In 1996 I was asked to play Queen Elizabeth in Friedrich Schiller's *Mary Stuart* at the National Theatre. It was an absorbing journey to undertake, and I was looking forward to the prospect of working with the great French actress Isabelle Huppert, who was to play Mary. In life the two queens never met, but Schiller has given them a wonderful scene at the end of Act One when Elizabeth, out hunting, comes upon Mary as if by accident, but immediately realises it is a trap. The scene is full of power and accusation, each minute fraught with danger.

Isabelle is extremely original. Her beauty off the screen is equally striking, the golden red hair, and the perfect peach-toned skin. She is very self-contained, and has a rather mysterious aura about her. I liked her from the start, and admired her throughout the five-month run. She is fiercely intelligent, quite wilful, and at first seems to be full of confidence. When we all assembled for the first read-through, it was quite clear that she had not studied the script, and had certainly not learnt her role. This I think was a mistake. English is not her mother tongue, and Mary is a mammoth part. Her scenes are emotional switchbacks, which only become possible if the lines are almost second nature. I know many people don't believe in learning lines before rehearsals start, and that is up to each individual, but if you are not completely at home with the language, I think a prior know-ledge of the text is an enormous help, if not a necessity. Rehearsals were difficult for her, and she had only just mastered the text before the first preview.

I really enjoyed working with the director, Howard Davies. He has formidable concentration and patience, listens to his actors, and the whole process is a wonderful mixture of ideas, which he then hones and shapes. He is totally in charge, but not a tyrant. The adaptation was by Jeremy Sams. I welcomed the cuts that were suggested, but Isabelle was less keen to lose a line. Tim Pigott-Smith was playing Leicester, and was not only excellent in the part, but a tower of strength and diplomacy within the company. But working with Isabelle from day one was exciting. She was wonderfully free and inventive, and she never let her difficulties with the language hamper her unique view of the character.

Howard had encouraged the comedy in some of the scenes, and urged me to relax a little and tone down the regal armour. I obeyed, and we came to the first preview. William (Bill) Dudley had designed the set and the costumes. Isabelle was thrilled with her wardrobe, but I was less happy with mine. The Elizabethan robes were so heavy and cumbersome. I am sure they looked terrific, but they hampered my movements, and I had to say to Bill during the previews that I was nearly sixty, small boned and only weighed seven stone twelve, and that if he added any more bum rolls or padding to my costumes, I would be unable to perform, and would probably faint.

The night of the first preview, Isabelle came to my dressing room and asked me if I was nervous. This was like asking a mouse if it likes cheese. I told her there and then of my long struggle with stage fright, and she confessed that in the theatre, she was the same. She said that sometimes it felt as though she was outside her body and looking at herself as a spectator. She said she had these 'troux', holes of blankness. I knew exactly what she meant.

We did five or six previews before we opened, and everybody was settling in. People who came round said they felt that Isabelle was talking too rapidly, and that it was not always easy to catch what she was saying, but they all admired her performance greatly. My agent Pippa Markham said that she felt the court were not enough in awe of me, and was there something that I could do about this. I talked with Howard and he agreed that we should up the ante of terror amongst the courtiers, and that I should be more commanding and awesome. Before the performance, he assembled the actors involved, and warned them that the atmosphere would be more charged. The performance that night was electric. There was terror on stage, and everyone responded to my icy authority. The audience sat like hushed mice.

I was so grateful to Pippa for having spoken, and to Howard for generously having let me change my performance so near to an opening night. Not all directors would have reacted similarly. It showed enormous trust, and I am delighted that it all turned out so well.

We played in repertory for five months, and often had quite long breaks between the blocks of performances. This is always difficult to cope with. The first show after a gap of two weeks or so demands courage. You have a word-run in the afternoon, but the cast, and the play itself, needs to be re-warmed. It takes at least two performances to settle in again, and then after three more shows, you're off on another break. The time off is enjoyable, but I always felt that the plays suffered from this system.

Isabelle and I played a large part of our big scene together right down front, centre stage. The lighting was mainly from the side, quite blinding at times, making it difficult to see the actor you were speaking to, and if you went too far down, you were in danger of not being lit. Positions on stage are not so critical as on film. On a couple of occasions, Isabelle had warned me that I had strayed too near to the edge of the apron. No great issue was made of this, and on the whole we really got on very well together. I admired her great ability to take an audience into the subtlest close-up with the minimum of effort. However, sometimes I was rankled because she seemed to upstage me rather dramatically, but I let it pass and kept quiet, sitting on any irate feelings.

On the Friday night before our last two Saturday performances, Isabelle went so far upstage that in order to speak to her, I had to turn my back completely on the audience. I was enraged, partly me, Anna, and partly Queen Elizabeth. The scene thereafter was electric. I came off the stage on fire. Tim was standing in the wings, and tried to calm me down. 'Let it be', he said, 'it is nearly over, keep calm and don't have words, for you will gain nothing, and only regret it.' I went to my dressing room and started to have my wig dressed and my costume changed. I was almost applying Sellotape to my mouth to keep all vituperation within. There was a knock on the door. It was Isabelle, saying as she entered, 'Anna, I have a note for you.' I could contain myself no more, and the Sellotape was ripped from my lips, and the feathers flew. Adrenalin flows rapidly through actors' veins during a show, and Isabelle and I shouted at each other with grand energy. By the end of the performance everyone backstage at the National knew about our screaming match, for news spreads there like a bush fire. Mary Stuart and Queen Elizabeth are at loggerheads, the rumour went.

Back at home, I tried to work out what had really happened. Her upstaging had appeared to me, without reasoning, wilful and selfish. But on reflection, I saw that Isabelle is a beautiful woman, and a great screen actress, and the lighting and how she looks to an audience really matter to her. I am not beautiful, nor do I care very much about lighting, and therefore I should have apologised to her unreservedly for having taken our scene out of the scheduled spot, even if only by inches. She had not upstaged me in the old-fashioned sense, she had merely been determined to find her light, and if that meant walking upstage behind me, then that was what she had to do. I now fully understood. I rang her the following morning and cleared the air, and I hope that she understood the situation and forgave me.

Mary Stuart was to be the last time that I have appeared on stage. In many ways I found the experience quite draining, and

I also realised that during the run I had seen little of Uri – I like to get into the theatre very early when I'm performing, which entails leaving home around four o'clock, and then not getting home till late, when the loved one has already gone to bed. This seemed rather stupid, as I had met someone I really wanted to be with. So I have decided that for the time being I shall give the theatre a rest and do film, television and radio, for they are for me much less stressful mediums. Who knows what the future will bring, but for now this decision comforts me.

In the early nineties, Daniel had gone to a doctor with a lump in his neck, and been told that it was a fatty cyst and nothing to worry about. He was advised to go out and play some golf, his great passion in life. Months later he had returned to the doctor complaining of itching, but no connection was made between the two symptoms. By the time he was correctly diagnosed, he was told he had Hodgkin's disease that had reached the tertiary stage. He embarked on an intensive course of chemotherapy. I knew from David that he was going through a very difficult time, but I knew that he was in good hands, and prayed that he would pull through.

At the end of the treatment, he was able to start rehearsals for *Taking Sides* by Ronnie Harwood. Harold Pinter, who was directing, had been determined to wait for Daniel, for he wanted him to play the conductor Wilhelm Fürtwangler. The play is about Fürtwangler's interrogation by an American army major working for the deNazification tribunal in post-war Germany. I think the thought of this role had enabled Dan to recover from the dreadful side effects of the therapy. The great love of his life was music, and the part had seemingly been sent from heaven.

Uri and I went to see the play in Richmond, where it was on tour prior to a West End run. We slipped in and slipped out, hoping that Dan had not seen us in the audience, for still he was not speaking to me. We were both enthralled by his performance. I really believed he was a conductor, the way he moved, and the way he held his head were utterly convincing. He had such dignity as he drew you into his defence of staying on in Nazi Germany, and the complex arguments as to whether art, music or culture can ever be divorced from politics. I had not always been impressed by Dan's performances. We were both harsh critics of each other's work, but his Fürtwangler was so moving, and such a triumph for him, that I decided to write him a letter, expressing my admiration and delight. I sent it to Bath, where they were to be the following week. I had a nice reply from him about a fortnight later, thanking me, and saying how much he was enjoying the play.

They opened in London and Dan had a tremendous success. But, alas, before the end of the run, he developed shingles in his eye and had to leave the cast. It was a bitter blow for him.

Soon after he recovered, David and Dan's daughter, Alice, arranged for the four of us to meet in a Chinese restaurant for a reconciliation dinner. It was a very tense occasion. So much time had elapsed, we couldn't slip back easily into the old light-hearted ways. Both David and Alice had worked so hard to bring us together, and I appreciated their thoughtfulness, but the evening was difficult, and I went home feeling very depressed. Dan had changed. He was guarded, and the old humour was veiled. I had been hoping for a rapprochement for so many years, and now that it had arrived I couldn't deal with it. Dan rang me a few days later. He was friendly, and we chatted away for some time. It was left that I would ring him and arrange a dinner at my house so that he could meet Uri. This never happened. I let time pass, and then it was too late, for he had gone to New York to appear with Ed Harris in the Broadway production of *Taking Sides*. By the time he came back, the drawbridge was pulled up once more. This time it was my fault for not having been more open and forgiving. I shall always regret that, but the pain of the ten-year silence had taken its toll, and I couldn't press the delete button as though nothing had happened. I should have been big enough to do just that, but I failed.

Time went by and I heard that he had to have an operation on his lung. The tumours had spread. Before he went into hospital, he married Penelope's sister, Linda Wilton, who had been his partner for the last few years. David went to the wedding, which looked to be a very happy occasion from the photographs.

After the wedding he went into the Brompton Hospital to have the operation. He recovered enough to come home and convalesce, but he was soon back in hospital with severe breathing problems. At this stage things were looking so grim that Penelope and Linda and their eldest sister, Rose, decided that it was time for me to come and see Dan. I had left him flowers at the hospital each week, with loving messages, and now I was to visit him. He greeted me with his old smile, but he looked so poorly and so frail that I found it hard not to burst into tears. This strong, tall, handsome man was shrivelled, and his body ravaged with illness. He was on strong painkilling drugs at this stage, and as I was leaving the room, he called out to me, 'Do you remember Ben?' Ben was our Great Dane that had run around Rosings when I was a baby. The Brompton Cocktail is a powerful mixture, and plays odd tricks with the memory. It was touching that he should have remembered something from so long ago.

I sat outside his room after my visit and sobbed and sobbed. I knew that he was being wonderfully cared for by the whole Wilton family, but I couldn't bear to see him suffer so. I felt the end was near. But he rallied, and for the next three months I went and saw him most days, and we became friends again. He once said to me that we hadn't talked through the past, and I said that it wasn't necessary, to which he replied, 'I don't really know why it happened.' He had pressed the delete button. Feelings had taken him over all those years ago, and he hadn't known how to deal with them, and now none of that mattered.

He asked to meet Uri, and so we went in one day, and it could not have been a nicer visit. Dan asked Uri if he would read to him from *The Three Sisters* in Russian. It was one of Dan's favourite plays, and I shall never forget the look of joy on his face, as Uri read a scene most movingly for him. How soothing it sounded. I know that they would have got on if they had been given the time.

Dan was allowed out of hospital in early January, but he had to have breathing apparatus with him all the time, and he was dreadfully weak. One evening I was sitting with him whilst Linda went out for a break. I stood behind him and stroked his head, and he said, 'Oh, Annie, what shall I do?' He had not called me Annie for so long, but it was the name of my childhood, and the one he had used until the silent years, and now he was using it again. All the pain of the past melted away. He was my dear brother again, and all the bad times were truly deleted. Oh, that he could have recovered, but that was not to be. He died in March after a valiant fight.

In June, Linda organised a memorial service for Dan at St Paul's, Covent Garden. It was such a warm occasion. Everyone there had adored him. Barbara Cook, his friend and co-star from *She Loves Me*, sang for him, and Ronnie Harwood paid him a tribute that was so amusing, affectionate and accurate about Dan's character that we all burst into applause at the end. I made a short tribute myself, for I wanted the congregation to know that after the turbulent years, calm had been restored between us, and no rancour was left in the air. He was, like a lot of us, extremely quixotic. But we had stood by each other at difficult times, and he was, and always will be, my special brother.

Our half-brother Geoffrey had come over from Canada for the service, and afterwards he and I walked for an hour and a half across the park, back to my house. I felt very close to Geoff that day. We spoke a lot about our strange family, and shared many memories. I thanked him for having been so kind to Mother when she had gone to stay with him and his wife, Ruth, and their children in Vancouver. Geoffrey was an architect, and Mother had told me how he had taken her up in a helicopter to see all the buildings that he had designed. When I repeated this to Geoff that day, he said that he had never been in a helicopter in his life, and had certainly never taken Mother on such an exciting excursion. This illustrates Mother's vivid imagination, and how it was always best to take her stories with a pinch of salt, if not a stiff drink.

The nineties came to an end, and many of the main players in my family were no more. However, good tidings were on their way.

EPILOGUE

ONE OF THE HAPPIEST TALES THAT I HAVE TO RELATE HAPPENED on 9 June 2001. This is the day when David married Madeleine Christie, and no mother could have acquired a more special daughter-in-law. Maddie was a fashion editor at *Vogue*. I did not know of her presence for quite a while after they met, but I did notice that David started to dress rather more smartly, and thought some new influence was at hand. My Christmas and birthday gifts also began to change, beautiful scarves and a pashmina entered my wardrobe, and I looked forward to meeting the person whom I suspected was responsible for the choice of these treats.

We did finally meet, and I knew at once that David had found his soulmate. Their wedding day was the joyous occasion that you would expect. At the time they lived in Jeremy's old penthouse in Clapham, and Maddie had decorated the entire apartment herself, softly coloured ribbons twined around the banisters, beautiful mobiles were suspended from the ceilings and there were flowers in every corner, imaginatively arranged. Guests wandered through all the rooms and on to the roof garden, and as dusk descended, soft lights gave an added glow to the proceedings. David had asked Uri to be his best man, which gave us much pleasure, and he made a short and touching speech to the couple. He was not used to public speaking, and had gone for a short walk on Clapham Common to calm his nerves beforehand.

David's speech had us all in fits of laughter. He spoke of their courtship, of how he had proposed to Maddie on one knee in the ocean at Goa, and how she had burst out laughing as a large wave came and knocked David off balance. The music was turned up at eleven o'clock and Uri and I crept away, but we heard that dancing had continued until dawn.

As in all novels with a happy ending, the young couple spent their honeymoon abroad, where mercifully no dramatic events took place, and on 1 November 2002, Master Dan Huggins entered this world and enchanted us all. A friend once told me that she didn't really know the meaning of the verb 'to dote' until she had grandchildren. I now know what she means. Dan has large luminous blue eyes, and fair golden hair, and he can get me to do anything that he commands. His father and I were once dressing him together, and David turned to me and said, 'What shall we put Dan in today?' And a little voice piped up, 'Casual.' He is definitely the son of a fashion editor. He has also taken to five-star life: staying as a treat at a rather grand hotel at two-and-a-half years old, while lying on his parents' bed after his bath, watching a video, he looked up at his father and said, 'I'm just relaxing Daddy.'

On 14 June 2005 a sister arrived for Dan. She is the most exquisite little girl called Iris, and all her gestures are delicate and mesmerising to behold, as I'm sure all grandmothers declare. I am again besotted. This little family now live in the country. I do regret that they are so far away, but I know that the fresh air and the seaside are far better for small people than the crowded and often dirty London streets, and I console myself that they are in England, and only a car trip away, and not in some distant land that would involve flying. When my grandson, Dan, is out somewhere having a good time he says, 'Please may I stay a little more while,' and that's exactly how I feel when I have to leave the family in Dorset.

★   ★   ★

So now I come to the end of my tales. The month-old infant perched in the palm of my father's hand has travelled through many decades, and looking back, I think that with all the ups and downs I have laughed more than I have cried, and certainly the last years with Uri have taught me the pleasures of just being with someone, of not having to struggle to have a good time, and to relish the solace that a warm relationship can bring.

INDEX

A la recherche du temps perdu (book) 187, 194

Abe Lincoln at Illinois (film) 31

Acton, Harold 26

The Admirable Crighton (film) 67

The African Queen (film) 159–61

Albery, Donald 79–80

Aldwych Theatre (London) 152

Alexander technique 125–6

Algonquin Hotel (New York) 35

Allen, Adrianne (Gladys) (Anna's mother) 205, 206; divorce and re-marriage 1–2; background 3; personality 3–4, 5, 30, 223–4, 225–6; social life 3–4, 11, 15, 19, 20–2, 29–30, 35–7, 42; wartime fun 11; dress sense 24, 29; decoration of houses and flats 35, 41, 82; co-writes cookery book 42; acts with Anna 61; and marriage of Anna 68, 70; move to Switzerland 82–4, 223; death of 222–3, 230; love for Raymond and Bill 226; visit to Geoffrey in Canada 244

Alliance Française 46

Almeida Theatre (London) 220–2

Andrea (daughter of Kate Whitney) 39

Andres, Tamara (Uri's sister) 211

Andres, Uri (Anna's husband) 51, 227; meets and marries Anna 207–10; character and background 210–12; visits to Russia 211–13; married life 213–15; meets Anna's mother 225–6; as best man to David 245–6

Andres, Victoria 211

Andrews, Henry 42

Annals, Michael 133, 134

Another Country (film) 192–3

Arletty 47–8

Armstrong, Alun 160

Armstrong-Jones, Anthony 70–1, 74

Arosa (Switzerland) 12

Arts Council 58, 202

Asquith, Anthony 180

Athlone, Countess of (Princess Alice) 19–20

Athlone, Earl of 19–20

Atkin, Pete 146

Atkins, Eileen 132, 134, 136–7, 141

Avedon, Richard 62

Awakenings (book) 180–1

Bagnold, Enid 78

Baker, George 96

The Balkan Trilogy (radio) 141

Ballantyne, Miss 53

Balliol College (Oxford) 117

Barrault, Jean Louis 47

The Basket (Dunsfold) 15–16

Bates, Alan 110, 153–4

Battye, Anne 126

BBC Broadcasting House (London) 145

BBC radio 140–3, 144–8, 202
BBC television 128, 131, 200–1
Beaton, Cecil 62
Beaumont, Hugh (Binkie) 20–1
Beckett, Samuel 162, 163
Bell, Gertrude 233
Bennett, Alan 116
Bennett, Jill 164
Benson-Gyles, Anna 183–5, 187, 189,
    194, 209
Berchtesgaden (Austria) 26
Berenson, Bernard 26–7
Berger, Senta 104
Bergman, Ingmar 142
Bergman, Ingrid 123
Berlin (West and East) 104–7
Berliner Ensemble Theatre (Berlin) 106
Bertish, Suzanne 165, 203
Best, Edna 61
Betsw-y-Coed (Wales) 158, 160
Betts, Miss 15
The Big Kiss (book) 231
Birmingham Repertory Theatre 107
Birtwistle, Sue 197–9, 200, 201
Blakely, Colin 132, 133, 134
Bloom, Claire 198
Bogarde, Dirk 17
Bogart, Humphrey 160, 161
Bond, Edward 175–8
Bonham-Carter, Helena 65
Boots the Chemist 182–3
Bradwell, Mike 220
Brantley, Betsey 173, 174
Bray, Barbara 162
Brecht, Bertold 106
Brett, Jeremy 51; character of 68, 71–2;
    meets and marries Anna 68–72;
    social life 73–4; death of mother
    75–6; changes in 76; breakdown of
    marriage 77, 79–80, 81; divorce
    84–5, 86; looks after son 102; acts
    in *Rebecca* 155–7; gives son a
    motorbike 156–7; moves to
    Clapham 164; as manic depressive
    165–6, 230–1; move to Beverly
    Hills 165; death of 230–1

Brillamont (Switzerland) 43–5
British Academy of Film and
    Television Awards (BAFTA) 201
Broadway Bound (theatre) 220
Brodsky, Joseph 213
Brookner, Anita 197–9, 200–1
Brown, Pamela 76
Browne, Coral 91–2, 202
Brown's Hotel (London) 67
Bruce, Nigel 31
Bryant, Michael 203
Bryceland, Yvonne 175–6
Buchner, Georg 141
Buckingham Palace 57–8, 74, 229–30
Bulgakov, Mikhail 215
Bunin, Ivan 215
Bunny Lake is Missing (film) 93–4
Burbidge, Gertrude (Nanny) 81, 147;
    character and background 7–9;
    comforting presence of 10, 11–12,
    15, 18; reaction to Royalty 20; helps
    with school work 24–5; at first
    night of *The Last Joke* 79; illness
    and death 99–100, 101
Burge, Stuart 170
Burton, Richard 92–3
Butley (theatre) 110
Buxton Spring Water 160

Callas, Maria 49
Camilla (daughter of Kate Whitney)
    39
Campbell, Alan 15–16
Canada 4–5, 244
Capote, Truman 64
Cardiff, Jack 159, 160
Carlyle, Kitty 34–5, 71
Carlyle, Thomas 46
Casson, Hugh 187
Cavaletti, Mary 49
Chamberlain, Richard 107
Chang, Jung 144
Chapman, Hester W. 50–2
Chekhov, Anton 141, 170
Chelsea 71
The Cherry Orchard (radio) 141–2

Cheshire 5
Chettle, Peter 86, 94
Chetwyn, Robert 99
Chiddingfold (Surrey) 15
Child Psychotherapy Trust 131
Christie, Agatha 144
Christie, Madeleine 245
Churchill, Winston 160
Clare, Anthony 214
Claridges's Hotel (London) 70
Clark, Sir Kenneth 58
Claudel, Paul 47
Cleopatra (film) 92
Close of Play (theatre) 11
Coe, Peter 79
Coleridge, Samuel Taylor 41
Collier, Constance 36–7
Collier, Patience 133
Comedy Theatre (London) 222
Compton-Burnett, Ivy 146
Confucius 123
Connecticut (USA) 31
Connery, Sean 173–4
Conville, Clare 232
Cook, Barbara 243
Cook, Miss 157
Cookson, Cherry 142, 147
Corfu 165
Corman, Roger 105–6
The Corn is Green (TV) 157–60
Cornell, Katherine (Kit) 61–2
Cornwall 8, 117
Cortina d'Ampezzo (Italy) 50
Cottesloe theatre (London) 175–8
Covent Garden (London) 117, 119
Coventry, Bishop of 71
Coward, Noel 1, 4, 17, 21, 42, 54,
    83–4, 93, 114–15, 150, 224
Cowles, Fleur 73
Crete 178–9
Cribbins, Bernard 119
Cukor, George 157–8
Cusack, Sinead 141
Cushing, Betsey 38, 39

Dark Blue World (film) 234

Daunt and Dervish (radio) 147
David, Joanna 157
Davies, Howard 236–8
Dean, James 216–17
Dear Delinquent (theatre) 64–5, 68
Déjà Vu (film) 227–8
Dench, Judi 126–7, 179, 181–3, 205–6,
    228
Dewar, Dr Millicent 130–3, 150–1, 168
Dews, Peter 107
Diamond, Gillian 176–7
Dickens, Charles 24–5
Dillane, Stephen 227
Dior, Christian 24
The Doll's House (theatre) 103
The Doll's House (TV) 198
Donkey's years (theatre) 99
Dorset 153–4, 246
Double Yolk (theatre) 57
Douglas, Michael 137
Douglas-Home, William 55, 61
Dr Kildare (TV series) 33
Du Maurier, Daphne 156
Dudley, William (Bill) 237
Dullea, Keir 93, 94, 104
Dunsfold (Surrey) 15–16

Eaglebrook (USA) 30
East of Eden (film) 216–17
Edinburgh Festival 75
The Elder Statesman (theatre) 74–5
Eliot, T.S. 74
Eliot, Valerie 74
Elizabeth II, Queen 54, 229–30
Elizabeth, the Queen Mother 74
Elliott, Denholm 198, 200
Emily (Bill's aunt) 13
Endfield, Cy 104–5
Englefield Green 21
ENSA 11
Evening Standard Awards Dinner 59
Everett, Rupert 193
Everyman Cinema (Hampstead) 216
Everyman Theatre (Hampstead) 2
Eyre, Peter 51, 143, 194, 197, 201, 204,
    209

Eyre, Richard 151–2, 201

Family Reunion (theatre) 97–8
Family Voices (theatre) 179
Farhi, Nicole 234
Faye, Janina 80
Fenton, George, affair with Anna
    108–11, 116, 117, 122, 123, 127
Ferber, Edna 34, 36
Fernandel 47–8
Ferris, Barbara 112, 114, 115
Feuillière, Edwige 47
Ffrançon-Davies, Gwen 96, 97–8,
    141–2
Finch, Jon 119, 122
First World War 6
Five Days One Summer (film) 173–4
Five Finger Exercise (theatre) 223
Flare Path (theatre) 29, 34
The Flipside (theatre) 99
Florence (Italy) 26–7
Fontanne, Lynn 21–2
Fonteyn, Margot 82
Food for Thought (book) 42
49th Parallel (film) 11
Forbes, Meriel (Mu) 89–90
Ford, John (Anna's godfather) 22–3,
    66–7
Forwood, Tony 17
Foster, Barry 119, 122
Foster, Giles 198
Fournier, Alain 140
Frayn, Michael 99
Fremantle, Peggy 2
Frenzy (film) 118–23
Freud, Sigmund 15, 30, 130, 133
Fry, Stephen 231
Fulham (London) 138, 149, 153, 162
Fürtwangler, Wilhelm 240

Galloway, Jack 153
Gander (Newfoundland) 35
Gardner, Ava 129
Garland, Judy 74
Garmisch (Germany) 26
Germany 25–6

Gertie, Countess of Dudley 93
Gibson, William 79
Gideon's Day (film) 22, 66–7
Gielgud, John 78, 79, 86, 88, 89, 223
Giles, David 153
Gill, Peter 154–5
Gish, Dorothy and Lillian 36
Gish, Sheila 143
The Glass Menagerie (theatre) 96–8
Glion (Switzerland) 82–4
Goering, Hermann 25
Goldwater, Barry 32
Gothenburg (Sweden) 19
Grace (theatre) 220
Grant, Cary 73
Grasshopper Films 207
Gray, Simon 11, 110
Greco, Buddy 74
The Green of the Year (TV) 66
Greene, Graham 59
Greentree Foundation 39
Greentree (Long Island) 38
Greenwich Theatre (London) 220
Griffiths, Melanie 137
Grossi, Grazia 48
Grossi, Lallo 48
Grossi, Laura 48–9
Grossi, Signor 48
Gstaad (Sweden) 19
Gulbenkian, Nubar 78
Gunters tea rooms (Park Lane,
    London) 147

Hagen, Uta 97
Haggar, Khaled Al 228
Hagman, Larry 37
Hall, Peter 179, 180
Halliday, Heller 37
Halliday, Jon 144
Halliday, Richard 37
Hamer, Robert 66
Hamlet (theatre) 107–9
Hammerstein, Oscar 37
Hampstead Theatre club 220
Hampton, Christopher 51, 165, 194,
    198–9

Hampton, Laura 165

Hamsun, Knut 215

Hanbury Tennison, Marika *see*
Hopkinson, Marika

Hancock, Sheila 125

Hardy, Thomas 153

Hare, David 51, 111, 112–13, 114–15,
177, 194, 202, 203, 233, 234

Harlem 64

Harris, Ed 241

Harrison, Noel 227

Harrison, Rex 105

Harrods (Knightsbridge) 22, 28

Harry (Bill's stepfather) 13

Hart, Jim 218

Hart, Moss 34–5, 71

Hartnell, Norman 21

Harty, Russell 160

Harwood, Ronald 240, 243

Havers, Nigel 179

Hawkins, Jack 22, 66

Haymarket Theatre (London) 86, 97

Heartbreak House (theatre) 127, 132–8,
155, 181–2

Heifitz, Jascha 81–2

Heller, Otto 77

Helpmann, Robert 21

Henry V (theatre) 92–3

Hepburn, Audrey 49

Hepburn, Katharine 36, 157–61

Hermitage (St Petersburg) 212–13

Higgins, Bill 195

Highgate (London) 198

Hitchcock, Alfred 117–23

Hitchcock, Alma 121

HM Tennent Ltd 20–1

Hockney, David 137

Hodge, Douglas 220

Hoffman, Dustin 137

Holland Park 180, 193, 213

Holland Park (London) 164, 167–8,
204, 205

Holland-Martin, Lady Anne 57–8

Holm, Ian 220–1, 222

Holmes, Sherlock 231

The Homecoming (theatre) 221

Honey Hill Farm (Connecticut) 31–2,
33

Hope, Bob 87

Hopkins, Anthony 202–4

Hopkins, Jenny 203

Hopkinson, Maria (*later* Marika
Hanbury Tennison) 24

Horton, Rima 178, 179

Hotel in Amsterdam (theatre) 164

Hotel du Lac (book and TV) 197–201

Hoten, Miss 15

House, Gordon 142

Howard, Ken 131

Howerd, Frankie 59

Hoyt, Victoria 227

Huggins, Dan (Anna's grandson) 246

Huggins, David (Anna's son) 75, 81,
92, 101, 241; at boarding school
102, 129, 138; relationship with
George Fenton 109–10, 116; moves
to flat near his father 149, 162; relationship with Anna 150; given
motorbike by Jeremy 156–7; and
death of grandfather 190; at Anna's
wedding 209; as successful illustrator
and graphic designer 217; relationship with grandmother 222, 224;
and death of father 230–1; as
successful novelist 230–1; marriage
and children 245–7

Huggins, Iris (Anna's granddaughter)
246

Huggins, Peter Jeremy William *see*
Brett, Jeremy

Hughes, Howard 35

Hugo, Victor 47

Hunt, Martita 93

Huppert, Isabelle 48, 236–9

Hurricane (film) 22–3

Huston, John 105, 161

Hutchinson, David 142

Huth, Angela 168–9

Hyde-White, Wilfrid 55

I Never Sang For My Father (theatre)
116–17

Ibsen, Henrik 103, 142, 198
The Iceman Cometh (theatre) 221
Imperial College (London) 227
The Importance of Being Earnest (theatre)
     179–80, 181–3, 228
In the Psychiatrist's Chair (radio) 214
In Which We Serve (film) 54
Innocent, Harold 160
Irish Club (Eaton Square, London) 113
Irwin, Alex 195
Italy 26–7
Ivy restaurant (London) 57

Jackanory (TV) 207
Jackson, Michael 218–19
Jaglom, Henry 227
Jamaica 83
Jarvis, Martin 179
Jeans, Isobel 17
Jefferies, Peter 151
Jenkins, Martin 142
Jewish Museum (Prague) 234
Jingo (theatre) 151–2
Jody (Anna's school friend) 43, 44
John, Gwen 183–7, 188
Johns, Glynis 17
Johnson, Celia 55, 56, 57, 60
Johnstone, Pinkie 89
Jones, Gemma 107
A Journey Into the Shadows (film)
     183–7, 188, 191
Judd, Profesor Denis 131
Judd, Dorothy 131

Kaniewska, Marek 193
Katya (Uri's granddaughter) 236
Kaufman, George S. 34
Kaye, Danny 35
Kazan, Elia 216
Keith, Penelope 99
Keller, Helen 79–80
Kelly, Grace 120
Kember, Paul 155
Kennedy, Jackie 61
Kennedy, John F. 61, 90
Kenwood (London) 41

Kilroy, Thomas 170
A Kind of Alaska (radio) 181
A Kind of Alaska (theatre) 179, 180–1
King Lear (theatre) 127, 202–4
Kinsman, Tommy 58
Korda, Alexander 67–8
Kubrick, Stanley 93

La Tour de Peilz (Switzerland) 83, 198,
     224
Lake Geneva (Switzerland) 82–3
Langton, Simon 155
The Last Joke (theatre) 78–9
Laura (daughter of Kate Whitney) 39
Lausanne (Switzerland) 17
Lawrence, Gertrude 84
Le Caprice restaurant (London) 183
Le Grand Meaulnes (radio) 140
Le Touzel, Boney 184
Leach, Archie *see* Grant, Cary
Lee, Christopher 145
Leigh, Vivien 4, 59
Leighton House (London) 204
Leighton, Margaret 71
Leningrad (St Petersburg) 212–13
Leonce and Lena (radio) 141
Lerminière, Madame 46–7
Les Enfants du Paradis (film) 47–8
Lesser, Anton 170
Leveaux, David 220, 221
Liesel (Anna's school friend) 43, 44
Lincoln, Abraham 123
Linley, Carol 93
Lintott, Ken 134
The Little Basket (Dunsfold) 15–16
Liverpool 11
The Living Room (theatre) 59
London, 49 Hill Street 11–12, 19;
     Berkeley Square 12; South Street
     (Mayfair) 19, 20–2; No.2 The Grove
     (Highgate) 41–3, 45, 58, 68, 69;
     Clipstone Street (Bloomsbury)
     50–1; Streatham 80; Notting Hill
     162; Clapham Common 164, 246
London Films 67, 68
Los Angeles 33

Lucie, Doug 220

Luddington, Dorothy (Anna's stepmother) 1; fearsome character of
10; unpopularity of 23; jealous
nature of 33; and marriage of Anna
70; reaction to George Fenton 117;
control of Anna's father 166–7;
death of 188

Lunt, Alfred 21–2

Luxury Amnesia (book) 232

Lydia, Duchess of Bedford 117

Mac (Gielgud's dresser) 89

Mac, Mrs 28

Macaulay, Rose 50–1

McClintock, Guthrie 62

McCowen, Alec 75, 97–8, 107, 120

McGrath, Leueen 34

McShane, Ian 96

McWhinnie, Donald 140, 141, 162, 163

Madeleine (housekeeper) 82–3

The Magic Flute 26

Maison Verlet (Paris) 46

Majorca 45

Maloney, Michael 233–4

Man and Superman (theatre) 75

Manchester 3, 208

Manhasset (Long Island) 38, 63

Manhattan Project 14

Mann, Thomas 215

Manning, Olivia 141

Margaret, Duchess of Argyll 53

Margaret, Princess 71, 74

Marion (Bill's aunt) 13

Markham and Froggatt agency 195–6

Markham, Pippa 195, 237–8

Marks, Leo 77

Marshall, Sarah 61

Martha's Vineyard (USA) 217–20

Martin, Mary 34, 37

Martin-Brown, E. 74

Mary Stuart (theatre) 48, 236–40

Massey, Alice (Daniel's daughter) 209,
241

Massey, Anna, birth and early memories 1, 2; need for love and security
6, 9; character of 8; wartime in
Wales and London 11–12; family
holidays 12, 25–7; hypochondriacal
tendencies 14–15; education 15,
16–18, 20, 24–5, 30–1, 37–8, 42,
43–50, 145–6; insecurities of 20, 25,
40, 46; relationship with Daniel 20,
130, 202, 242–3; undergoes analysis
21, 30, 130–3, 135, 150–1, 168; love
of dressing up 28, 28–9, 29; prowess
in detection 28–9; visits father in
USA 31–3; learns facts of life 44;
learns French 47–8; and art of
makeup 49–50; learns Italian 49; has
voice lessons 50; love of reading
50–1, 86, 193–4; becomes a debutante 53, 57–8; early acting experience 53–4, 55–7; learns to drive 54;
first play 55–7, 60–4; social life
58–60, 64, 73–4; photographic
sessions 62; disastrous second play
64–5; film career 66–8, 104–6,
117–23, 173–4, 183–7, 188, 192–3,
227–9; meets and marries Jeremy
Brett 68–72, 77; birth of son 75–6;
breakdown of marriage 79–80,
81–2; recovers from marriage and
divorce 82–5, 86; affairs 86, 94–5,
103, 108–11, 116, 122, 123, 127;
reaction to death of Nanny 101–2,
103; becomes anorexic 104; as
follower of fashion 109–10; and
difficulties of acting 125–7; depression 129; wins Plays and Players
Award for Best Supporting Actress
134; use of imagination 135–6;
radio work 139–43, 144–8;
recording of books 143–4; TV
work 66, 157–60, 197–201, 207;
advertising work 160; last visit to
her father 165–7; obtains US work
permit 165–7; stays with Jeremy in
Beverly Hills 165–7; nominated for
Best Actress in *Summer* 178; wins
Best Supporting Actress in *The
Importance of Being Earnest* 180; and

death of father 187, 188–91; has hysterectomy 189, 191–2; out of work 194–5; joins Markham and Froggatt agency 195–6; wins BAFTA Best Actress for *Hotel du Lac* 201; fiftieth birthday party 204–6; takes stock of life 205–6; meets and marries Uri 207–15; and death of mother 222–6; becomes a grandmother 246

Massey College (Canada) 98

Massey, Daniel (Anna's brother) 2, 7, 187; Noel Coward as godfather to 4; character of 9; relationship with Anna 20, 130, 202, 242–3; in Italy 27; in analysis 30; education 30; visits father in USA 31, 32–3; auditions for film part 54; twenty-first birtday 58; acts with sister Anna 86, 87, 88; depressive nature 87–8; relationship with parents 87; turns down stage part as father's son 116–17; gives Anna a cookbook 167; and death of father 187, 189, 190; sends wedding gift to Anna 209–10; estrangement from mother 225; illness and death 240–4

Massey, Geoffrey (Anna's half-brother) 2, 32–3, 189, 243–4

Massey Harris company 5

Massey, Raymond (Anna's father), divorce and re-marriage 1–2; character and background 3, 4–6, 23; Anna's wartime visit to 9–10; and filming of *Hurricane* 22–3; visit to Dunsfold 23; as actor 31–2, 33, 216–17; and naming of children 32; as woodworker 32; mistress of 33; gives Anna an opal fan 56–7; and marriage of Anna 69–70; on the London stage 116–17; and signing of Anna's green card 166–7; illness and death 187, 189; proposes to adopt Wendy 188, 189; childhood 189; gifts to Adrianne 224

Massey, Vincent (Anna's uncle) 5, 98–9

Matalon, Vivian 96–7, 99, 108, 116

Mathilde (cook) 82

A Matter of Life and Death (Stairway to Heaven) (film) 32

A Matter of the Soul (radio) 142–3

Maugham, William Somerset 58–9

Mauretania (ship) 10–11

Maw, Janet 153

Maxim's (Paris) 47–8

The Mayor of Casterbridge (TV) 153–4

Me Me Me (book) 232

Menuhin, Yehudi 41

Merchant, Vivien 110

Meredith, Guy 147

Messel, Oliver 41, 42

Messrs Lesley and Roberts (tailors) 117

Meyer, Tom Montagu 73

Miller, Arthur 59–60

Millie (cook) 42

Minster, Jack ('Jolly Jack') 55, 56, 64

The Miracle Worker (theatre) 79–82

Mitchell, Julian 192

Mitford-Colmer, Dorothea 16

Mitford-Colmer, Lillian 16

Mitford-Colmer School (London) 16, 18, 20, 39–40, 43, 45

Monroe, Marilyn 59–60

Montreux 81

Moonlight (theatre) 220–2

More, Kenneth 67

Moscow 211–12

Mount Whitney 13

Mozart, Wolfgang Amadeus 26

Munich (Germany) 26

Muscanto, Madame 38

Museum of Modern Art (USA) 39

Naismith, Laurence 88

Nancarrow, Marion 142, 143

Nanny *see* Burbidge, Gertrude

National Art Gallery (USA) 39

National Theatre (London) 11, 48, 127, 132, 174, 175–8, 179, 182, 183, 202, 203

National Velvet (film) 93

Nelligan, Kate 132
Neville, John 86
New Haven (USA) 13
New York 17, 30–1, 34–5, 61–4, 165;
    Plaza Hotel 1, 7; Anna's visits to
    9–11, 30–9; Hampshire House 9;
    270 Park Avenue 35–7
Newport (Monmouthshire) 3
'The Night of a Thousand Stars' 87
Niven, David 34
Noce, General 25
Notley Abbey (Oxfordshire) 59
Nottingham 182
Novello, Ivor 4, 21
Nuremburg trials 42

Oak Bluff (Martha's Vineyard) 217
Oberon, Merle 63–4
O'Brien, Edna 218
Old Vic Theatre (London) 68, 90–1,
    132, 138
Olga (Uri's daughter) 211, 234–236
Olivier, Laurence 4, 59–60, 90–1, 93–4
Olivier, Tarquin 59
Olivier Theatre (London) 204
Osborne, John 164–5
Osborne, Paul 121
Other Places (theatre) 179, 183

Pacino, Al 228
Palermo (Sicily) 191–2
The Pallisers (TV) 128, 129
Palmer, Lilli 105
Paolozzi, Eduardo 234
Paris 46–8
Parker, Dorothy 16, 36
Parker, Oliver 228
Partage du Midi (theatre) 47
Paterson, Bill 147
Peck, Gregory 31–2
Peeping Tom (film) 32, 76–7
Philip, Prince 99, 229–30
Philippe, Gerard 47
Phipps, Nonie 63
Phyllis (Katharine Hepburn's
    companion) 159

Pickup, Ronald 162
Piggott-Smith, Tim 237
Pinter, Harold 110, 179, 180, 181, 183,
    220, 222, 240
Pitti Palace (Florence) 26
Play (theatre) 162–4
Plimpton, George 64
Ponte Vecchio (Florence) 26
Ponte Vedra (Florida) 32–3
Pontresina (Switzerland) 173–4
Port Hope (Batterwood, Canada) 98
Portmeirion (Wales) 128
Potter, Dennis 153
Powell, Michael 32, 76–7
Power, Tyrone 87
Prado art gallery (Madrid) 128–9
Prague 233–4
Pravda (theatre) 203
Preminger, Otto 93, 94
Presley, Elvis 153, 154
Pride and Prejudice 2
The Prime of Miss Jean Brodie (theatre)
    99
The Prince and the Showgirl (film) 59–60
Private Lives (theatre) 1–2
Proust, Marcel 187, 194

Quadrille (theatre) 21
Quayle, Anthony 55–6, 91
Queen Charlotte's Ball 58

RADA Annual Matinee 54
Ramsay, Peggy 178
Randall, Stephanie 195
Randolph, Elsie 121
Rattigan, Terence 29, 34, 71
Ray, Andrew 66, 67
Rayner, Eric 168
Rebecca (TV) 155–7
Redgrave, Lynn 112, 114, 115
Redgrave, Michael 11, 90–1
Redgrave, Vanessa 99, 227–8
Reid, Sheila 173–4
The Reluctant Debutante (theatre) 55–7,
    60–4, 68
Renaud, Madeleine 47

The Resistable Rise of Arturo Ui (theatre) 106
Richardson, Ralph 78–9, 86, 89–90, 204
Richmond Park (Surrey) 209
Richmond Theatre 240
Rickman, Alan 56, 170, 173, 178–9, 180, 192
The Right Honourable Gentleman (theatre) 91–2, 94
Riley, Jon 232
Ritz Hotel (Madrid) 128–9
River Café (Hammersmith) 209
Riverside Studios (Hammersmith, London) 154–5
Rodgers, Dorothy 37
Rodgers, Richard 37
Rodin, Auguste 185–6
Rogers, Demelza 200
Rogers, Paul 74, 179, 180
'Roman Fever' (radio) 143
Rome 48–51
Romeo and Juliet (theatre) 124
Room to Rent (film) 228–9
Roosevelt, Franklin and Eleanor 38
Roosevelt, James 38
Rosings Farm (Sussex) 2
Roth, Joseph 215
Roth, Philip 220
Royal Court Theatre (London) 111, 112, 162, 170
Royalty Theatre (London) 80
Russia 208–9, 211–13
Rutherford, Margaret 87, 179
Ruy Blas (theatre) 47

Sacks, Oliver 180, 183
Sade, Marquis de 104
St James's Cinema (London) 3, 65
St Michael's Church (Highgate) 69
St Paul's church (Covent Garden) 243
St Petersburg (Leningrad) 212–13
Sallis, Peter 164
Salter, Marjorie 42
Salzburg (Austria) 26
Sams, Jeremy 237

Sargent, Sir Malcolm 59
Savoy Hotel (London) 71
Saynor, Ian 159
The Scarlet Pimpernel (film) 31
Schiller, Friedrich 48, 236
Schlesinger, John 132, 133–4, 137
The School for Scandal (theatre) 86–9
Schuman, Howard 51, 194
Sea Cow restaurant (Weymouth, Dorset) 154
The Seagull (theatre) 170–3
Searcy and Tansley restaurant (Sloane Street, London) 147
Second World War 11, 16, 19
Shaffer, Anthony 223
Shakespeare, William 155, 203
Shannon Airport (Ireland) 35
Shaw, George Bernard 132, 155
Shaw, Glen Byam 78
Sheen, Michael 220, 221
Shepherd, Jack 141
Sheridan, Richard Brinsley 86
Simon, Carly 218–20
Simon, Neil 220
Skinner, Claire 220–1
Slag (theatre) 111, 112–16
Smith, Reginald 140–1
Sneden's Landing (USA) 61
Society of West End Theatre Managers 178, 180
Socrates 101
Something Unspoken (radio) 143
Sophie's Choice (film) 220
South Pacific (musical) 37
Spandau 105
Spiegel, Sam 160
Stafford-Clark, Max 111, 112–13, 116, 170, 171, 172, 173
Standing, John 151
Stanislavski 97, 170
Start the Week (radio) 160
Staunton, Imelda 146–7
Sting 41
Stock, Nigel 140
Stratford 80
Styler, Trudie 41

Styron, William 219–20
Summer (theatre) 175–8, 180
Sussex 2
Sverak, Jan 234
Sweden 19
Sweeney, Frances 53
Switzerland 17, 81, 82–4, 173–4, 198,
    199–200, 206, 224
Sylvia (voice coach) 119

Taganka Theatre (Moscow) 211
Taking Sides (theatre) 240, 241
A Tale of Two Cities (TV) 208
Tana Delta (Kenya) 160
Tanner, John 75
Tanya (Uri's granddaughter) 234–236
Taubman, Mary 184–5
Taylor, Elizabeth 92–3
Te Kanawa, Kiri 137
Tenerife 79–80
Théâtre National Populaire (TNP)
    (Paris) 47
This Sceptred Isle (radio) 145–6
Thomas, Frank 39, 217–18
Thorndike, Dame Sybil 60
Toynbee, Arnold 233
Tracy, Spencer 159
Troilus and Cressida (theatre) 68
Trollope, Anthony 128
Turpin, Gerry 76
Tutin, Dorothy 59
Tydeman, John 141
Tyrwhitt, Ursula 185

Uffizi Gallery (Florence) 26
Uncle Vanya (theatre) 90–1
United Nations 39

Vacani, Madame 53
Variations on a Theme (theatre) 71
Verlet, Françoise 46
Verlet, Madame 46
Vevey (Switzerland) 222
Victoria (Uri's elder daughter) 211
Victoria Station (theatre) 179
Vilar, Jean 47

Virginia Fly is Drowning (TV) 168–70
The Vortex (theatre) 17
Voyage á Biarritz (film) 47

Waldeck, Colin 186
Walter, Harriet 170, 172–3
Warren, Iris 71, 75, 126
Wayne, John 67
Weigel, Helene 106
Wendy (proposed adoptive daughter of
    Anna's father) 188, 189, 190
West, Rebecca 42
Westminster Theatre (London) 3, 65
Wharton, Edith 143
When We Dead Awaken (radio) 142
Whitby, Joy 207, 208
The White Devil (radio) 140
Whitemore, Hugh 155
Whitney, Dorothy (Anna's step-sister) 2
Whitney, Hassler (Bill's brother) 13,
    14
Whitney, John (Jock) Hay 38, 39
Whitney, Josepha (Bill's mother) 13
Whitney, Kate 38–9, 63, 217, 218
Whitney, Margaret (Anna's step-sister)
    2
Whitney, Roger (Bill's brother) 13–14
Whitney, Sara 9, 38
Whitney, William (Bill) Dwight (Anna's
    step-father) 1, 12, 30; background
    13–15; character 13–15, 24, 42; and
    marriage of Anna 69–70; move to
    Switzerland 82–3; illness and death
    183; love for Adrianne 226
Wild Swans (book recording) 144
Wilkinson Tom 228
Williams, Emlyn 4, 157
Williams, Hugh and Margaret 57, 99
Williams, Michael 151
Williams, Tennessee 96, 143
Williams-Ellis, Sir Clough 128
Wilson, Lambert 173
Wilson, Richard 169–70, 178–9, 191–2,
    209
Wilton, Linda 242, 243
Wilton, Penelope 88, 162, 209, 242

Wilton, Rose 242
Witznau (Lake Lucerne) 199–200
Wolcott, Alexander 35–6
Wolf, Sir John 160
Wolfenden Report 85
Wood, Charles 151, 152
Wood, Peter 99
Woolton, Lord 20
The World of Yesterday (book) 194
Worth, Irene 136
Wortley, Richard 142

Wyler, William 90
Wyndhams Theatre (London) 231

Yale University Art Gallery (USA)
39
Young Indiana Jones (film) 233–4
You're Not Watching Me Mummy (TV)
164–5

Zinnemann, Fred 173–4
Zweig, Stefan 194